DIALOGIC CONFESSION

Dialogic Confession
Bonhoeffer's Rhetoric of Responsibility

Ronald C. Arnett

With a Foreword by Clifford Christians

Southern Illinois University Press / Carbondale

Printed in the United States of America
08 07 06 05 4 3 2 1

Library of Congress Cataloging-in-Publication Data

Arnett, Ronald C., 1952–
Dialogic confession : Bonhoeffer's rhetoric of responsibility / Ronald C. Arnett ; with a foreword by Clifford Christians.
p. cm.
Includes bibliographical references (p.) and index.
1. Bonhoeffer, Dietrich, 1906–1945—Ethics. 2. Christian ethics—History—20th century. 3. Dialogue—Moral and ethical aspects—History—20th century. 4. Dialogue—Religious aspects—Christianity—History of doctrines—20th century. I. Title.
BJ1231.A76 2005
230'.044'092—dc22
ISBN 0-8093-2640-X (cloth : alk. paper)
ISBN 0-8093-2641-8 (pbk. : alk. paper) 2004022527

Printed on recycled paper. ♲

The paper used in this publication meets the minimum requirements of American National Standard for Information Sciences—Permanence of Paper for Printed Library Materials, ANSI Z39.48-1992. ∞

CONTENTS

FOREWORD

Clifford Christians

Dialogue has emerged as a centerpiece of contemporary communication theory. It reflects most deeply the nature of human interaction and stands in contrast to the overwhelming one-way, monologic character of communications in our technological age. But the concept "dialogue" has become distended and typically invoked without much academic rigor and sophistication. The idea needs exactly the kind of serious scholarship that this book represents. In developing Bonhoeffer's dialogic emphasis and relating him to cognate work, Arnett makes fine-honed distinctions that matter and distinguishes center from periphery. Dialogic communication emerges from this book with a richness and complexity unmatched anywhere. It is treated both psychologically and sociologically in classical terms, but in novel and provocative ways as well. This book is a tour de force in insuring that the dialogic is understood as *public* communication. Arnett's earlier work distinguished him as a premiere scholar of the dialogic tradition, and this sophisticated volume advances his intellectual leadership to the forefront.

In their book *Dialogic Civility in a Cynical Age,* Arnett and Arneson argue for a dialogue of story, and *Dialogic Confession* brings that framework into its own. While the agrarian age rooted the dialogic principle in local culture, and the industrial age made the self preeminent, the era of information needs stories to systematize it. Arnett understands narrative as the ordering process of information, and in a postmodern age of arbitrary interventions, the narrative process of telling coherent stories is of paramount importance. In these terms, Bonhoeffer's dialogic confession provides a phosphorescent pathway, a third alternative beyond provincial attachments to place and self. In an age of diversity, dialogic *confession*—not *telling*—enables difference to meet, formed not by the self but in story. Story provides a communicative home for Bonhoeffer's engagement with a "world come of age." He shows us the interplay of story and historical moment. He understood the power of competing stories in struggling against Nazi domination, and enables us to privilege the notion of storytelling in an era of extreme conflict but without agreement on unifying narratives.

Bonhoeffer's own discourse is one of death, pain, and suffering, but respect for life and gratitude too. Giving it coherence is the Christocentric faith story. Phenomenology is situated within chronicles of belief, and this faith is creatively applied in the concrete historical situation. As a result, Bonhoeffer's communication is not reduced to the therapeutic. And he avoids psychologism by refusing to make individuals the fulcrum. The faith story guides but does not keep us from ongoing temptation and sacrilege. In Bonhoeffer's narrative, optimism is tempered by undeserved suffering and the inevitability of sin. But living with a faith story opens the promise of continual learning.

With a craftsman's skill, Arnett shows us how this faith story is not threatening to the disinterested or condemnatory of its nonfaith despisers. It cannot be limited to religious communicators, and they must beware of the assumption that they can see the face of God. Bonhoeffer's own worldview is Christocentric, but for those uneasy with God-centered language, he insists on "religionless Christianity" and nonreligious language about the faith. While he himself was embedded in a spiritual sphere, we are all embedded within existential obligation to the Other who is made in the image of God. In Bonhoeffer's terms, only if we bring the story of faith to authentic engagement with the historical moment do we invite the possibility of revelation. The ultimate reserved for God alone and the restraint of human penultimates take effect in history through God's governance of the world.

In Arnett's astute summary, "Bonhoeffer's interpersonal ethic of dialogic confession reaches out to others while firmly surrounded by a story that connects one to others through the 'bridges' of service and awareness of other perspectives" (chapter 10). Thus, without requiring that we imitate him directly in content, Bonhoeffer makes inescapable the need to begin with a position in a dialogic framework. Without an interpersonal ethic guided by a center, we cannot embrace a diversity of others in today's world of narrative and virtue confusion. He "suggests a story of conviction that places ground under one's feet without embracing an inflexible ideology" (chapter 2).

Those who theorize about dialogue, as Arnett does here so brilliantly, cannot escape the central antinomy of humanistic studies generally, that is, the status of the notion of norms. On the one hand, values appear as spontaneous activity, creatively or oppressively ordering our worldviews. On the other, values break upon us in essentialist terms, as mechanisms of orientation that are discovered and not constructed. Paul Ricoeur insists correctly that this problematic of social life is an antinomy in the sense that both sides independently can be justified as self-evident. The nature and logic of norms is a genuine dilemma in social philosophy. No knowledge is presuppositionless, but what then is the status of context-dependent, everyday discourse? And wherein can language as a medium of domination and power be critiqued outside of a commitment to norms? In terms of the classic paradox that Karl Mannheim delineated against relativism, the centrality of discourse is itself incapable of being grounded hermeneutically.

While these queries and Mannheim's argumentation point to the validity of the values-as-discovered modality, true to the character of antinomies, the values-as-created trajectory is not thereby discredited. And in terms of this classic formulation, Bonhoeffer's Christocentric narrative receives validation and contributes dramatically. His dialogic version is a reconstructive strategy discontinuous from the modernist goal of transcendental arguments established as conceptually unique. By inscribing his faith in story, Bonhoeffer is not a foundationalist. He shares the skepticism in contemporary epistemology for unconditional first philosophy. His dialectic view of faith engaging history is reconstitutive in character. His starting point is not a fixed human nature or ontological a prioris. Dialogue shares the conditions for understanding articulated by Max Weber, that is, our capacity as discursive beings to take a deliberative attitude toward the world and lend it significance.

Thus Bonhoeffer's story-formed dialogue represents a radically different approach to the norms-as-discovered motif than does philosophical or theological prescriptivism. In his dialogic as both strategy and theory, Bonhoeffer shifts the Christocentric from a metaphysical, vertical, punctiliar plane to the horizon of community, world, and being, but a transcendental domain it remains nonetheless. On this view, societies embody discourses that are recognized internally as legitimate. Without them the social order becomes, as a matter of fact, inconceivable.

Bonhoeffer's faith narrative affirms an unmitigated human dignity in terms that are non-negotiable. Through his faith story, he can justify an ethics of human mutuality in the face of anarchy and equivocation. Since his discourse is more-than-contingent, he can condemn oppression and dehumanization without personal prejudice or emotional diatribe. Absent a defensible definition of the good, praxis will be vitiated by arbitrariness. In an ironic twist on conventional skepticism, normativity is not a medieval remnant but the catalyst for empowerment. Bonhoeffer issues a manifesto on dialogue's behalf, a declaration so penetrating that without a commitment to it, our academic quarrels seem scandalous in a postmodern age of sliding signifiers and fragmented narratives.

The dialogic lineage of Martin Buber, Paulo Freire, and Emmanuel Levinas to which Bonhoeffer through Arnett contributes most directly insists on emancipatory struggles and transformative action. This trajectory stands opposed to mainstream procedural liberalism and offers a critique of Western culture's individualism. Together they make their normative commitments unequivocal. In Freire's language, only through dialogue do we fulfill our ontological and historical vocation of becoming more fully human. Under conditions of oppression rendered silent in an invaded culture, we can gain a critical consciousness as an instrument of liberation through communication as dialogue. For Buber, restoring the dialogic ought to be our primary aim as humankind. Buber's philosophy of communication is not content with empirical claims regarding socially produced selves or lingual assertions about symbolic constructions. He speaks prophetically that only as I-Thouness prospers will the I-It modality recede. Levinas's interaction between the self and the Other makes peace normative—nonviolence not only a political strategy but a public philosophy.

Within this category of unapologetic normativity, the dialogic paradigm alone escapes both the rationalist and distributive fallacies. Rationalist ethics endorses the central role of reason while presupposing an a priori of duty. This cognitivist ethics falls prey to the rationalist fallacy in which reason determines both the genesis and the conclusion. Nor does the dialogic paradigm from Buber to Bonhoeffer commit the distributive fallacy by presuming that humanity as one empirical subject can be represented by one particular group. Their appeal to everyday life, and Bonhoeffer's dialogical confession with stunning clarity, precludes them from the distributive fallacy of assuming that one strategic human position in the social structure represents the whole. Within their normative claims, a revolutionary working class, or a persecuted minority, or religious sects by a faulty logic of substitution are not made universal.

Dialogic theory brought to maturity in Bonhoeffer advocates a politics of empowerment that diverges fundamentally from a system of power elites, whether their elitism is gained by violence or subterfuge and even if they control by default. This is a normative approach that simultaneously makes the ideological penultimate and enables us to endorse dialogue as the apex of normative communication theories.

In the process of Bonhoeffer's establishing a normative dialogic theory, Arnett through Bonhoeffer resolves a fundamental problem in narrative ethics. Narrative ethics has turned the ethics of rationalism on its head. It has contradicted the metaphysical foundations on which the modernist canon has been based. It has worked from the inside out, from the back-yard and grass roots. Social constructions have replaced formal law systems. Moral values are now situated in the narrative context rather than anchored by philosophical abstractions. The moral life is developed through community formation and not in obscure sanctums of isolated individuals. Contextual values have replaced ethical absolutes.

Our task in narrative ethics is understanding those problem situations where we distinguish good conduct from bad. Conflict and a tangle of incompatible impulses prompt us to ask the question, "What is good?" These are the clues we need for a conception of values that is nonfoundational. Goodness and badness are not objective properties of things in themselves. On the other hand, as Hume argued, values cannot be mere sentiment either. In our value judgments, we say something that is true about the world and not merely express subjective attitudes. Thus narrative contextualism challenges both metaphysics and emotivism as possible homes for values. It does not seek an ultimate normative standard but investigates the social conditions under which we consider our assertions warranted. Interpretation rather than pure reason or divine revelation is the only appropriate method. The narrative level constitutes our best shot for values such as community formation, shared rituals, inclusive language, and human fulfillment to prosper and authoritarianism in all forms recede. In narrative, we rehearse our common doubts, affirm our mutual contingencies, and push away fundamentalisms that purport to be the final answer. From this perspective, as Richard Rorty argues, truth does not correspond to reality but is what we come to believe.

This is an ethics closer to the ground where the moral life takes place. As Arnett articulates so clearly in chapter 2, the shift from principle to story, from formal logic to community formation, is an attractive option for the communications enterprise. Stories are symbolic frameworks that organize human experience. Through stories, we constitute ways of living in common.

For Walter Fisher, we are narrative beings, inherent storytellers, *homo narrans.* Narratives are linguistic forms though which we think, argue, persuade, display convictions, and establish our identity. Storytelling cuts through the endless details of the disorderly world and enables us to think imaginatively and publicly about them. Stories contain in a nutshell the meaning of our theories and beliefs, and Bonhoeffer demonstrated dramatically how non-utopian stories of faith can accomplish this signification in the marketplace.

The stories of Nelson Mandela's twenty-six years in prison, Martin Luther King's letter from the Birmingham jail, the demolition of the Berlin Wall, Bonhoeffer's hanging from Nazi gallows, the loving embrace of a Down syndrome adult, firemen rushing the World Trade Center inferno are the fodder for political revolution and a life of hope. Cardinal Bernardin of Chicago told us how to face an accuser with integrity and death itself with dignity. Stories oral and visual from Iraq's Abu Ghraib prison reverberate around the globe. Great storytellers probe deeply into our belief systems and shape the social landscape. Accordingly, the narrative turn in the human disciplines has produced a multiple collage that enriches our life together.

Taking ethics out of the ether and situating values contextually is a paradigm revolt of historic proportions. But upon decentering ethical rationalism, conventional narrative ethics is co-opted by the status quo. After providing a thick reading of how societies work in a natural setting, narrative ethics can be mute in its own terms on which valuation to value. Whatever is identified experimentally cannot in itself yield normative guidelines. If phenomena situated in immediate space and present time are presumed to contain everything of consequence, the search for values outside immediacy and particularity is meaningless. The standard narrative paradigm yields arbitrary definitions of goodness, as if to say, "This is good because the stories of a people-group identify it as good." From David Hume through G. E. Moore, we have recognized the fallacy of deriving "ought" from "is." To assert prescriptive claims from an experiential base entails a contradiction.

Bonhoeffer offers another kind of narrative ethics. While celebrating the antirealism of mainstream narrative ethics, he points instead to a morality at odds with rationalistic ethics. He represents an army of intellectuals not content with contextual values and the narrative ethics derived from it. Through this stimulating book we can join them in rejecting a narrative ethics of the empty center. A morality of collective values only allows us exhortation and busy maneuvering. But Bonhoeffer refuses to opt for a society that is contingent all the way through. What if the context within which values are supposed to percolate is fractured and tribalistic? Values clarification distinct from matters of ultimate importance is meaningless.

Instead of appealing to rational abstractions or to the social order, this book argues for a dialogic paradigm in which faith stories inform action and give meaning to our otherwise fragmented and ephemeral lives. Without a starting point, ethical imperatives are always indeterminate. Bonhoeffer demonstrates that if moral claims are presuppositionless, the possibility of doing narrative ethics at all is jeopardized. Without a shared sense of right and wrong, how can we despise Bonhoeffer's assailants and support him instead? If following Michel Foucault, we conclude that moral discourse is only rhetoric for securing power, then we undercut our opposition to sexism, military megamachines, torture, and today's obvious evils, as Bonhoeffer opposed Nazi evil in his time. With a commitment to faith narrative, our moral claims are not merely emotional preference. Obviously not every community ought to be celebrated. Through Bonhoeffer's dialogic confession, we resist social values that are exclusivistic and divisive. His model, so luminous in this splendid book, responds to the human yearning for a lever long enough to move the earth.

ACKNOWLEDGMENTS

This work is dedicated to the story of diversity and affirmation lived by the First United Methodist Church in Pittsburgh, particularly to the choir and to their willingness to accept persons in brokenness.

I offer thanks to Rob Anderson and Cliff Christians for their insightful comments and to Karl Kageff for his assistance at SIU Press. I am most fortunate to have such colleagues. Additionally, I am grateful to the discipline of communication, which permits so many diverse voices. It is a welcoming discipline; the field of communication is a postmodern refuge, providing a scholarly home on shifting ground.

I am thankful for the support of family in this project—my wife, Millie, and our children, Adam and Aimee. Watching children become adults is a confession of thanks in itself. I am honored to be a dad.

I do not know if I would have completed this project without my research assistant, John Prellwitz, and my friend and colleague Janie Harden Fritz. They both read and commented on the manuscript. Janie provided numerous thoughtful suggestions that enhanced the quality of the work.

Finally, I offer thanks to all those who work from a story of conviction with the courage to meet, listen to, and learn from stories contrary to their own. In their hands and hearts lies our hope. Lives that confess conviction with openness to Otherness keep the texture and diversity of human life before us—permitting us to learn, permitting us to understand, and permitting us to acknowledge the limits of our own insights. For such persons who expand the human story, I offer my thanks.

INTRODUCTION

Dialogic confession: the key metaphor of this project was never used by Dietrich Bonhoeffer. The term connects Bonhoeffer's "world come of age" to this historical moment of narrative and virtue contention. Postmodernity was foreshadowed by Bonhoeffer's "world come of age."

This communicative engagement of Bonhoeffer relies upon philosophical hermeneutics, bringing the metaphor of dialogic confession as a bias to the text of Bonhoeffer's scholarship and life. The first principle or privileged bias of this work is the term *dialogic confession.* Additionally, Bonhoeffer's insights are met by six interpretive standpoints central to this project but not explicitly claimed by Bonhoeffer. First, the interplay of communication modes (rhetoric, dialectic, and dialogue) opens conversation with Bonhoeffer's work. Second, the assumption that our postmodern moment of narrative and virtue contention is foregrounded by the Nazi attack on difference illuminates the "why" for engaging Bonhoeffer's struggle. Third, understanding the faith story and historicity in dialectic points to how a person with a narrative position must meet a "world come of age," a world not in agreement with the particulars of one's own position. Fourth, Bonhoeffer details what happens in a moral crisis; he, like Alasdair MacIntyre today, understood the pragmatic need for ethics to rest on narrative ground, not the whim of an "emotive" self. Fifth, communication ethics in action personifies Bonhoeffer's rhetoric of responsibility. Finally, Bonhoeffer points to the importance of blurred vision—we do not see the face of God or "the good." Even as one engages a narrative to the best of one's ability in a given historical moment, there is constructive doubt that accompanies the conviction.

Bonhoeffer asked who Christ is for us today. Following that question, this work asks how one engages a religious narrative in a time when many disagree or dismiss positions of conviction. How can one communicate from a point of narrative conviction with a world of difference, indifference, and even hostility? Modernity brought us the experiment of meeting the historical moment from the stance of the self. In moral exhaustion, such a position collapses from lack of ground or support under one's feet. Postmodernity is a metaphorical critique of both the notion of metanarrative (universal) and an understanding of agency or the self abstracted from a petite story or sense of ground. The self is not lost in postmodernity but returned to narrative ground with full knowledge that other stories and ground shape the life of others. What differentiates the postmodern turn of an embedded agent from traditionalism is the recognition of multiplicity of narratives. Modernity was an effort to make a particular form of tradition—reliance upon the self and confidence in inevitability of progress—universal. Postmodernity assumes the pragmatic necessity of encountering clashing rhetorics that represent differing narrative traditions with dialectic giving insight into alterity and dialogue permitting the meeting of difference. Postmodernity assumes persuasion, learning, and coinforming at the heart of identity in a time of difference. Postmodernity is a communicative era where constant learning guides knowledge of one's own stance and that of another.

This work takes a communicative look at Bonhoeffer as an author of this foretold moment. Bonhoeffer's world come of age points to a rhetoric of conviction meeting disparate and contrary positions. To honor Bonhoeffer's communicative horizon, this work openly refers to God and uses Christocentric language. To engage difference, one must meet and learn the particular, whether one is in agreement or not. Modernity assumed we could bypass learning the tradition of another. Postmodernity does not assume such magic. This work turns to Bonhoeffer to observe a communicator of conviction engaging what is alien to him. One can learn from his engagement without agreeing with Bonhoeffer's first principles. One cannot meet an age of difference if one simply dismisses another due to contrary points of entrance into the conversation. First principles still matter in a postmodern world; we simply recognize that there are many more first principles than "my" or "our" own.

The book invites two readers: (1) the religious communicator wanting to meet what Bonhoeffer knew was coming, "a world come of age," and (2) the nonreligious reader interested in how narrative conviction meets a world of difference. Bonhoeffer has kinship with Camus, Buber, Arendt, Levinas, Gandhi, M. L. King Jr., Freire, Benhabib, and many others seeking a "good" that has temporal conditions, a "good" in a given historical moment. Postmodernity does not give up on the "good." We simply must acknowledge that the notion of the "good" is in contention amidst the vying of multiple narrative and virtue structures. Bonhoeffer would not deconstruct a modern world. He witnessed its own self-deconstruction. The task of postmodernity for Bonhoeffer would be engagement with difference, ever learning—meeting the Other in rhetoric, dialogue, and dialectic. This work does not claim authorial intent of Bonhoeffer but rather claims that there is a story of communicative implications of Bonhoeffer's work that provides a model for a constructive hermeneutic meeting a world of difference from a narrative of conviction. Postmodernity does not eliminate the self or narrative; it only rejects the imperial self standing above history and narrative and a single narrative vision (metanarrative). Communicative life begins in story that meets the story of another. The religious communicator turns to Bonhoeffer not for answers, but for a reminder that in the beginning was the Word and the nonreligious reader reads the importance of "word" without the implications of its capitalization. Today in a world without one ground or narrative point of agreement, we still begin with word meeting word—the revelation of that ongoing meeting is the task that shapes our life together in a "world come of age."

I

CONFESSION

Pragmatic Communicative Relevance

Emmanuel Levinas on the interplay of theory and practice in attending to the presence of the Other:

> The traditional opposition between theory and practice will disappear before the metaphysical transcendence by which a relation with the absolutely other, or truth, is established, and of which ethics is the royal road. Hitherto the relation between theory and practice was not conceivable other than as a solidarity or a hierarchy: activity rests on cognitions that illuminate it; knowledge requires from acts the mastery of matter, minds, and societies—a technique, a morality, a politics—that procures the peace necessary for its pure exercise. We shall go further, and, at the risk of appearing to confuse theory and practice, deal with both as modes of metaphysical transcendence. (*Totality and Infinity* 29)

Dietrich Bonhoeffer on the attentiveness to the present:

> For above all the gospel must deal with the present—and that means at this moment the proletarian mass—in a concrete way, "serving the Lord" (Rom. 12.11). But let there be no apotheosis of the proletariat! It is neither the bourgeois nor the proletarian which is right, but the gospel alone. Here there is neither Jew nor Greek. Nevertheless the gospel must be concretely proclaimed in history, and that is why it brings us today face to face with the problem of the proletariat. It is not very easy to offer a proof for something which is more instinctive than conceptual, in this case to prove that our modern church is "bourgeois." The best proof is that the proletariat has turned away from the church, whereas the bourgeois (the petty official, the artisan and the merchant) have remained. [. . .] There can be no evangelical message without knowledge of the present. (*The Communion of Saints* 191–92)

Bonhoeffer's commitment to communicative relevance begins with a public confession; the concrete moment, the historical situation, shapes understanding and implementation of a living story of the faith that is attentive to the call of responsible service. Levinas points to the unity of theory and practice, and Bonhoeffer details the place of application in dialogic response to the demands of the historical moment.

The historical moment is a communicative demand, calling forth attention and response. It is a moment that calls clearly. Communication does not rest with us alone; the historical moment speaks. It is our response that furthers the conversation. History is marked by public points of memory. Awareness of the significance of a given historical moment begins with a rhetorical interruption, calling us from the routine of everyday life into response, into what both Bonhoeffer and Levinas would call responsibility.

The religious communicator has a moral obligation to address the concrete moment, not mere wishes nor the formation of youth, or theory or practice alone; otherwise one misses the needs of the present, the needs of the Other echoing within the call of the historical moment. Focus upon one's own wishes and one's own historical formation invites narcissism, missing concrete application of the faith story responsive to the demands of today.

Bonhoeffer's life and scholarship suggest a faith story that connects one to the historical moment, framing a religious communicative ethic as the dialectical product of a faith story meeting the historical situation with fitting response.

Bonhoeffer considered it important for a person of faith to meet the everyday, the present situation, with a guiding faith story. Bonhoeffer never ventured far from "fighting the battle of the day" (*Life Together* 89). His commitment to Christian fellowship and meditation on the Word reconnected him daily to the story of the faith that prepared him for engagement with the historical situation. Dietrich Bonhoeffer's life and scholarship point to a religious rhetorical charge—to meet and address the world before us, not the world we demand of God. Bonhoeffer never forgot that this is God's world. Our communicative charge is to respond and meet the moment, foregoing the demand of a reality more to our liking. Change emerges in genuine encounter with the real, not in lament of the unwanted.

Bonhoeffer provides us with relevance, with a call to attentive application of the faith story that shapes religious communication as responsive, not based within the impulse to "tell." Bonhoeffer walks between conviction and attentiveness to the present moment, learning, change, and adjustment. He shifts positions in order to address changing circumstances without abandoning the fundamental mores and storyline of the faith.

Such willingness to learn from the unknown permits Bonhoeffer to provide communicative insights illustrative for a postmodern world. Bonhoeffer met diversity and difference as he grappled with a "world come of age" (*Letters and Papers from Prison* 326) and "religionless Christianity" (280). Bonhoeffer penned a faith story capable of meeting the world outside the sanctity of the Church.

Bonhoeffer responded to the rise of Nazi power, offering a language capable of addressing a time of disruption and change. Within his dialectical spirit, he also warned us that no set of ideas or insights captures reality for all time. The historical moment, not wishes, pet theory, or accepted routine, can drive appropriate application of the faith story. Temporal application of the faith story situates Bonhoeffer within a rhetorical understanding of communication that finds truth in application, not in abstract theory and self-centered wishes. Bonhoeffer finds truth in the gray zone of theory and practice, within the interplay of idea and application.

If terms such as "religionless Christianity" and a "world come of age" assist in meeting a historical situation of disruption, they are useful. However, Bonhoeffer would shift his vocabulary if a different historical situation called for alternative communicative engagement. Rhetorically, there is no final communicative answer when engagement of the faith story with the temporal demands of a given historical moment shapes religious communication.

There is pain, suffering, and death in Dietrich Bonhoeffer's personal and theoretical story, as well as love of life, respect for life, even respect for meeting the unwanted and painful. Bonhoeffer's communication invites a profound sense of joy through responsibility and gratitude in thoughtful and faithful response to the historical moment, whether liked by him or not. Bonhoeffer, like Levinas, points us to joy in the midst of genuine meeting of the undesired.

> Being unhappy is destiny, but wanting to be unhappy—that is sacrilege and a serious illness of the soul. Man has gorged himself on happiness; now for a change he hankers after unhappiness, just from curiosity. I can't imagine anything more jaded, anything if you will—although I dislike seeing the word misused—more bourgeois than flirting with unhappiness. It is a dangerous product of boredom and profound ingratitude. (Bonhoeffer, *Novel* 126)

Bonhoeffer embraces a faith-laden story of happiness that permits meeting God's world with courage, conviction, and openness, openness to what is, while rejecting the demand for life to conform to "my" wishes. Attentiveness to God's world unites the dialectic of the faith story and the historical situation, providing a beginning base for a religious communicative ethic, textured by a responsive rhetoric of discernment.

A Responsive Rhetoric of Discernment

Bonhoeffer connected theoretical insights from theology, philosophy, and sociology with the historical moment, situating practices with the dual demands of theoretical ideas and historical necessity. The uniqueness of his theory-informed insight assisted his popular writing centered on religious communication themes appropriate for concrete needs of his time, suggesting a religious rhetoric that seeks to discern communicative action in an era of confusion and fear, an era without agreed-upon theory or agreed-upon understanding of a given historical moment. Rhetoric for Bonhoeffer is not a "telling," but a responsive discerning of the faith story engaged with the Other and the historical situation. Bonhoeffer lived a rhetoric of *phronesis,* a practical wisdom emergent from the meeting of the concrete moment and the storyline of faith ever responsible for the Other.

Bonhoeffer's faith story of responsibility does not fall prey to an individualistic humanism and place undue confidence in the individual. Yet, on the other hand, he does not discount the importance of the person. The faith story and the historical situation in dialectic encounter offer interpretive insight for discernment. Discernment is the place of agency, the window of faithful decision making. One finds oneself situated or embedded in the story of the faith and within the demands of the historical situation. The faith story comes from tradition, and the historical situation comes from the immediacy of the demands of the moment. Alternatively, discernment, situated within a person's agency, sorts through the meeting of faith and situational demand. Bonhoeffer points to a person of faith as an embedded agent—a person situated within a Christocentric story responding to a communicative call to discern appropriate action faithful to both the story of the faith and the demands of the historical moment. The result is not a final truth, but a temporal rhetorical answer, responsive to the interplay of faith story and historical moment. Bonhoeffer understood a world in which "both the reality of God and the reality of the world" (*Ethics* 200–201) are equally important, to be taken seriously. Bonhoeffer meets a reconciled world, a world where faith and attentiveness to the call of today live together.

Bonhoeffer rejected a view of the world as remote and distant. His religious communication begins with a Christocentric story and naturally meets the concrete demands of everyday life. The dialectic of faith story and historicity suggests the dual importance of limits *and* freedom. A story guides (limits), yet does not dictate (freedom). The historical moment guides (limits), yet does not dictate (freedom). An embedded agent, situated within story and historicity, discerns action within the dialectical engagements of everyday life. Discernment is the engine for religious communication, combining the fuel of freedom and restraint. Neither the story of the faith nor the historical situation functions as law; both guide and restrict, calling for a rhetoric of discernment that prepares one for the responsibility of decision.

A responsive rhetoric of discernment involves the interplay of persons, story, and historical moment; this interplay unites faith and creative application in the concrete historical situation. The responsibility of communicative discernment among and with the interplay of persons, story, and historical moment permits communication to avoid the extremes of a priori answers situated in rigid ideology and "emotivism," decision making by personal preference (MacIntyre, *After Virtue* 11–14, 16–35).

The rhetoric of responsive discernment rests outside of determinism and the whim or will of the communicator.

> "Telling the truth," therefore, is not solely a matter of moral character; it is also a matter of correct appreciation of real situations and of serious reflection upon them. The more complex the actual situations of a man's life, the more responsible and the more difficult will be his task of "telling the truth." (Bonhoeffer, *Ethics* 364)

The more complex the situation, the more one needs to know and the more thoughtfully one needs to apply the information. Discernment within Bonhoeffer's communicative project keeps a communicator informed from multiple vantage points, encouraging nimble communicative action. The rhetoric of responsive discernment begins with one basic assumption: finding a space between a faith story and the historical situation where a temporal truth, an appropriate action, emerges that guides without false conviction of absolute certainty. A responsive rhetoric of discernment need not shy from engagement with communicative complexity, life contrary to one's own wishes and accepted routine.

Communicative Complexity

Foregoing easy answers relies upon knowledge that informs and guides application. Bonhoeffer's communicative discernment begins with *phronesis* (Aristotle 1141a20–1142a), "practical wisdom" discerned from the dialectic of a priori knowledge and the demands of the historical moment. Communicative complexity in the rhetoric of discernment presupposes that we can misread both the story and the historical situation, yet this knowledge cannot stop the process of addressing and responding to one another in our limitations. Communicative complexity rejects a universal solution, a "pure" and correct answer, inviting the best temporal possibility available in a given setting.

From the interplay of story, historicity, embedded agency, and ongoing self-questioning, Bonhoeffer situates discernment that calls for the risk of decision within the "good," not the pure, within the realm of "maybe," not the certain. Bonhoeffer had little patience for persons unable to risk action under uncertainty. "[Such persons] take pleasure in making problems. They hear no word without lots of reflection" (Bonhoeffer, *Spiritual Care* 42). Bonhoeffer called for communicative complexity that grounds discernment, action, and the responsibility of decision.

Bonhoeffer's communicative complexity permitted him to originate ideas such as a "religionless Christianity" and "nonreligious" (*Letters and Papers from Prison* 300) language about the faith, without adopting the ideas as his own or constructing a "Bonhoeffer position." Communicative complexity permits the dialectic of faith story and historical situation to give birth to different ideas as the situation and needs of a moment shift. Bonhoeffer's commitment to application keeps his communicative complexity informed by competing forces. One cannot freeze Bonhoeffer in time; his work is responsive, not exhaustive of possibilities. Bonhoeffer raised the question of "who Christ really is, for us today" (Bonhoeffer qtd. in Bethge, *Dietrich Bonhoeffer* 767). We might ask, "What would Bonhoeffer do today as a religious communicator?" Would he call for renewal of the faith story, historicity, or agency?

Bonhoeffer, of World War II Nazi Germany, engaged his moment; he would do likewise today with similar integrity and intensity of discernment. Unreflectively freezing Bonhoeffer into a single moment reifies the metaphors that guided him as the central feature of Bonhoeffer's communicative discernment. However, Bonhoeffer's dialectic of the faith story and the historical moment shift from one key idea to another when necessary. Bonhoeffer did not forget that this is God's world, calling for us to attend to the needs of God's world in the moment—calling us not to utopia, but to "deputyship" (Bonhoeffer, *Ethics* 224–27). Bonhoeffer's communicative complexity is akin to Emmanuel Levinas's "interpreting otherwise" (Manning 48), contrary to normative expectations. Bonhoeffer's greatest insight rests not in what he said, but in engagement with the situation that provides an example for meeting a changing historical moment as a religious communicator. It is the saying of Bonhoeffer, his genuine responsiveness to the historical moment, not the said (concepts reified outside engagement with the demands of a given historical moment), that assists a communicative era of narrative and virtue contention.

Interpreting Otherwise

Bonhoeffer "interprets otherwise" in his understanding of the dialectic of "faith" and "material history"; these two ideas coinform one another (*The Communion of Saints* 233). The "otherwise" for Bonhoeffer invites an engagement with historicity, meeting a "world come of age" without losing a Christocentric base. Worldly engagement and a Christocentric emphasis shape Bonhoeffer's dialectical effort to interpret otherwise. Bonhoeffer places responsibility on the religious communicator to discern the temporally appropriate connections between the story of the faith and the demands of the historical moment.

The Christocentric framework from which Bonhoeffer attends to the historical moment finds support in the story of the faith rather than through focus upon the self or the individual in isolation. He situates the person within a Christocentric story of the faith. Bonhoeffer equates an individualistic view of the world with temptation—a temptation that disembeds the person from the given issues of the day. Such is the reason for Bonhoeffer's insight: "Lastly, in gratitude for temptation overcome I know, at the same time, that no temptation is more terrible than to be without temptation" (*Creation and Fall* 126). The person cannot rise above life, living without temptation and sin. The faith guides, but it does not keep us from ongoing temptation, sin, and the need for confession and redemption.

The individualistic communicative temptation for the religious communicator rests in the placement of too much confidence in the individual and the communication process. Both the individual and the communication process itself live embedded within the historical situation, neither controlled by individual demand. As a counter to an individual focus, Bonhoeffer stressed community, and instead of communication process, he stressed communicative content, a Christocentric admission. "The basis for the formation of religious community lies in the individual's need to communicate. The church is the satisfaction of this need" (*The Communion of Saints* 223). Communication does not begin with an individual or process, but with an embedded person—a person embedded in a faith story, the historical situation, and a community of persons. In a culture that privileges individualism, Bonhoeffer offers communicative insight that "interprets otherwise."

A focus on individualism, like its counterpart, the universal, requires a world of certainty, a realm that seeks pure decisions. The notion of universal places control within the a priori, and individualism places control within the self. Bonhoeffer called for an alternative to these two differing places of communicative decision. He suggested a concrete communicative decision-making style that weighs contrasting positions dialectically, unwilling to enact the "pure," the abstract, the universal, and unwilling to place control within the self. Concrete communicative decision making looks for the "good," the concrete, the temporally appropriate answer in response to a given historical moment. Instead of privileging the individual and/or a universal, Bonhoeffer emphasized guidance of a faith story that responds to the dialectical relation of the historical situation and an embedded decision-making agent. Within this dialectic framed against the background of the faith story lives Bonhoeffer's understanding of religious communication. The interplay of a faith story, the demands of the historical moment, and situated agency shape Bonhoeffer's communication with intentional complexity.

The communicative impulse to "interpret otherwise" goes beyond Bonhoeffer's questioning of individualism and the universal with his linking of the faith story and historicity. He questioned the use of privatized language. "There is no place to which the Christian can withdraw from the world, whether it be outwardly or in the sphere of the inner life" (*Ethics* 200). Bonhoeffer rejected privatized communication. Edwin Robertson states that Bonhoeffer limited "private language" (*Bonhoeffer's Legacy* 96), a message in concert with Alasdair MacIntyre's critique of "emotivism," decision making by personal preference. Bonhoeffer privileged public discourse, working dialectically to protect the public domain as he rejected the private that masqueraded as public discourse.

Bonhoeffer loved the work of the Old Testament prophets, but he did not place them within a framework of private motive attribution, which would have missed public conversation that renews the story of the faith. Bonhoeffer understood that Old Testament prophets called people back to a story, a story necessary when there is narrative and virtue "collapse" (Bethge, *Dietrich Bonhoeffer* 115). The public-reminder function of the prophets assisted in Bonhoeffer's questioning of privatization, leading him to a public turn. Bonhoeffer's public turn took him from an academic life back to the parish, from the safety of American soil back to the struggle in

Germany. Bonhoeffer "interpreted otherwise," leaving safety for conviction of commitment. He lived a call of public accountability, understood not as a technique, but as response to the demands of a given historical moment. Bonhoeffer's public turn took him from security to faithful loss of his life on the Nazi gallows. Like the prophets of old, Bonhoeffer continually rediscovered reminders of the faith story that increased his call to responsibility and his exposure to danger.

Bonhoeffer rejected the individual as the fulcrum point of communication, which kept him from the trap of psychologism, an attempt to ascertain the "real" meaning of someone's action. Bonhoeffer went so far as to suggest that a pastor should not try to pass himself or herself off as someone who can be trusted. Trust should be in the "Word, Christ, alone" (*Spiritual Care* 37). Trust in the Word keeps the story as the key to faith and service, lived out in the concrete demands of the historical situation.

Bonhoeffer embraced a communicative style of prophetic humility that pointed to God, not to himself. As he stated: "Spiritual care is quite modest" (*Spiritual Care* 39). This modesty of communication with another permitted Bonhoeffer to acknowledge the demanding task of communicating with another. One begins with the faith story meeting the historical situation and the Other, calling for particular interpretation and implementation. The dialectical reading of faith story and historical moment comes not with complete assurance, but with the call for confession to aid in avoidance of partial knowing and misapplication. Such pragmatic modesty permits one to understand religious communication as "looking through the glass darkly." Responsiveness to the historical moment requires reading and responding, not in light of clarity, but in story-guided response to varying degrees of dusk.

Looking Darkly

"Looking darkly" offers insight into the fuzzy nature of communicative connection with another; we need to be careful about the promise of undue clarity. Religious communicators must beware of the assumption that one can grasp the face of God; such certainty does not come with Bonhoeffer's understanding of the faith. The distinction between the concrete and the abstract assists us in understanding the importance of "the blurred" for understanding real living within the uncertainty of concrete life. The concrete functions like loosely clasped hands, permitting sand to fall between one's fingers. The abstract, on the other hand, is logical, cut and dried, and clearly understood. The abstract has no frayed edges and has little correspondence to lived life.

What we typically call concrete is often abstract when connected to the give and take of real life. The terms "fuzzy" and "blurred" point to concrete life more accurately than does the term "clarity." A nationally known magazine wanted to write an essay on the ten steps for ethical communication. What they sought under the popular guise of the "concrete" was the "abstract." There are no ten universally applicable steps to communication ethics when historical moment, players in the communication, and topic shift what is and is not important in a given exchange. What is possible is to offer a story that guides. Bonhoeffer functioned like a prophet of the Old Testament, not giving *the* answer but pointing the way "home," back to God, telling a story about the faith. "The poet in exile sings his people to homecoming" (Brueggemann 130). The poet, as storyteller, connects a given story to the historical demands of a given moment; otherwise, one cannot understand revelation that assists a people. A poetic story of the faith offers guidelines for behavior responsive to given situated and concrete demands.

A "concrete" focus of attention rests within blurred vision, forever limited—looking for God, interpersonal meaning, and answers discerned between persons, the historical situation, and the faith story. Bonhoeffer went out of his way to permit ideas, application, and answers to retain a concrete sense of fuzziness. Beyond Bonhoeffer's obvious commitment to the dialectic, he sought out information from unfamiliar positions, welcoming new ideas and diversity. He contended with Nazi assurance—their unwillingness to learn from the Other, the different. Bonhoeffer cautioned against the advancement of knowledge propelled by false assurance. Bonhoeffer offered such a warning to the Church.

> It is not good when the Church is anxious to praise itself too readily for its humble state. Equally, it is not good for it to boast of its power and its influence too soon. It is only good when the Church humbly confesses its sins, allows itself to be forgiven and confesses its Lord. Daily must it receive the will of God from Christ anew. It receives it because of the presence of the incarnate, the humiliated and the exalted one. (*Christ the Center* 113)

Too much assurance in any vision loses focus from the center of the Church, Christ, the story of the faith, and focuses attention upon oneself. The poet of the faith, an image called forth by Bonhoeffer's life and work, and the insight of New Testament scholar Walter Brueggemann (94) suggest the power of pointing toward without dictating a position. A communicative poet points to the story of the faith in concrete application, seeking "some" clarity in the midst of the ambiguity of enactment. Such responsiveness, like *Fiddler on the Roof,* suggests the limits of tradition-bound decisions.

Bonhoeffer's willingness to engage ideas without undue assurance from tradition permitted him to read outside the conventional limits of theology at that time. Bonhoeffer connected sociology to the study of the Church and the faith in *The Communion of Saints* long before such study was fashionable. Additionally, Bonhoeffer studied the work of Husserl and Heidegger, who questioned basic assumptions within Western philosophy. Bonhoeffer followed the work of Dilthey on hermeneutics and the humanities into discussion of Husserl's "idealistic" project that brackets existence for a world of "pure consciousness" (*Act and Being* 62), and then continued onto the work of an emerging scholar, Heidegger. Bonhoeffer found Heidegger necessary for understanding the disclosure of "Being itself" as a concrete temporal act (*Act and Being* 68). Heidegger's idea of being did not rest within the conventions of a pure consciousness. Today, discussion of phenomenology (attentiveness—focus of attention), existential phenomenology (responsiveness—historicity), and philosophical hermeneutics (meeting—the engagement of the biased horizons of interpreter and text) are part of the history of ideas. The wisdom of Bonhoeffer is that he embraced these ideas during their emergence; he took the faith story into novel terrain. Bonhoeffer understood that revelation happens in moments of blurred vision, not in times of undue assurance. A poet of the faith understands that encountering the new opens the door to blurred vision, the home of revelation and insight.

Without the dialectic of conviction and blurred vision, Bonhoeffer might have ignored the work of such authors as Darwin. Bonhoeffer pragmatically asserted that Darwin's correctness or incorrectness was not the issue; whether right or wrong, neither outcome tested the faith (Bethge, *Bonhoeffer: Exile and Martyr* 341). The door to revelation of God and the story of the faith depended on whether or not one forgot who is ultimately in charge—God. God could have orchestrated any option, Darwin's view of evolution or a stricter Biblical interpretation. How God chose to reveal his plan to human beings remains a mystery, a mystery that God directs, not us. For Bonhoeffer, God is in charge of the beginning, the middle, and the end of life. Bonhoeffer did not fear Darwin, nor did he fear new ideas. Bonhoeffer met the new with knowledge that Christ's "energy is not dissipated in a series of historical events, but progresses undiminished through history" (*Christ the Center* 43).

As an academic and a pastor, Bonhoeffer was a learner without a temperamental or delicate faith. He encountered the unexpected, the different, from the standpoint of a Christocentric faith interested in engagement and application, not protection from ideas capable of blurring his vision. Bonhoeffer's faith-centered position of conviction, tempered by responsibility to learn, to question, and to reevaluate, shapes a communicative style that encourages texture in decision making and evaluations. Bonhoeffer unifies a Christocentric story of conviction with learning and temporality, a commitment to discerning "who Christ really is, for us today" (Bonhoeffer qtd. in Bethge, *Dietrich Bonhoeffer* 767). Bonhoeffer did not work with a static understanding of knowledge or the faith; he engaged learning. "What can and must be said is not what is good once and for all, but the way in which Christ takes form among us here and now" (*Ethics* 85). Learning and responsiveness, not recitation or imitation, guides Bonhoeffer's faith communicated in action with changing circumstances and persons.

The implications of Bonhoeffer's unification of Christocentric assurance and temporality are the union of provinciality without fear of change, conviction tempered by listening to and learning from the Other and the historical moment, temporal answers textured by the dialectic of the faith story and the historical demands of a given moment. Bonhoeffer suggests a religious communication style that unites moderated conviction and humility that calls us to question and to learn: "'God opposes the proud, but gives grace to the humble'" (*The New Oxford Annotated Bible,* 1 Pet. 5.5). The cross of Jesus Christ, which shows that God is with the weak and the humble, is God's rebuke to the insolent" (Bonhoeffer, "Meditation on Psalm 119" 144). Religious communication, as suggested by Bonhoeffer, walks within the dialectic of conviction and humility, of the expression of position and questioning of oneself, and of the transcendental and the temporal, shaping a communicative texture worthy of revisiting in an era of narrative complexity and contention. Bonhoeffer's intentionally blurred vision fits within an Old Testament tradition of not looking directly into the face of God, but seeing darkly.

Bonhoeffer's communication works with the dialectic of temporal conviction taken into communicative action. A student asked, "How could Bonhoeffer write *The Cost of Discipleship* and then assist in an effort to assassinate Adolph Hitler?" Understanding Bonhoeffer's dialectic communication style of temporal conviction within the guidelines of the story of the faith and responsive to fuzzy clarity in real life application answers such a question: he was open to learning, change, and responsiveness to the historical moment. Bonhoeffer acted with conviction and appropriate doubt wondering whether the action was "correct" (Kelly and Nelson 38). There is little "cheap grace" (*The Cost of Discipleship* 43) in Bonhoeffer's assurance: each act guided by temporal conviction and historical application could be wrong, making a call for confession a pragmatic extension of his religious communication.

Confession is a pragmatic and faithful path out of the crippling impact of undue complexity, reminding one of a guiding story and understanding the inevitability of error, sin, and misapplication. Confession permits the religious communicator to reject the temptation of rejecting the responsibility of decision due to too much complexity. The everyday importance of confession permits Bonhoeffer to engage faith story and historicity with the goal of application, not indecision. If one errs, the act of confession permits a spiritual and practical regrouping, permitting communicative reflection and redirection.

Temporal Conviction

Bonhoeffer's consistent focus on the authority of Christ in response to the historical situation creates a communication style receptive to revelation, vulnerable to error, and open to correction. Such a communicative style engages confession as the means for realignment of action and the faith story. Confession keeps one accountable to a narrative structure, framing the "why" and the communicative limits for meeting and engaging the Other and the historical situation.

Bonhoeffer's confession assumes an ultimate focus of attention (Christ) that guides the faith story in meeting with the Other and the historical situation. Confession announces the ground or standpoint upon which Bonhoeffer stood, reminding him of a communicative first principle—"Christ as Center." Dialogue begins with a stance, a position one takes into encounter with the Other and the historical situation. Confession is the initial communicative move that permits Bonhoeffer to meet a troubled world in need of dialogue. Confession is a communicative act that results from the engagement of story and the historical moment. When faith story and historical moment meet, the chance of pure application of the faith evaporates into the mud of everyday life, making confession the guiding metaphor of application.

Adding the notion of "dialogue" to "confession" makes explicit a communicative entrance into Bonhoeffer's work. Dialogic confession is not a term used by Bonhoeffer, but privileged in this work and within the horizon of Bonhoeffer's project, suggestive of his communicative engagement of faith story and historical moment. Framing Bonhoeffer's responsive story-framed view of communication around the metaphor of dialogic confession offers intentional lack of precision, privileging the notion of complexity in communicative encounters. A metaphor suggests "fuzzy clarity" (Arnett, "Dialogic Civility" 316). Fuzzy clarity, unlike an operational definition, assists philosophical hermeneutical inquiry to explore multiple possibilities within the horizon of a given phenomenon. At best such metaphors guide without telling the way or manner of engagement—one must find one's way with limited assistance and lighting and at the end of a given journey rest with cautious questioning assurance of following the "right" path. Confession suggests both clarity of admission and a hope for a change of heart and action not yet clearly envisioned. Dialogue suggests a ground or position from which one encounters and listens to the Other while permitting undiscovered answers to emerge between persons in conversation. Together, confession and dialogue guide without giving us a template for accuracy or appropriateness; they point without telling or assuring beyond doubt.

Both confession and dialogue suggest a dialectic of fuzzy clarity. Confession suggests knowing admission of a current position and a willingness to respond to the possibility of change. Dialogue begins with a known position, responsive to possibilities emerging between persons and the historical situation. Dialogic confession suggests admission and knowing, from which there is a willingness to respond to the unknown, emergent in the interplay of faith story, persons, and the historical situation. Dialogic confession begins in story-laden admission that opens the door to uncertainty that is responsive to the demands of persons and the historical situation. Dialogic confession, like any communication concept, finds life in the agency of communicators. However, this agency lives embedded within a Christocentric story, ever-attentive to the demands of the Other and the historical situation.

Dialogic confession is a metaphor of fuzzy clarity pointing and suggesting, foregoing preaching and dictating. Dialogic confession admits limits of position while reconnecting a person to the story of the faith and opening oneself to revelation and new possibilities. Dialogic confession is a fuzzy metaphor, reminding us of the importance of admission of sin and error, the reality of yet unknown changes and possibilities in a life and action, propelled by reconnection to the faith.

This work uses the term *dialogic confession* as a communicative metaphor offering spiritual care to those in the Church and a "world come of age." "Spiritual care does not want to bring about competence, build character, or produce certain types of persons. Instead it uncovers sin and creates hearers of the gospel" (Bonhoeffer, *Spiritual Care* 32). Like Bonhoeffer's notion of spiritual care, dialogic confession does not rest in individual confidence, but in uncertainty, redirecting one back to the story of the faith. Dialogic confession is a metaphor that seeks to put temporal ground under a person's feet without offering false assurance.

Bonhoeffer used confession as communication ground that united conviction and change. Confession and uncertainty emerge as we discern how to assist the Other; every person and every situation comes with unique needs, requiring a different communicative gesture situated in an act of faith. A faith-centered confession in communication begins with uncertainty of action; such a beginning lessens false confidence in a "self" blinded to the Other and the unique situation, helping us avoid the pitfall of attraction to our own image. For Bonhoeffer, keeping the focus on God permits one to see the other person and the historical situation, lessening our natural tendency to blind ourselves by our own artificial light. By not beginning with the self, one finds a story of the faith that provides ground upon which the "I" can stand, taken into service for others.

Bonhoeffer offers communicative caution and limits with one hand as he calls attention to God with the other, rejecting a pregiven answer from God; instead, he embraces the dialectic of a faith story and the historical situation. In a "world come of age," we must discern the "best" or "right" way to assist another in a given situation in a temporal, not universal, fashion. Undue confidence in the individual self misses the authority of Christ, the place where the charge of responsibility rests, the place where the "why" for action and the "how" of service gather definition and meaning. Undue confidence in the self misses the importance of the historical situation, failing to listen to its demands. Yet, out of lack of self-confidence, an embedded agent finds ground of position and conviction within a responsive story. Bonhoeffer unites uncertainty and conviction-tempering religious rhetoric with dialectical responsiveness to the world, which then makes dialogue possible. Bonhoeffer's communicative complexity gives us a concrete picture of the interplay of rhetoric, dialectic, and dialogue informing and tempering one another. This interplay of communicative texture is a dance that enriches a story ever-responsive to life before us. Bonhoeffer's work embraces a dance of story and historical demand played out in the intertwining of rhetoric, dialectic, and dialogue. His work is neither tradition-bound nor relativistic but offers a third alternative of responsible engagement of a faith story with a given moment—opening the way for a communicative poet of the faith to enter the dance of everyday life.

A Communicative Dance

The dance of texture and complexity permits honest communicative engagement with temporal, situation-based decision making. The textured unity of rhetoric (conviction/position) with dialectic (intentional questioning with alternatives) and dialogue (responsiveness to life "between" persons and between one's ground and the demands of the moment) brings communicative life to a temporal dance with guidance and emerging new steps. Take, for example, the following issue, not uncommon or unknown in church life. A worship committee in a Protestant church struggled with contrary visions of two copastors; the two pastors contended with civil disagreement over the morning greeting in church. The first pastor wanted to open the service with a greeting of hello and hand shaking, an interpersonal welcome. The second pastor wanted a traditional call to worship without the initial interpersonal greeting. Both pastors desired a closing centered on the passing of the peace of Christ to one's neighbor. The first pastor wanted interpersonal recognition of persons to begin the service, ending with attentiveness to one another within the faith story. The second pastor called for attentiveness to the story of the faith with a traditional call to the worship of God and the faith story with an interpersonal recognition (passing the peace in the name of Christ) at the end of the service.

Both pastors were well meaning, differing on first principles in the enactment of welcome. One begins with a Christocentric story and the other with the body of believers. Both are theologically appropriate options. Bonhoeffer's position on this disagreement would call for the story of the faith first out of which would come the greeting (passing the peace) at the end of the service: "May the peace of Christ be with you" connects one to the story of the faith. Bonhoeffer would keep the focus of church life clear—Christ as first principle. However, if one fights only to win the dispute, then the focus of attention goes once again to self, away from God. Bonhoeffer would understand that not only are theological issues at stake, but so are practical issues of focus of attention. God does not rest in interpersonal celebration or in theological purity; the key is not to lose one's focus of attention, attentiveness to God, as we attend to serving others. The rhetoric of conviction is tempered by the dialectic of questioning even one's own position, without forgetting the necessity of meeting the Other in dialogue on a issue or principle that is of the highest importance and simultaneously ceases to be of assistance to the faith when embraced without concern for the Other. Bonhoeffer calls for communication situated in the faith, which "transcends the medium of the pastor's personality" (*Life Together* 51).

In light of the above discussion, spiritual care transcends the personality of the parishioners, as well. Dialogic confession is admission of a loss of an ultimate focus of attention, a repositioning of a focus of attention on the story of the faith, and a connectedness to the ongoing demands of the historical moment. Bonhoeffer's story takes a communicator into service for the Other. However, the story never forgets the beginning place of the call to service. Bonhoeffer's world does not begin with humanism, centered upon individual wishes, but with a Christocentric call to service with and for human beings. Bonhoeffer situates ultimate authority within a Christocentric framework. For Bonhoeffer, "Genuine authority realizes that it can exist only in the service of Him who alone has authority" (*Life Together* 109). Dialogic confession, as a metaphor, works within Bonhoeffer's project—a story that begins with God, not with me, you, or even the historical situation, but is responsive to each.

Living the story of the faith engages persons and historical events with a persistent call back to a Christocentric fulcrum point. Dialogic confession, understood within the spirit of Bonhoeffer's story, reminds one of first principles—a Christocentric story and honest engagement with life before us. Bonhoeffer, like Levinas, understood the importance of beginning points, first principles. Levinas claimed ethics as first philosophy (*Totality and Infinity* 304). Bonhoeffer suggested Christ and meeting life before us as first philosophy, the primary place that initiates communicative life. Dialogic confession moves us from the limits of self to reconnection to the story of the faith, permitting us to see the Other and the historical moment, ever open to a glimpse of Christ and to direction from a faith commitment.

Dialogic confession works within the spirit of Bonhoeffer's project and engages a phenomenological communication style that goes to the "things themselves" (Husserl 120–21), keeping the focus of attention on the object at hand. In Bonhoeffer's case, Christ is a phenomenological focal point, as is the reality of life before us. "Between" the faith story and application in the historical moment, the communicator works to find temporal answers through the contrasting unity of rhetoric, dialectic, and dialogue. The sacred lives not just in the story of the faith, but in honest connection of the faith to the Other and historical moment.

Bonhoeffer invests us in the sacred meaning connected to a story of the faith, particularly in his discussion of the I-Thou relationship. Bonhoeffer understood life beginning with attention to the Other. "[S]elf-consciousness arises only with the other" (*The Communion of Saints* 44). Bonhoeffer did not ignore this phenomenological fact. Bonhoeffer confessed, however, that response to the Other does not necessarily imply a Thou. The Thou rests within a different sphere—a spiritual sphere, understanding the Other as made in the image of God. Bonhoeffer understood the human being as "embedded, not just within phenomenological obligation to the Other, but within the sacred space of the faith story" (*The Communion of Saints* 45).

Bonhoeffer understood an embedded person of faith responsive to the Other as a Thou situated within a spiritual sphere. A person is an individual situated within a given story—for Bonhoeffer, the person of faith lives within a Christocentric story.

> [W]e must not confuse this [phenomenological recognition of the Other] with the Christian I-Thou relation. Not every self-conscious I knows of the moral barrier of the Thou. It knows of an alien Thou—this may even be the necessary prerequisite for the moral experience of the Thou. (*The Communion of Saints* 44)

Bonhoeffer's confession about the I-Thou of dialogue is that the story within which one's life is "embedded" makes all the difference—the story of the faith turns phenomenological recognition of the Other into the spiritual space only when one answers the call for responsibility, "deputyship" (*Ethics* 224–27), and service for others. Bonhoeffer understood phenomenology and went one step further into an existential phenomenology—existence shaped by the interpretive bias of an embedded agent. Bonhoeffer concurs with a basic phenomenological assumption: one's focus of attention defines the place of consciousness; he then embeds the person within a story of the faith and meeting of the demands of daily life, affecting everyday interpretation and understanding of existence.

Bonhoeffer's Christocentric/responsive focus permits him to reach out to Others, attending to the unique demands of a given historical situation within the story of the faith. Bonhoeffer's focus of attention, his ongoing communicative Christocentric confession, frames the "why" of concern or responsibility for the Other, a given reason for acts of "discipleship" (*The*

Cost of Discipleship 61–114). The metaphor of discipleship points to a focus of attention on God that additionally calls one to connect with others. This focus of attention gives definition to words such as "obedience" and "forgiveness" (*Spiritual Care* 42). Bonhoeffer's focus of attention on the story of the faith gives one the "why" for obedience and the reason for forgiveness, as do the concrete circumstances of persons. Bonhoeffer does not suggest that phenomenology propels service, but rather that a story of a responsive faith makes such a life a necessity. Bonhoeffer takes phenomenology and situates it within a faith story and the concrete call of the demands before us, doing what is more akin to philosophical hermeneutics of a later German scholar, Hans-Georg Gadamer (*Philosophical Hermeneutics* 18). Dialogic confession is a metaphor dependent upon the whole of Bonhoeffer's story, ever-responsive to the Other and the historical moment.

Between the Particular and the Story of the Faith

Dialogic confession is the part of social practice that connects us to the whole. Paul Ricoeur's understanding of philosophical hermeneutics as requiring a movement from part to whole and whole to part (*Time and Narrative* 1: 66–70), this "configuration," points to how dialogic confession works—the stance or standpoint (the large interpretive text) meets the Other and historical situation (particular parts of life) with each informing the other. Part and whole coinform one another in the communicative engagement of dialogic confession, uniting the particular needs of a given moment and the story of the faith.

Ricoeur's emphasis on the importance of part and whole in interpretation connects the particular and the larger story of a given communicative text, the doing of philosophical hermeneutics. Bonhoeffer does philosophical hermeneutics from a faith perspective, witnessing as he interprets the temptation of Christ.

> Jesus is tempted in his flesh, in his faith and in his allegiance to God. All three temptations (parts) rest within the "whole" of the faith that must not be put at risk—to separate Jesus from the Word of God (*Life Together* 105).

The guiding metaphor is God from this primary focus of attention, engaged in the genuine meeting of everyday trial and tribulation. The metaphor of dialogic confession works as entrance into Bonhoeffer's communication project, if understood as always pointing to a larger whole, an ultimate metaphor, a Christocentric focus of attention.

Ricoeur's assessment of part and whole in the interpretive process serves two purposes within this work. First, dialogic confession extracted from the larger Christocentric focus of Bonhoeffer's work no longer carries the same meaning. Second, dialogic confession extracted from the demands of the historical moment no longer carries the same meaning.

Dialogic confession takes on significance as a part of the faith only because it points to the whole of a responsive faith story. Dialogic confession is a metaphor that reminds one of communicative social practices—foregoing self-justification, speaking to another about one's weakness, and foregoing the temptation to psychologize sin in oneself or the Other. Sin moves one from communicative focus on God and the world before us to focus upon the self.

Bonhoeffer's early work *The Communion of Saints* frames confession as a practical guiding metaphor, placing primary stress upon confession as an essential communicative practice in a faith community.

> [T]he greatest task at the moment is to make private confession once again into a living source of strength for the church. In it the one man assumes the status of a priest for the other, by virtue of Christ's priesthood, as the church that makes intercession and forgives sins. The fact that such an act does not take place only generally in worship, but particularly in the affliction and anxiety of a concrete encounter between two persons, is of great significance for the realization and experience of the Christian idea of community. (*The Communion of Saints* 240)

If the life of the faith is understood as a responsive text or story, then the whole and the part, in this case the "ultimate" and the "penultimate" (Bonhoeffer, *Ethics* 125–32), inform one another. The ultimate is God and the penultimate the world before us in a given moment, including our communicative response/action. In Bonhoeffer's faith story, God is the ultimate, but without the near ultimate, the penultimate of response to everyday life, dialogic confession is eclipsed by a priori tradition or subjective wish/demand.

Bonhoeffer's communicative style is a form of dialogic confession, moving from a self focus to a Christocentric focus, making attentiveness to Others and the historical situation more likely. In *Letters and Papers from Prison,* one finds Bonhoeffer doing what this work calls dialogic confession, moving the focus of attention from himself to reconnection with the faith.

> [T]hat I'm "suffering" here, I reject the thought. It seems to me a profanation. These things mustn't be dramatized. I doubt very much whether I'm "suffering" any more than you, or most people, are suffering today. Of course, a great deal here is horrible, but where isn't it? Perhaps we've made too much of this question of suffering, and been too solemn about it. I've sometimes been surprised that the Roman Catholics take so little notice of that kind of thing. Is it

> because they're stronger than we are? Perhaps they know better from their own history what suffering and martyrdom really are, and are silent about petty inconvenience and obstacles. (*Letters and Papers from Prison* 232)

Bonhoeffer discussed the role of Christ in our lives, which frames the meaning of suffering. His dialogic confession moves the focus of attention back to the faith, connecting with the Other, and as a by-product resituates himself within the guidance of faith. Such a form of confession assists the self as a by-product as one keeps a proper focus of attention.

The metaphor of dialogic confession situated within the story of the faith reminds a religious communicator to understand communicative social practices of conviction, caution, listening to and learning from the Other and the historical situation, and finally the importance of decision. Dialogic confession combines conviction and caution in listening to and learning from the Other and the historical moment as one seeks to discern temporally appropriate action, to learn by recognizing revelation. Bonhoeffer questioned pride unwilling to attend to new insight. "God hates the insolent, those who are content with themselves, who care nothing for justice and mercy, who despise the Word of God and the faithful. Pride before God is the root of disobedience, all violence, all irresponsibility" ("Meditation on Psalm 119" 143). This view of religious communication suggests the fundamental importance of willingness to shift and change; attentiveness to God requires attentiveness to God's world.

Dialogic confession points to an engagement with the Other that does not rest on the importance of the self or the motives of either communicative party. Reconnection to the story of the faith minimizes the impulse to psychologize. David Hoy in *The Critical Circle* offers Gadamer's and Ricoeur's understanding of hermeneutics as an alternative to a psychologizing impulse: "[F]usion of horizons [is] Gadamer's alternative to a psychologistic account of historical understanding. The term 'horizon' is an attempt at describing the situatedness or context-bound character of interpretation" (Hoy 95–96). The horizons represent the meeting of the bias of the interpreter's standpoint and the text's position. In the case of Bonhoeffer, the faith story meets the Other and a historical situation with communicative social practices of conviction, listening to and learning from the Other and the historical moment, admission and decision/action that reconnect one to the faith without focus upon psychological analysis. Bonhoeffer, as a member and pastor of the Confessing Church, wrote of the Church in the following fashion, pointing to the importance of the dialectic of God and the Other, the neighbor, no longer bound by the past because of tradition or comfort. Both new and old ideas must meet the demands of a "world come of age."

> [T]he Confessing Church: the theology of revelation [. . .] over against the world, involving a "factual" interest in Christianity; art and science searching for their origin. Generally in the Confessing Church: standing up for the church's "cause," but little personal faith in Christ. "Jesus" is disappearing from sight. Sociologically: no effect on the masses—interest confined to the upper and lower middle classes. A heavy incubus of difficult traditional ideas. The decisive factor: the church on the defensive. No taking risk for others. (*Letters and Papers from Prison* 381)

Bonhoeffer works with a Christocentric framework that embraces an Old Testament warning—to be cautious of any revelation that claims to see clearly the face of God. Revelation points without complete assurance of interpretive accuracy. Answers are found not in old or the new, but in the emerging between of the faith story and a "world come of age."

Dialogic confession includes not only a Christocentric focus of attention, but an awareness of the danger and the limits of claiming clarity in communication with God. We see darkly with cautioned conviction into the face of the faith. Dialogic confession is a metaphor that tempers the rhetoric of the faith with the dialectic counterpart of uncertainty and caution, permitting one to learn from the Other and the changing historical situation, ever responsive to the ongoing revelation and relevance of the faith story in action. Dialogic confession offers the relevance of admitted confusion, engaged from a story perspective, ever responsive to the Other and the historical situation, working within a hope that answers can be found as we keep the conversation going. Or, in Bonhoeffer's terms, if we can keep bringing the story of the faith to unique and authentic engagement with any historical moment, we invite the possibility of revelation that directs and calls us in particular ways at a particular time in service to Others.

2

COMMUNICATIVE GROUND

From Dictate to Story Guidance

Walter Fisher on coherence and fidelity of stories:

> [C]oherence brings into focus the integrity of a story as a whole, but the principle of fidelity pertains to the individuated components of stories—whether they represent accurate assertions about social reality and thereby constitute good reasons for belief or action. ("Human Communication" 105)

Dietrich Bonhoeffer on veracity and honest lessons:

> Little Brother was holding a young bird. "She pushed it out of the nest," he said, tears streaming down his face, when he saw the grandmother.
>
> "Who, the cat again?"
>
> "No, much worse; the mother herself, the bad, mean beast."
>
> The young bird twitched once more, then died in the boy's hand. That was too much for him. Frightened, he involuntarily open his hand and dropped the dead little robin. Then he felt shame, reached again for the little bird, stood up, and showed it to his grandmother.
>
> "Put it under the earth," she said; "it'll feel most comfortable there."
>
> Erich wordlessly took a big spade, punched it deep into the soil, and Little Brother laid the bird into its grave and covered it up. The grandmother took her small grandson's hand and went to the house with him. Erich stayed for a moment and then quickly ran out to the street.
>
> "Why did the mother do that?" Little Brother asked when the grandmother came to his room with him to wash his face and get him ready for Sunday dinner.
>
> "Probably because the young bird was weak and sick," Frau Brake answered calmly. She would have disdained using such an elemental experience as a dishonest lesson, perhaps by saying, "Because the young bird was naughty." In any case, Frau Brake considered the truth better pedagogy than subterfuges and tricks. [. . .]
>
> "[Remember] there is not one sparrow forgotten before God [. . .]"
>
> "Then that's good," said Little Brother. (*Novel* 66–67)

Walter Fisher provides the theoretical reminder of the importance of story for communicative guidance. Story requires engagement with the situation before one; it is not philosophically or practically stagnant. A story keeps a story line with multiple possibilities available in the telling. It guides without dictating. Bonhoeffer understood the power of such pointing, in an era increasingly calling for responsibility to connect the faith story to the demands of the times meeting a communicator. While in prison, Bonhoeffer wrote a drama wherein the main character, Little Brother, asked profound questions about life and death, framing story guidance for the importance of attentiveness to the unexpected and unwanted events that meet us.

Little Brother's constant questions received honest, realistic answers from his grandmother that invited this young person into a world of adult realism—life does not always conform to our individual wishes, demands, or efforts at agency. The grandmother did not placate Little Brother, just as Bonhoeffer did not placate his readers or himself. Easy answers typify neither Bonhoeffer's theology/philosophy nor his personal courage and conviction. The drama takes us into a story of engagement unwilling to forego honest exchange for acts of self-protection.

Bonhoeffer's project, understood through the lens of a story-centered understanding of communication, underscores the importance of a guiding faith story responsive to the realities and difficulties of life and responsive to the demands of the historical moment. Walter Fisher's emphasis upon the fidelity of a narrative suggests the importance of "good reasons" within a given story. The fidelity, the "good reason" that constitutes the narrative fidelity, of Bonhoeffer's communicative implications is his ongoing commitment to a Christocentric worldview and honest engagement with a world come of age. One can judge fidelity in three ways in a postmodern world. First, if one assumes such a narrative position, one asks whether the actions propelled by a given narrative direction make sense in response to the unique moment before one. In short, narrative agreement permits one to engage Vico's notion of *sensus communis*—common sense. This form of common sense is responsive to a narrative, not necessarily to an empirical community. Second, if one does not agree with Bonhoeffer's narrative background beginning, one can ask whether he stays within the horizon of his project and, when he deviates, whether there is a clear reason for the digression. Third, one can look at Bonhoeffer's narrative project in a larger fashion, asking: "How does Bonhoeffer assist in understanding postmodern engagement of narrative difference from a stance of relative narrative assurance and conviction?" This question links Bonhoeffer to a postmodern world without abandoning a Christian narrative.

Bonhoeffer implicitly works within Fisher's simple, yet profound, assumption—stories make a difference in communicative lives. Fisher framed a story-laden nature of human life, referring to the person as an inherent storyteller, *homo narrans* (5–6). It is not just communicative foreground application that requires attention, but background stories that guide foreground application. A narrative provides a temporal background for communicative engagement.

Narrative conviction engaged in a postmodern world works within the interplay of telling, discernment, and responsive engagement—or, in communication terms, within the interplay of rhetoric, dialectic, and dialogue. This comprehensive view of communication makes Bonhoeffer's communicative implications a story worth revisiting in a postmodern age. Bonhoeffer suggests a story of conviction that places ground under one's feet without embracing an inflexible ideology.

The complexity of Bonhoeffer's communicative work offers a story that works as ground that makes a difference: "Give me ground under my feet, give me the Archimedean point to stand on—and all would be different" (*Drama* 47). The story-laden ground that Bonhoeffer offers is a story of dialogic confession, temporal assurance ever-situated in the humility of faith that engages the Other and changing historical circumstance.

Bonhoeffer works from a nonutopian story of the faith, linking a Christocentric story with an emerging story of a "world come of age" (*Letters and Papers from Prison* 326–29). Bonhoeffer frames how a person of story-laden conviction can meet a world of difference, a "world come of age," offering a story line situated in thoughtful complexity—a story with a dialectic heart in which conviction and openness meet.

The complexity of Bonhoeffer's story line lives within his writing and his actions, such as wanting to meet Gandhi and finding himself unable to do so due to responsibilities at home, as he contended with Hitler's Germany. *The Cost of Discipleship* provided a major reason for his hope of meeting Gandhi. Bonhoeffer's pacifism guided that book, but the complexity of his story line indicates that his response to the concrete moment later required violation of its tenets. Interestingly, the following statement about Gandhi reflects Bonhoeffer: one should not confuse a person of conviction with a person of closure (Rokeach 392). Bonhoeffer, Gandhi, Martin Luther King Jr., and Dorothy Day shared the capacity to live a dialectical unity of conviction and openness. A dialectical story line guided their work and contributions to others.

A Dialectical Story Line

This work constructs a story-formed understanding of communication responsive to Bonhoeffer's dialectical embrace of a Christocentric faith story and an understanding of an emerging "world come of age," a world in which responsibility rests with us without hope of an intervening God. Bonhoeffer rejected deus ex machina witnessing instead the revelation of narrative and virtue contention before his eyes.

Bonhoeffer begins with a story, a Christocentric story, seeing competing stories vying for acceptance in a "world come of age." Bonhoeffer situates his own story within a multitude of stories, ranging across family, academic insights, cultural life, interpersonal life within the Church, and attentiveness to the particular situation. Bonhoeffer understood that historicity offers a test of veracity of a story line in a given moment. The necessity of historicity is that it counters both subjective and objective readings of a given moment.

Such a reading of historicity takes one from relativism to encounter with the concrete implementation demands of a given story-framed moment. Bonhoeffer understands historicity as something that has its own power, a story-guiding influence. We cannot "reify as an object" nor view as "accidental" the story line of a given historical moment (*The Communion of Saints* 88). The story of persons, institutions, and the historical moment speak to us. We cannot offer objective interpretation of a story, but we can avoid manipulation of a given story line, encountering it on its own terms, its historical place in time.

Awareness of a complex collage of story themes and remnants permitted Bonhoeffer to meet the demands of the historical moment with texture and thoughtfulness, foregoing the temptation of an a priori assurance of what is "right" prior to meeting the necessities of a unique set of circumstances. Bonhoeffer walked a textured story into a historical moment full of social tension and narrative confusion that called him to pen the phrase "a world come of age."

Bonhoeffer's unique commitment to a faith story, textured by diversity of other story remnants within an era of obvious narrative contention, permits him to speak to this postmodern moment. If one accepts postmodernity as a moment in which there is general disagreement on what should be the guiding narrative structures, then Bonhoeffer offers insight for such a moment in which no one story frames the narrative and virtue structures of a people. Bonhoeffer, like Lyotard (7, 18–23) today, reminds us to choose a story with care. Stories must contend with other stories. Persons find their strength within stories that guide and offer insight. This work meets a moment of narrative disagreement, not with the notion of the self, but with the call to search for stories worthy of shaping persons capable of meeting a "world come of age."

Bonhoeffer met narrative contention with a universal narrative commitment that engaged a world of competing "petite narratives" (Lyotard 60). One of Bonhoeffer's central contributions to religious communication in a postmodern age is the assumption that from the stance of a universal conviction of the faith one can out of pragmatic necessity meet and learn from a world of multiple narrative and virtue structures. Recognizing a moment of narrative disagreement does not imply the end of narratives of conviction. Such a moment simply signals awareness that others may not agree with one's assumptions; this is the end of the blind presupposition that all people adhere to a given narrative structure. Bonhoeffer lives with narrative ground under his feet without assuming others follow the same path.

Bonhoeffer brought the story of the faith into a marketplace of narrative contention, a place of competing stories, in a "world come of age." Bonhoeffer's contemporary relevance rests with his life and scholarship that continue to witness to the possibility of walking the story of the faith into an era of narrative contention, even in times of supreme anger and hatred. Bonhoeffer's work is both contextual and guided by and within a narrative structure, which separates his work from a relativistic communicative structure. His story reminds us of the importance of fidelity between a faith story and our actions and the importance of veracity between a lived story and the historical moment. Fidelity calls for faithfulness to a given narrative, and veracity calls for a truthfulness that makes sense for a given situation. Bonhoeffer's life and work suggest a story-formed view of communication situated in a textured understanding of story and attentiveness to the historical moment, working within fidelity of conviction and veracity of response.

Interpretive Depth

A story-laden perspective on communication understood within Geertz's notions of thin and thick interpretation (6–7) embraces a thick interpretation requiring depth of understanding. A thick interpretation requires knowing understanding of the story that frames the standpoint of a given communicative agent. An unreflectively agreed-upon understanding of communication implies a taken-for-granted story-laden background, requiring only a thin interpretation. With unreflective grounding in the story of the faith, one misses the thick interpretation pointed to by Bonhoeffer that requires dialectic engagement of a faith story meeting the emerging story of a "world come of age," resulting in a penultimate story of guidance in a given situation.

Bonhoeffer's work implies that a thin view of religious communication misses the story-laden texture of communicative life that includes such diverse realities as irony, joy, and tragedy in human life. An American colleague of Bonhoeffer's, Reinhold Niebuhr, in his work *The Irony of American History,* reminds us of the story of being human—the irony of turning good to evil when texture and a light touch are lost.

> There is, in short, even in a conflict with a foe with whom we have little in common the possibility and necessity of living in a dimension of meaning in which the urgencies of the struggle are subordinated to a sense of awe before the vastness of the historical drama in which we are jointly involved; to a sense of modesty about the virtue, wisdom and power available to us for the resolution of these perplexities; to a sense of contrition about the common human frailties and foibles which lie at the foundation of both the enemy's demonry and our vanities; and to a sense of gratitude for the divine mercies which are promised to those who humble themselves. (174)

Bonhoeffer situates religious communication within the content of a faith story that acknowledges the limits of human action, the inevitability of "costly grace" (*The Cost of Discipleship* 45–60), the necessity and risk from responsible concern for one's neighbor. The irony of religious communication is that there are limits of reward for "right" action—costly, not cheap, grace frames Bonhoeffer's communication. Cheap grace expects little other than reward. Costly grace calls one to do the right thing with knowledge and discovery of consequences. Bonhoeffer's insight into the demands of everyday life, suffering from human responsibility, adds yet another voice to a theology that recognizes the ontology of suffering in everyday life, so painfully penned by a Jewish compatriot unknown to Bonhoeffer, who suffered and framed meaning within the spirit of a sense of costly grace, Viktor Frankl (*Man's Search for Meaning* 178–79).

From Bonhoeffer's understanding of the faith story, limits temper undue optimism, acknowledging the inevitability of human sin. Limits are part of all persons, institutions, and ideas, requiring counter perspectives, keeping good ideas from running amok without counter questioning from other perspectives. Situating an individual within a faith story begins with limits, with suffering and sin, and with tempered conviction, calling us to continual learning as we engage others and changing historical circumstances.

Limits acknowledged and engaged offer depth of insight, forcing us to understand differently. Few find depth and multiplicity of insight from a trouble-free life—the movie and book *Pleasantville* drive this simple point home. Routine life without acknowledged limits offers little opportunity for change or wisdom. One seldom benefits from the wisdom of another who has lived a life without crises, suffering, and knowledge of that person's own sin.

Bonhoeffer's story-centered view of communication rejects undue optimism about talking; he placed limits on the role of communication in a life of faith. Bonhoeffer would not utter, "If you only take more time to talk, I am sure you can work out the issues." Communication engaged as a technique moves us far afield from the interpretive insight of Dietrich Bonhoeffer. The first principle for Bonhoeffer is not communication, but confession of a given narrative position—a responsive Christocentric worldview. Without a story, a narrative, a common place that guides one's own standpoint and response to another's standpoint that beckons one to learn new and different insights, the chances of enacting a thin interpretation increase. A thin interpretation assumes the Other is simply another "me" with both of us working from an unreflective set of assumptions, offering a thin interpretive story of communicative optimism. Bonhoeffer offers a story-framed view of communication that keeps before us the limits of sin and guilt, within a story of forgiveness, love, and "deputyship" (*Ethics* 224–27), responsibility for others. Limits remind us that we work to carry out the story, in spite of our limits.

Jacques Ellul suggested that if Karl Marx were to write today, the danger he would point out to us is technique, not capital (*The Technological Society* 150). From the perspective of this work, interpersonal technologies that embrace unduly optimistic assumptions about communication work to lessen "costly grace," trying to find a technique to make communication work out. Bonhoeffer suggests that "costly grace" is a responsibility that assumes the inevitability of sacrifice and responsibility, not just painless fulfillment. A thin view of communication works with interpersonal technological assumptions, striving to fix, solve, and invite a sense of routine, rather than understanding the characteristics of differing stories that move communicative life in competing directions.

Bonhoeffer avoided a thin view of religious communication, rejecting easy answers; instead, he took a demanding path, accepting responsibility to learn from one's own story, the historical moment, and the story of another. He understood that the Promised Land requires a journey through the night, through what one does not know or understand; such journeys require a faith story willing to engage the unknown territory of "a world come of age."

> That the way of all of us into the land of promise leads through the night; that we also only enter it as those who are perhaps curiously scarred from the struggle with God, the struggle for his kingdom and his grace; and that we enter the land of God and of our brother as limping warriors—all these things we Christians have in common with Jacob. (Bonhoeffer, "Thy Kingdom Come" 47)

A religious communicator enters a "world come of age" as a wounded warrior, ever aware of the limits of self, others, and institutions, with the conviction to continue. Bonhoeffer offers us the grace of cost—the grace of a "limping warrior" willing to extend a hand to an ailing world. Like a flawed parent attending with responsibility to the needs of the child, Bonhoeffer offers us a religious communicator of interpretive depth unifying conviction and pragmatic humility.

Interpretive depth discovered in a journey without guidance of clear light calls for learning from each encounter with Others and the historical situation. Religious communication in a "world come of age" privileges learning more than talking and telling. Interpretive depth requires a willingness to attend to temporal glimpses of light revealed in the temporal engagement of story, persons, and historical situation. Such interpretive action is responsive; it modifies, augments, and changes in the meeting of persons and the historical situation. This emphasis on change and responsiveness, learning from the Other, distinguishes this form of communication from expressivism, the impulse to speak first. Depth of interpretation rests in multiplicity, in the interchange of stories, persons, and the historical moment. Bonhoeffer points to a trinity of interpretive significance in the meeting of story, persons, and historical moment that offers guidance without the assurance of a static faith situated in deus ex machina.

Interpretive Action

Interpretation makes a difference in what we see and our understanding of action. Bonhoeffer penned and lived a story of faithfulness responsive to the historical moment. In the face of tyranny, Bonhoeffer's work recasts the question of how to react "when bad things happen to good people" (Kushner) to *How does a story of the faith offer some freedom and meaning as bad things happen?* Bonhoeffer's critique of deus ex machina puts responsibility upon the person in a "world come of age." He understood Nietzsche's call for courage and responsibility, not passive acceptance (74–79). Nietzsche rejected a church that calls one into weakness and bad faith. Bonhoeffer agreed without losing confidence in the faith story: "We're apt to acquiesce in Nietzsche's crude alternatives" (*Letters and Papers from Prison* 239). Bonhoeffer accepted Nietzsche's critique, not his solution. Bonhoeffer stayed within the story of the faith *and* framed an interpretive key of courage and responsibility responsive to the horizon of the faith. Bonhoeffer was responsive without falling prey to easy answers within a static faith.

Bonhoeffer could have ministered to our campus at the death of our provost, who died one month after retirement. The campus mourned the loss of the provost, his energy, insight, and courage. Many asked: Why do bad things happen to good people? The sound of Bonhoeffer's realistic call of responsibility unified this Catholic campus. The campus found meaning in the midst of this painful and sad moment for our provost's family and this academic community as people remembered a life of responsibility.

The Vice President for Student Life, a priest, ministered to the family and the academic community from a faith story that openly acknowledged responsibility in moments that seem so unfair. There was no effort made to ignore the feeling of theft in this moment, no attempt at well-intended lying to the community. Father stated with a simple eloquence, "This is not right and the wrongness of this death cannot diminish the light of responsibility that shines before us." No placating, just open doors for persons in the community to lament a premature death and reflect upon the demands of service and responsible ministry to the community.

Such a life of faith and responsibility Bonhoeffer understood, and such a ministry in the midst of seemingly unfair death he would acknowledge.

> Particular care must be taken with the proclamation of comfort. One should not extend comfort where it is not desired. One should not describe the pain of the mourners. People take simple pleasure in solitary grief. Grief is one of the secular forms of immortality: "[. . .] as long as there is grief the dead live on." As false comfort, it is a flight from discomfort. The truly concerned and healthy person wants no one who offers comfort to understand comfort as a substitute for that which is his responsibility. (*Spiritual Care* 73)

Bonhoeffer would understand a faith stating, "This is not right," while being ever loyal and responsive to God. Bonhoeffer understood the faith "touched down in reality" (*Spiritual Care* 69).

Tragic moments remind one of human irony. Hawthorne's story "The Great Stone Face" begins with observation of the Great Stone Face carved upon a mountain. Many wanted to be seen as the incarnation of the Great Stone Face. One person who never wished to be what he was not simply went about his work, quietly affecting the people around him. One day when people gathered around him near the end of his life, they looked upon him only to find the image of the Great Stone Face reflected in his countenance.

Standing in line waiting to pay respects to the provost's family, I recalled the Hawthorne story, thinking of one more image of a great human face. The power of service and responsibility, of doing one's job, offers meaning to those who remain to witness a life of "costly grace" (Bonhoeffer, *The Cost of Discipleship* 45–60) and "discipleship" (61–114). The story of the faith with an interpretive key of responsibility does not lessen the reality of a sudden death, the authenticity of our feeling of pain and injustice, the starkness of the sense that "this is not right." The grace of a responsible life lived within the story of the faith reveals the power of "costly grace," not in the abstract, but in life embedded in a story of faith consisting of service and responsibility to the Other. Bonhoeffer's metaphors of costly grace and discipleship do not shield us from tragic moments but return us to a story capable of framing meaning for a family and for a campus community—framing a faith story of service and responsibility.

Bonhoeffer understood that interpretative action cannot deny reality but must offer a story that contends with evil, oppression of the Other, and unearned privilege for oneself. The battle Bonhoeffer waged (interpretive action) is too often associated with the evil of Hitler alone, yet the lasting power of Bonhoeffer's interpretive key of responsibility is capable of contending with ordinary, everyday evil. Bonhoeffer understood that within everyday evil one finds soil that nourishes the ground for larger evils that eventually contend for public acceptance.

Renate and Eberhard Bethge in the introduction to Bonhoeffer's *Fiction from Prison* describe the interpretive story line of Bonhoeffer's writing and life as the courage to discern evil in the everyday, not just in "significant" public questions and events.

> But Bonhoeffer was also convinced that the basis for all really great evil was already to be found in banal evils, and that the two cannot be separated. "I detest

> such behavior. Much evil, much unhappiness will come from it in our country," he has the major in the novel say about the forester's assistant, the representative of "banal" evil. Again he writes: "These tormentors of men that you find everywhere nowadays, in schools, in offices, in the military. One must engage in battle against them, in pitiless, ruthless battle." And a little later: "Many right-minded people of our class have acquired the habit of smiling about these petty tyrants and of regarding as fools those who have declared total war on them. But smiling about them is as foolish and irresponsible as smiling about the tiny size of bacteria." (9–10)

Bonhoeffer took the story of the faith within a call to costly grace and discipleship into the historical situation before him, engaging the banality of evil in everyday life.

Bonhoeffer questioned and countered the lure of destructive stories that avoid meeting the historical moment. Like Viktor Frankl, a holocaust survivor, stated, our final freedom is the attitude we take as we meet the inevitable (*Man's Search for Meaning* 178–79). Even when there is no hope, there is a call of responsible action framing a life within direction that keeps meaning alive. The responsible action is finally the "*stand we take* toward a fate we can no longer change" (Frankl, *Psychotherapy and Existentialism* 15).

Bonhoeffer's story is nonutopian. There is no end game where responsibility and cost to the person of faith ceases; a story-guided faith centered on responsibility keeps the feet of the person of faith on solid ground, situated away from both a rigidified story and a relativistic and an objectivistic understanding of the present historical moment. Bonhoeffer's interpretive key of responsibility begins with a story of the faith and attends to the uniqueness of persons and historical situation, resulting in responsible action—action that does not, however, preclude the possibility of pain. Bonhoeffer points to a communicative story that requires tenacious patience, gritty optimism, and a realistic sense of the demands of service for God's people.

Bonhoeffer's faith story, with an interpretive key of responsibility, works with a "horizon of possibilities" (Gadamer, *Truth and Method* 302), a set of parameters, without dictating a singular perspective or worldview. The parameters provide the necessary interpretive keys to avoid relativistic responses to changing contexts, while permitting a nimble responsiveness to the historical situation. As Gadamer suggests, a horizon of possibilities offers the opportunity for both wrong and multiple "right" interpretations. Multiple insights within the horizon of possibilities enrich us with movement outside the horizon of possibilities of the taken-for-granted set of assumptions. The horizon of a given story offers ground, a sense of a communicative home from which one meets the world before us.

Story as Communicative Home

Bonhoeffer's communication began within a story that provided a communicative home for his engagement with difference, a "world come of age." The Christocentric story of the faith was Bonhoeffer's communicative home, from which he met a world come of age. Bonhoeffer's story embraces the importance of responsibility and service, unlike common religious life within the German churches at that time (Bonhoeffer, "Our Way According to the Testimony of Scripture" 170).

Bonhoeffer's story of responsibility lived within an ongoing engagement with new ideas and change, offering texture, not blind legalism. Bonhoeffer begins with a textured understanding of story that results from a primary story meeting other story remnants (e.g., family and intellectual life) that suggest responsibility. Bonhoeffer's story finds increasing texture as the particulars of the historical moment meet the story of the faith. He meets the demands of reality before him, rejecting the impulse to hide within the confines of abstract theory and ideas. Finally, Bonhoeffer's story embraces the texture of learning through engagement with the Other. Bonhoeffer's story of faithful responsibility begins with the story of the faith only to find increasing texture via education and engagement tested in the historical situation and in encounter with others.

In a postmodern culture, there is no one guiding story that all can agree upon. This does not suggest, however, that one forego bringing a story to such a moment. The communicative genius of Bonhoeffer is his textured story of conviction connected to the story of responsibility and service engaged in a historical moment of differing perspectives and story standpoints. Bonhoeffer understood the power of competing stories as he engaged in struggle against Nazi domination. He understood the necessity of questioning problematic stories from a faith perspective. Bonhoeffer's textured story of conviction, situated with a call for responsibility, shapes his understanding of the faith story.

To recognize the importance of story does not require embracing a hegemonic metanarrative; an emphasis on story acknowledges the presence of both good and bad stories, in which embedded agents meet the given and offer change in the public arena. An emphasis on story recognizes that we cannot agree uniformly on what constitutes a good life; there are multiple stories vying for the chance to offer definition—hate groups, self-help individualistic pop therapies, blind greed and consumption, and the counter stories of faith and responsibility.

Privileging the notion of story in this historical moment assumes the confoundedness of the notion of story in an era without agreement on a universal story, a common communicative background agreement to guide discourse between persons. The inability to agree upon one story or a limited number of stories leaves little guidance except one's own insight. In postmodernity, we weave a story about fragmentation and difference—providing, ironically, a sense of coherence about a story that engages disruption and fragmentation.

This work considers times of narrative contention as moments for story construction, finding together textured story understanding. An ordinary understanding of "story" includes commonplace elements, such as context (historical situation), plot (direction), main characters (embedded agents), and events that capture and maintain our attention (communicative practices). This modest understanding of story stresses the importance of a communicative account larger than an isolated, self-driven perception centered upon an imperial self as expressed in Philip Reiff's *The Triumph of the Therapeutic: Uses of Faith after Freud* and Richard Sennett's *The Fall of Public Man* and *Authority.* The "self" is necessary, but insufficient as the final arbiter of meaning.

Paul Ricoeur suggests that a narrative organizes and provides coherence situated within historicity. Time/historicity moves a story from narcissism, simply telling, to the possibility of story embodied in life and time. Time embodies simultaneously the past (memory), the future (expectation), and the present (attention). This three-fold view of time that Ricoeur adapted from Augustine rests not in chronology, but in situatedness within time. A past event is a present event when it continues to shape decision making and discourse. Ricoeur addresses narrative as organized time with characters, events, and plot and describes Bonhoeffer's story of the faith.

Maria von Wedemeyer published the following from Dietrich Bonhoeffer's last letter, written to her near Christmas 1944, vividly reminding us of Bonhoeffer's engagement with time and story in a particular historical moment.

> It is as though in solitude the soul develops senses which we hardly know in everyday life. Therefore I have not felt lonely or abandoned for one moment. You, the parents, all of you, the friends and students of mine at the front, all

> are constantly present to me. Your prayers and good thoughts, words from the Bible, discussions long past, pieces of music, and books,—[all these] gain life and reality as never before. It is a great invisible sphere in which one lives and in whose reality there is no doubt.
>
> [. . .] Therefore you must not think that I am unhappy. What is happiness and unhappiness? It depends so little on the circumstances; [. . .] (*Letters and Papers from Prison* 419)

At the end of his life, Bonhoeffer reminded us of the power of story—of main characters in life in which attentiveness and responsiveness to the historical moment invite new insight, revelation, and creative application. Bonhoeffer understood that the story we take to the historical moment shapes our response to a given context.

We stand within a story, not atop or outside a story; it is our standing within a story that makes time understandable in relation to events within the story, whether the story of a family, church, or Bonhoeffer's imprisonment. Situated within a given story as within a given historical situation, a communicative agent responds to both stories and the historical moment that situates and embeds us. Heidegger suggests that language is the "house of being" (217–18). This work assumes that story, narration, is the first human home. Language may be the house of being, but story is the home of the person. It takes a story to move a house to a home; unless we narrate our lives, we miss the interpretive meaning and learning that emerge from communicative practices understood in time and organized within a sense of plot and direction. Heidegger's metaphor of language as the house of Being misses a sense of home that story provides, a communicative background that frames interpretation of communicative foreground issues.

Bonhoeffer's story weaves hope and disappointment (Arnett, *Dialogic Education* 113) with what Christopher Lasch called a "realistic sense of hope" (*The True and Only Heaven* 80–81). This nonutopian story accepts a determined optimism working to assist God's community without illusions about the difficulty of the task, moving us from a life of ease and comfort. Bonhoeffer finds one way after another to narrate a story of faith that attends responsibly to the demands of everyday life.

Bonhoeffer's story of Christian service incorporates the metaphors of "discipleship," "costly grace", "religionless Christianity," "a world come of age," "Christ the Center," "life together," "penultimate," and "deputyship" into a story of faith that frames a gestalt, a story greater than the sum of its constituent parts. The individual parts of this story—faith story, characters, historical situation, direction/a sense of organized plot and communicative practices/events—keep religious enthusiasms tempered by multiple commitments and contributions to a story-framed view of religious communication.

One of the founders of conflict theory, Georg Simmel, in 1904 and later, discussed how healthy relationships capable of withstanding intense conflict must possess a "web of group-affiliations" (137, 141). This work situates Bonhoeffer within a weblike set of communicative commitments—a responsive, story-formed view of communication situated within a web of constituent parts that offers a textured story of faith-guided service and responsibility. A story assists a person in the task of walking into crisis and doing what is necessary and appropriate. One finds Bonhoeffer narrating a responsible faith response to deep disappointment in the church communities' inability to offer resistance to Hitler's march into the culture and the pews.

> How can Christ become the Lord of the religionless as well? Are there religionless Christians? If religion is only a garment of Christianity—and even this garment has looked very different at different times—then what is a religionless Christianity? (*Letters and Papers from Prison* 280)

Bonhoeffer lost his life before his story matured; yet one finds a story engaged with the historical situation framed in responsible response: first, reminding the religious communicator that one is not alone, offering guidance even when the exact action is unclear; second, responding to the historical moment with responsible action in response to a given temporal moment.

One can, however, sense Bonhoeffer's ongoing story—one connected to the faith, engaged in the demands of life, and moderated by a prayer of confession that acknowledged the limits of understanding the story and the moment. Bonhoeffer lived the hermeneutic circle of his faith story—a story of a prayer of confession, connecting responsibility to prayer and then back to responsibility again.

> The prayer of the morning will determine the day. Wasted time, which we are ashamed of, temptations that beset us, weakness and listlessness in our work, disorder and indiscipline in our thinking and our relations with other people very frequently have their cause in neglect of the morning prayer. The organization and distribution of our time will be better for having been rooted in prayer. (*Life Together* 71)

Bonhoeffer's Christocentric story of responsibility began with prayer and moved into organization and action for the day, the concrete place of responsibility.

Responsibility: Meeting the Historical Moment

Bonhoeffer's story responds to the requirements of his historical situation, offering us similar insight in our own; his story connects organically with his own time. Bonhoeffer's story offers us a model unlike that of Jonah. Bonhoeffer freely returns to Germany by sea, leaving the safety of the United States, answering the call of the faith, responding to his historical moment. Without hesitation, he left the safety of the United States to fight for the soul of his country.

It is possible for persons operating from contrary philosophical convictions to agree on a general reading of the historical moment. However, agreements on the general characteristics of a historical moment do not presuppose similarity of response to the historical situation. A story situates one's response, guiding the interpreter, shaping the nature and limits of a response to the historical moment. The historical moment is not some "objective" or pure entity. The historical moment comes to light through the window of a story, whether the story is singular, an interactive composite of multiple stories, a knowing construction of a new story from various story remnants, or the act of "emotivism" (MacIntyre, *After Virtue* 11–14, 16–35), which depends upon unreflective use of various story remnants. In each case, some form of story guides response to the historical moment. When a story guides response to a given historical moment, both the story *and* the historical moment make a difference in the communicative outcome.

Bonhoeffer understood that a story-shaped life permits us to escape the singular power of the historical moment; we meet the historical moment within the guidelines of a faith story—living within the interplay of historicity and a faith story of responsibility. Bonhoeffer understood the key to temporal transcendence of the historical moment. Through the story of faith engaged with the historical moment, transcendence emerges. Such is his response to Heidegger's *Dasein.*

> If in Adam *Dasein* was violated by the form in which it actually exists *[Wiesein]*—through the encapsulation of human beings in themselves—then the solution to this problem comes as humanity reorients its gaze toward Christ. Dasein becomes free, not as if it could stand over against its being-how-it-is *[Wiesein]* as autonomous being, but in the sense of escaping from the power of the I into the power of Christ, where alone it recognizes itself in original freedom as God's creature. (*Act and Being* 150)

We cannot change the historical moment, but the story within which we meet the particulars of life makes a fundamental difference in our interpretation, understanding, and response to the historical moment. We are not at the mercy of the historical situation or Being itself. The story within which one lives and interprets the world offers the possibility of transcendence. A historical moment is a horizon containing multiple possibilities, not just one. The historical situation demands response to a given horizon but does not and cannot be understood as calling for one particular response. A story-laden faith gives us the opportunity to engage the historical moment on terms that can turn the horizon of a historical moment toward new possibilities. The story makes a difference in response and in the eventual historical moment that emerges after the meeting.

The interplay of story and historical situation with each informing the other is central to Bonhoeffer's ongoing conversation about the humanities. Bonhoeffer understood a faith story of responsibility within a humanities spirit of meeting, encountering, and reshaping as one adjusts to the historical situation and new information. He did not limit the humanities to memorization but brought the story of the humanities to the particulars of life.

> [O]ne of our tasks is to see that our contacts with other peoples and countries reach out beyond politics or commerce or snobbishness to something really educational. In that way we should be tapping a hitherto unused source for the fertilizing of our education, and at the same time carrying on an old European tradition (*Letters and Papers from Prison* 231).

Bonhoeffer understood that the humanities in story form require engagement with the historical moment and, reciprocally, a story makes a difference in the outcome of a given set of historical demands.

The humanities, understood as living story, can engage and change historical moments. Bonhoeffer would reject a "great books" tradition based in abstract reification of the good. He would insist that great books must continue to meet the historical situation, offering hermeneutic beginnings of new insights, opening new possibilities. Ideas were alive for Bonhoeffer; ideas were not items for collection and our amusement, but for propelling action. Neil Postman's title, *Amusing Ourselves to Death,* suggests an obsession unresponsive to the concerns of the historical moment. Studying the humanities without connection to the needs of a people would permit Bonhoeffer to use the phrase "amusing ourselves to death." Small evils can fester into serious issues as one memorizes ideas unconnected to the particular needs of a people at a particular time. Bonhoeffer understood the connection of a story-laden life to new historical realities as a responsibility that results in the creation of new stories. Engagement with the historical moment expands our story options. If a given story version of the humanities or any story fails to meet the particulars of a given time, that story risks anachronistic status—being out of place and out of time. Story-laden encounter illuminates options not yet understood or considered, framing yet another story only when engaged with the historical moment.

A textured story as the home or interpretive background for making sense of communicative foreground issues shapes how we listen to voices within a given historical moment. Listening to voices embedded within a story is the key to the story-centered therapy of Robert Coles. "Good" stories empower and assist us in meeting difficult moments. In the *Spiritual Life of Children,* Coles assisted a child, Avram, in understanding prayer with comments about story.

> I remembered a prayer I once heard Dr. Martin Luther King make in Alabama—one in which he asked God to speak to him at a time of great danger, so that he would in turn have some idea of what to say to others, who were paying him the closest of heed and who were also scared and in clear danger. "Speak to us, dear God," Dr. King implored repeatedly, "so that we can hear you, and thereby ourselves." (76–77)

A good story inspires yet another story, not as a static reproduction, but as an authentic creation. Continuing story creation finds life in the space between an initial story and the needs of a particular situation. This creative story contribution lives on through the story of the work and life of Martin Luther King Jr. He moved the attention of a nation from unwillingness to address the reality of racism as he brought a Judeo-Christian story to the historical moment of racism, framing a creative story about human freedom and civil rights. This ongoing story creation through textured response of persons engaged in the historical situation is central to Gadamer's differentiation of craft from art, with the latter being ongoing story creation and the former technical competency (*Truth and Method* 95).

Just as King began with a story and left us with yet another important story, Bonhoeffer's work offers a story about engagement with a moment of narrative contention. Good stories provide temporal ground from which to meet the historical moment, keeping us from being at the mercy of the rigidity of a determined reading of the historical situation, while permitting the demands of the historical situation to continue to enhance the texture of a communicative background story.

Bonhoeffer, like King, understood that good stories counter bad stories. Stories contend for ongoing shaping of the "reading" of a given historical moment. The Nazi model of demand for a uniform metanarrative displayed evil masquerading as a story of the "good." The legacy of learning from Bonhoeffer's moment is recognition of the danger of bad stories. Today, we enter conversation about historicity with wariness about interpretive stories. Historical agreement and narrative disagreement guided Bonhoeffer and Hitler. Each understood the historical moment of German life calling for change; however, the stories that guided these two German responses to the historical situation made all the difference. Bonhoeffer's story invited human responsibility and service, while Hitler privileged the Nazi story dependent upon religious and ethnic scapegoats bearing blame for disappointment and failure of a lost war and a failing economy. The Nazi story vividly indicates that both good and bad stories must contend with one another; when bad stories reign, good stories must enter the fray to counter them. A story guides communicative action, representing both philosophical and practical consequences for the human community (Bernstein, *Beyond Objectivism and Relativism* 209). Choosing a story to follow makes all the difference; it is a map detailing the importance of given social practices and the places they must be found to ensure clarity of communicative action.

The questioning and rejecting of particular stories with other stories suggests that contrary story-laden responses offer the rhetorical alternatives while rejecting the assumption that morality rests within the goodness of an individual. Good ideas emerge from good stories, disrupting bad stories. In a postmodern world, one contends that education is a public commitment to figure out what are and what are not good stories for meeting an era of a multiplicity of stories; working to find temporal answers among competing stories is an act of responsibility.

One can view the story of the faith engaged with historical circumstances as a chance to offer another faith-based story, a story of responsibility in "a world come of age." A story keeps the notion of historicity as part of life, not the determining factor. What permits a story to engage the historical moment and what permits the historical moment to engage a story is the creative act of a storyteller. Bonhoeffer assumes the role of storyteller, offering a story figured out in existential result of living the dialectic of engaged story and responsiveness to historical particulars. The storyteller works as an embedded agent, located within and responsive to the horizon of a given story and to the historical situation.

Storyteller

Bonhoeffer, as a storyteller, began with the story of the faith, added other narrative remnants, and then responded to the historical moment and the Other, from which his own story continued to evolve. Christianity, as a storytelling faith, begins in John 1.1: "In the beginning was the Word." The story of the faith is incarnate in the living Word of Christ. The Word forms, limits, and embeds the person within the story of the faith. The Word permits discovery of "light," clarity of understanding, through the insight of the faith story: "*Let there be light; and there was light*" (Bonhoeffer, *Creation and Fall* 24). Light announces the beginning of creation; a good story brings the light of interpretive clarity. The Word continues creation and the story of the faith continues to shed light. Creation is central to Bonhoeffer's story, tied to the Word; the story of the faith is the fulcrum point for a story of ongoing creation, light, and a call to responsibility.

A storyteller does *phronesis,* engaging in practical wisdom. Linking the notion of story and historical moment through the role of storyteller, an embedded agent doing *phronesis* recognizes the importance of constructing new stories and offering texture to the old as a by-product of responsiveness to the historical moment.

Connecting the story of the faith to the historical moment does not occur miraculously; such a union requires an agent embedded within the story of the faith and the historical situation. Bonhoeffer, as an embedded agent—embedded in the historical moment of Nazi evil and embedded within a textured story of the faith—avoided the extremes of emotivism and ideological reification. An embedded agent respects the horizon of a given textured story, permitting guidance without relativistic application or historical command. A storyteller engages the historical moment with knowledge of the possibilities for error in application of a given story, rejecting too much flexibility as well as historical rigidity. A storyteller respects the horizon of the story and in the act of *phronesis* engages the historical situation.

Respecting the Horizon of the Text

Gadamer offers insight into a respectful way to engage a text, showing deference to the "horizon of significance" (*Truth and Method* 302–7) of a text or story. Bonhoeffer worked respectfully with a text, the story of the faith. While respectfully engaging the Word, he did not fall prey to legalism or reification of the text. Bonhoeffer understood that the story of the faith works within a horizon of significance, an intentionally fuzzy definition that permits multiple right interpretations while recognizing the existence of incorrect interpretations.

Respect for the horizon of a text engages part of a text, knowing fully well that other possibilities go unheeded and unseen, recognizing that our interpretation depends upon the question or questions we take to the horizon of the text. Without respect for the horizon of significance of a text, one can seek one answer from a text or one can use one's own voice to obscure an interpretation. A horizon of significance does not imply a canon of interpretation or a set standard; it is not objective, nor is the horizon a mere subjective call of what one wants to see in a given text. To use Bonhoeffer's language, the horizon of significance rests "in between" an objective and a purely subjective reading.

The notion of a "horizon of significance" is another intentional form of fuzzy clarity; such ambiguity lives between the extremes of too much interpretive freedom and too much restraint. A dialectical reading of the term "horizon of significance" suggests creative discovery and restraint as descriptive of Bonhoeffer's way of encountering ideas.

Knowledge of hermeneutics and use of interpretive insight typify Bonhoeffer's scholarship. He was conversant with work in phenomenology and hermeneutics, from Schleiermacher to Dilthey to Heidegger and, of course, the work of Barth and Bultmann. He used multiple story remnants to frame a story of the faith responsive to the particular demands of the historical moment, tested in action, not just in abstract academic debate. Even in one of Bonhoeffer's most academic works, *Act and Being,* the connection to concrete life announces itself as he describes Heidegger's work with Dasein or "Being" connected to the importance of act. The revelation of Being announces itself in concrete acts. "Genuine transcendentalism" (Bonhoeffer, *Act and Being* 34) is a story of Being announcing itself in the concrete everyday events of life. Acts offer visibility for Being. Recognition of Being occurs in revelation through concrete acts, permitting a glimpse of Being, which for Bonhoeffer and unlike Heidegger has theological significance. Being, for Heidegger, is the a priori ontology, the essence or spirit of human possibilities. Bonhoeffer understood acts that disclose Being as offering a glimpse into the face of God. Genuine transcendence gives one a glimpse of the face of God. Nevertheless, the notion of a "horizon of significance" in no way grasps the meaning or the totality of God.

The dialectic of *Act and Being* permits "genuine transcendence," a penultimate glimpse or trace of God, the ultimate sense of Being. Genuine transcendence suggests that only in acts of life does Being manifest itself and make itself visible. Such acts permit temporal glimpses of the living Word that require flexible, careful, and humble application in action. Bonhoeffer's story points to meeting the face of God in the concrete acts of everyday life. God's face finds visibility in the concrete acts of human beings, in the deeds of genuine responsibility willing to violate laws that obscure the face of God.

Story-Guided Phronesis

Bonhoeffer's story is neither static nor relativistic. In order for a story to avoid the rigidity of ideology, it must address the needs of the historical moment. On the other hand, for a story to avoid relativism, the basic story line cannot be lost. Aristotle's notion of *phronesis* (1140b10–1141b20) underscores such a description. The flexibility required by *phronesis,* practical wisdom, works within the limits of a general story of Athenian virtues, first articulated by Homer, then detailed by Aristotle in the *Nicomachean Ethics. Phronesis,* practical wisdom, responds to the historical situation, the particulars, within the general story line of a "not fully written" story. Story guidance situates *phronesis* outside of relativistic and emotivistic responses. *Phronesis* is both story-informed (limited) and attentive to the particulars in a given situation (responsive to change).

The wedding of *phronesis* with historicity/particulars and story rejects story as an ideological entity unable to respond to changing historical circumstances and likewise rejects story as "emotivism," decision making by personal preference. Bonhoeffer points to storytelling as *phronesis* that walks dialectically between extremes of rigidity and undue fluidity. He worked from the story of the faith and recognized a change before him that he termed a "world come of age," and he used other story remnants to understand and meet his historical situation. Bonhoeffer begins with a single story of the faith, bringing additional story remnants into the story of the faith, to frame his own story about a "world come of age." Bonhoeffer learns from the church, the family, the culture, and from the life of ideas. He takes story lines, ideas, and remnants from multiple sources. His story begins with a clear foundation and then additively brings new story-laden insight to his developing story. Bonhoeffer displays how *phronesis* works within limits while creatively adding new ideas responsive to the historical moment.

The resultant interaction of story and historical situation is partially dependent upon the creative ability of the storyteller. The storyteller doing *phronesis* knows that we must choose our stories with care, attending to the particular situation, while recognizing that embedded agency still makes a difference as we engage practical wisdom that frames an appropriate story-guided response to a unique set of circumstances.

Practical wisdom moves us from the pure rationalism of idealism and from utopian demands of the historical situation to application of story within a concrete historical moment, guided by an embedded agent, a storyteller. Doing *phronesis* as a storyteller does not assume a final right answer; embedded agency makes a difference in both the story and the historical circumstances without assurance of the "correctness" of the resolution of a given struggle. The *phronesis* of the storyteller comes with no guarantee, only with risk and creative potential of engagement.

Bonhoeffer points to a storyteller doing *phronesis* "in between" (*Act and Being* 35) a faith story and the historical moment. Bonhoeffer's notion of the "in between" is a theological framing of the dialectic of the story of Christ as center and the particular situation. He understood the dialectic of limitation and openness. In his *Ethics,* flexibility and creativity of response remind us that "the question of the basis of the concrete warrant for ethical discourse still remains open. And the question, therefore, also remains open why the ethical must be understood not as a timeless principle but as being locally and temporally restricted" (276). Bonhoeffer rejected a systematic theology that leads to "inertness in real life" (*Ethics* 276). Bonhoeffer's flexibility rests with a companion commitment—a commitment to a story of faith within discipline and boundaries. He understood the possibility of commitment tied to flexibility. He rejected being "legalistic" and additionally cautioned against "the ruin by mere activism" ("On Meditation" 39). Bonhoeffer understood disciplined attentiveness to the dialectic of restraint and freedom of interpretation. The dialectic of restraint and freedom respects the story line in relationship to the particular. *Phronesis* does not work in complete freedom, but within dialectical respect for a story and the needs of the historical moment and the Other. Dialectically, an embedded agent doing *phronesis* works within the horizon of the text—both the horizon of the faith story and the horizon of the historical moment. Respect for the horizon of the text, whether story, historical particulars, or the Other, keeps *phronesis* from becoming a mere act of subjective or willful interpretation.

> Whether or not an action arises from responsibility or from cynicism is shown only by whether or not the objective guilt of the violation of the law is recognized and acknowledged, and by whether or not, precisely in this violation, the

> law is hallowed. It is in this way that the will of God is hallowed in the deed which arises from freedom. But since this is a deed which arises from freedom, and is not torn asunder in deadly conflict, in certainty and in unity with himself he can dare to hallow the law truly even by breaking it. (*Ethics* 262)

Bonhoeffer understood the notion of act as more than behavior; it includes the attitude we take into the event. Behavior itself does not define an act; such is the critique leveled against the Pharisees. Revelation breaks into the "law" calling for acts that reveal Being, the essence of the faith, not the letter of the law. Bonhoeffer's respect for the horizon of the significance of a faith story and respect for the historical moment invites a reflective action that points to a genuine glimpse of God found in our midst. This engaged faith story calls for a storyteller, a storyteller doing *phronesis* with respect for the horizon of the story and responsiveness to the historical situation. Within such a dialectic rests the possibility of temporal transcendence, revelation, and hope even in the midst of the worst of human crisis. Bonhoeffer's witness left us such a story—the possibility of revelation in the darkest of times.

3

ATTENTIVE RESPONSE

Silence, Listening, and Meeting

Jacques Ellul on the mystery of silence:

> The mystery is silence as a break in discourse, not silence in the sense of something that discourse fills up! The enigmatic, disturbing, saddening silence of the other person is an inconvenience as I wait. I expect a response, an explanation, or a statement from him. He falls silent, and I no longer know where or how to take my place in relationship to him. More precisely, I no longer know how to be as I face him. I find myself faced with a mystery which eludes me when there is a lull in the conversation. I expect words, but this silence constitutes a chasm in the word, which continues unspoken. It is unheard, but it cannot be eliminated. Thus in all sorts of ways the word is related to mystery. It engulfs us in mystery. There is a reason mythos and logos go together. (*Humiliation of the Word* 25–26)

Dietrich Bonhoeffer on silence:

> Teaching about Christ begins in silence, "Be still, for that is the absolute," wrote Kierkegaard. That has nothing to do with the silence of the mystics, who in their dumbness chatter away secretly in their soul by themselves. The silence of the Church is silence before the Word. [. . .] To speak of Christ means to keep silent; to keep silent about Christ means to speak. When the Church speaks rightly out of a proper silence, then Christ is proclaimed. (*Christ the Center* 27)

Bonhoeffer and Ellul detail meeting that honors the Other by encountering and attending to the mystery before us, beginning in the silence and listening before interrupting communicative space with one's own voice. In this moment of restraint, one opens the door to revelation and learning, hearing what one has not yet met or understood, withholding the impulse to tell and impose upon the Other prior to meeting or understanding the demands of the historical moment.

Bonhoeffer's religious discourse begins with listening, silent, attentive responsiveness to the story of the faith, the historical moment, and the possibility of revelation in the form of the temporal presence of Christ. For a postmodern reader uncomfortable with Bonhoeffer's Christocentric first principle, there is the communicative importance of listening and silence, countering the ongoing impulse to tell without genuine engagement with Otherness. Bonhoeffer listens to the story of the faith, the historical moment, and the Other, looking for a revelation or glimpse of the face of Christ offering a sense of direction for a life. Bonhoeffer's religious commitment begins with listening, a listening well underway before speaking begins. Not only does his religious framework point to the importance of communication, it points to the connection between a dialogic view of communication and revelation between persons in a given concrete moment.

Bonhoeffer points to religious communication that interprets otherwise than conventional interpersonal discourse. Generally, we assume that interpersonal possibilities begin when talk between partners commences. However, for Bonhoeffer, and perhaps the defining key of religious communication, there is one basic presupposition, an a priori assumption: the presence of a third partner, Christ. This third party is not always visible but is always present. Revelation suggests visibility, a visibility that permits persons in the exchange to glimpse the face of Christ, offering a direction for discourse and for life. Bakhtin's notion of "superaddressee" (126–27) illuminates interpersonal exchanges. The "superaddressee" is a third presence with whom conversation begins and continues; the third is present before and after an exchange between persons. The third, the presence of Christ, is the conviction, the basic presupposition that one takes into communicative encounter with the Other: meeting the Other and the historical moment in silence, listening before offering one's voice.

Bonhoeffer assumed a third party in religious communication. For most of us it is difficult to sort self-will from the Other and the Eternal Thou, the third party, in the discourse. Such attempts are fraught with error, inviting religious fanaticism. The difficulty of such listening necessitates linking listening with humility. The line between hearing what one wants to hear and hearing what emerges in revelation from the superaddressee requires caution against unquestioned assurance.

Listening with the companion of humility does not eliminate one's own voice but tempers conviction. One's own wishes color what one hears. Listening is not an objective task; it is a task of conviction tempered by humility in religious discourse. Listening includes attending to the ground of one's own position, which partially frames the hearing, and attending to the demands of the concrete moment and the Other, making listening akin to Buber's notion of the "between" (*Between Man and Man* 202–3). Listening does not discern what is actually present. Listening is interplay between the story we take to the event and the event itself. One listens for an answer emerging between one's own position and that of the Other.

Bonhoeffer's religious communication suggests attentiveness to Otherness, an Otherness that includes one's communicative partner and the unique demands of the historical moment, inviting a transcendental glimpse of Christ. This glimpse of Christ offers a reminder for humility in listening, attending to the events of this world. Christ did not come as a conquering Messiah; hopes and convictions of such a view died with the presence of a humbled Christ: "The meaning of history is found in the humiliated Christ" (Bonhoeffer, *Christ the Center* 62). A Christocentric position for Bonhoeffer offers a reminder of conviction, but not conviction alone—conviction situated within a humbled Christ. Religious communication begins with listening without forgetting one's own involvement. Our own presence in listening frames our hearing, reminding us not to confuse what is from within with assurance from God. Listening frames how we interpret; the quality of interpretation begins with listening and with the story we take to the text. Not only does Bonhoeffer begin in silence and listening; he begins with caution.

Cautionary Conviction

Dietrich Bonhoeffer countered boredom; he rejected profound ingratitude, embracing a faith story of responsibility and service. Instead of ingratitude, he lived and invited human appreciation of God's world. He began each day with dialectical interplay of conviction and the necessity of humility. Dialectally, Bonhoeffer stresses conviction countered by humility, with humility countered by the conviction of the faith story. The first principle of religious communication that separates religious communication from secular discourse is the superaddressee, the Eternal Thou (Buber, *I and Thou* 123), or in Bonhoeffer's case, Christ, who lives within communicative life.

Bonhoeffer discussed the power of listening associated with "secular education" (*Life Together* 98) aimed at assisting others. He warned: "Christians have forgotten the ministry of listening to them by Him who is Himself the great listener" (*Life Together* 99). The interpretive ground from which one listens and from which one then either invites or precludes a third party frames the difference between secular and religious communication. Bonhoeffer then quickly adds another ingredient, humility; he was ever wary of the fanatic. He cautions against "excuses for self-justification" (*Life Together* 93). Again, Bonhoeffer reminds us of both conviction of the faith and humility.

As Bonhoeffer engaged a "world come of age" (*Letters and Papers from Prison* 326–29), he listened and responded while cautious of telling. He met a "world come of age" not with relativism but with conviction situated in humility. Religious communication does not begin with "self-ownership" of ideas, but with listening, listening to the story of the faith, the historical moment, and the Other in hopes of discerning temporal answers in daily communicative social practice. The first communicative habit of religious communication rests in the dialectic of a faith story and humility that acknowledges the possibility of confusing genuine listening with self-justification. A religious communicator does not begin communication with neutrality, but with ground under the feet, with knowing interpretive bias of a "superaddressee," with humble caution that one must forever watch for one's own actions disguised as sanctioned by God, ever reminded of the pragmatic importance of humility and caution. The union of humility and caution permitted Bonhoeffer to forge a view of communication around the actions of a guest—someone not quite at home and therefore responsive to those about him or her.

A guest works with two basic assumptions: hospitality in response to the Other and a willingness to attend to the guidelines of the home owner. Bonhoeffer suggests, "The congregation is willed by God [an act of hospitality.] [. . .] There is an organic link between the congregation and the individual, brought about by gratitude" (*The Communion of Saints* 159). One begins by listening to a basic question and answer: "Whose home is this?" and the answer is simply, "God's home." One listens with the ears of a guest, not with those of the owner of the home.

Within the spirit of Bonhoeffer's work, communicative religious interpretation begins with three basic assumptions, situated within the metaphor of "guest." First, Christ is the interpretive "Center." From the existence of Christ comes the possibility of Christian discourse. A religious communicator assuming the role of guest does not act as if he or she owns someone else's house. Second, a guest does not attempt to control all that happens in a given environment. A guest is responsive to a whole "host" of items beyond the guest's own control, involving the interplay of the story of the faith, one's communicative partner, and the historical moment. Finally, the religious communicator working as a guest must question the self, recognizing the danger of imposing wishes masked under the false cloak of God. Assuming a Christocentric understanding of religious communication as a guest avoids beginning with "me," the self; the faith stance of a guest is cautious of one's own "wishful" readings. A religious communicator working as a guest accepts the dialectic of Christocentric assurance and the pragmatic necessity of caution in implementing the faith. Such a person is wary of the sin of self-imposition.

Bonhoeffer's religious communication assumes a Christocentric interpretive bias taken as a guest into the interplay of the faith story, historicity, and the Other. This communicative style accepts this world as God's home, ever wary of our desire to claim accurate discernment of action within someone else's home. Bonhoeffer never forgot whose home, whose world, he inhabited; he understood his role as a guest in the Master's home. Levinas uses the language of "hostage" (*Time and the Other* 108); we are indebted by the face of the Other that calls us into responsibility. Bonhoeffer understood this indebtedness, a gratitude that moves first to respect the home and then to assist the inhabitants. A guest is responsible for another's home out of gratitude, thankful for the generosity of the owner. Bonhoeffer reminds us, "Even routine mechanical work will be performed more patiently when it is done with the knowledge of God and His command" (*Life Together* 71). God's home is the entire world. Our task is to repair and help restore God's home, while remembering that we do not have the skill, knowledge, or interpretive wisdom of the original architect.

Bonhoeffer never forgets who owns the home and places responsibility on the guest tending the house, reminding the guest of the demands of the task. The owner does not come to rescue as deus ex machina; the guest works to assist, repair, and restore the home without expecting rescue at every wrong action. Bonhoeffer's dialectic includes knowledge that this is God's house with equal knowledge that we are responsible. We assume responsibility as we listen to an ongoing warning for a guest—to be wary of one's own skill and insight. A guest listens out of respect, understanding that one stands in the house of another, refraining from "saying much that occurs to him" (Bonhoeffer, *Life Together* 92). One listens, tempering one's own assessments, putting forth comments only after careful consideration.

Religious communication as a guest assumes an interpretative base situated within the following assumptions: 1) this is God's world, 2) we are not the center of the discourse, 3) we are responsible, and 4) implementation needs caution; we are fallible. Bonhoeffer reminds us that to "forego self-conceit and to associate with the lowly means, in all soberness and without mincing the matter, to consider oneself the greatest of sinners. This arouses all the resistance of the natural man, but also that of the self-confident Christian" (*Life Together* 96). Both the "natural man" and the "self-confident Christian" begin communication with telling. Bonhoeffer, on the other hand, begins with listening, remembering he is a guest in someone else's home, that his stay requires listening, responsibility, and caution. Religious communication embraces interpretation from the standpoint of guest, from the act of listening, with the cautioned confidence in response, and with knowledge of a dangerous impulse—the "telling" instinct. Bonhoeffer suggests an interpretive understanding of religious communication that offers guidance, not unwavering assurance, control, or possession of the truth. Bonhoeffer begins the interpretive process in communication within the dialectic of Christocentric assurance and the gratitude and caution of a guest. A guest understands the pragmatic necessity of tempering as one admits the limits of one's knowing in a new environment.

Tempering Interpretive Response

The metaphor of guest tempers conviction in Bonhoeffer's understanding of religious communication; he does not work with the self-assurance of a settler, one who by virtue of historic presence no longer functions as a guest and begins to engage unreflective social practices. The notion of guest permits a view of interpretation situated within "philosophical hermeneutics" (Gadamer, *Philosophical Hermeneutics* 18). Bonhoeffer's work fits well within the framework of German philosopher Hans Gadamer, whose *Truth and Method* cites scholars that Bonhoeffer also referenced. Clearly, Bonhoeffer understood the importance of interpretation, along with the history of and emerging contributions in phenomenology and hermeneutics. At the age of twenty-four, Bonhoeffer penned *Act and Being;* this work outlines his knowledge of phenomenology and hermeneutics, demonstrating interpretive sophistication that shaped his scholarly journey and his understanding of the communicative process.

Bonhoeffer understood "act" as a phenomenological focus of attention—act is intentional consciousness. Focus of attention, the act of intentionality, frames the object claiming attention. If one talks to another while tapping one's fingers, the focus of attention shifts from the act of conversation to the act of finger tapping. The focus of attention on a given act explains why dripping water is not an irritant until the water claims one's attention, lessening focus on other attentive possibilities. Bonhoeffer understood "Being" as a transcendental glimpse of possibilities. As we make Being visible, we make the possibilities of our humanness visible. Within the language of the Church, "act" assumes a "doing" focus of attention, and Being is a transcendental glimpse of Christ pointing to new insight and possibilities. For Bonhoeffer, phenomenology includes focus of attention and attentiveness to transcendental glimpses of the Being of Christ.

Bonhoeffer openly situated phenomenology within a presupposition of the importance of God and the Church. He placed a rhetorical spin upon phenomenological language. "The dialectic of act and being is understood theologically as the dialectic of faith and the congregation of Christ. Neither is thought without the other; each is "taken up" or "suspended" [. . .] in the other" (*Act and Being* 31). Within the language of the faith, he understood act as intentionality (phenomenological focus of attention) and Being as a transcendent glimpse of Christ. Focus of attention (act) and learning from the different, the unexpected, the transcendent, frame Bonhoeffer's interpretive understanding of communicative life.

Bonhoeffer's phenomenology frames religious communication within a focus of attention and transcendental glimpses; the former keeps ground under one's feet (the story of the faith), and the latter permits new insights, new learning, the revelation of Christ within the Church. Bonhoeffer's engagement with phenomenology reflects contemporary hermeneutic work. He publicly announced bias or "interests" that he took into the interpretive process, the bias of a Christocentric standpoint. Bonhoeffer's Christocentric interpretive bias frames communicative meeting of any text, event, conversation, or person within a focus of attention and transcendental insight. His announced bias shapes his focus of attention and his willingness to attend to the transcendent. Interpretation lives outside the world of the pure, of the objective; at best, interpretation is the dialogue of horizons, consisting of the bias we bring to a given reading and the horizon of the text or situation claiming interpretive attention.

For Bonhoeffer, religious communication assumes interpretation within a hermeneutic circle of the faith. "Our thinking, that is, the thinking of those who must go to Christ to know of God, the thinking of fallen man, has no beginning because it is a circle. We think in a circle. We feel and will in a circle. We exist in a circle" (*Creation and Fall* 14). There is no beginning, no end, in a Christocentric interpretive assumption; the start and the finish are with Christ.

Bonhoeffer acknowledges that one's heart rests with one's focus of attention. A Christocentric focus of attention shapes religious communicative engagement. Bonhoeffer does not envision transcendental glimpses of a secular Being, but transcendental glimpses of the Being of Christ. What permits Bonhoeffer's Christocentric position to meet a postmodern world is the caution he brings to conviction. Consistent with Bonhoeffer's dialectic impulse is the assumption that transcendental glimpses rest in ambiguity, finding shape through an interpretive lens functioning as a primary focus of attention, a first principle—a Christocentric engagement with the world. Bonhoeffer assumes Christ as the "ultimate" (*Ethics* 125–32) focus of attention accompanied by wariness of one's using God as a form of "self-justification." Christ is the ultimate focus of attention, and with an appropriate sense of caution Bonhoeffer models engagement with a complex and changing world, which required him to offer insight into a "world come of age" and "religionless Christianity" (*Letters and Papers from Prison* 280–82).

The religious communicator asks, "How does one assume a Christocentric position to a 'world come of age?'" Bonhoeffer's dialectical insights offer a framework for such an action. He points to interpretation that rests with a both/and, not an either/or. Bonhoeffer unites contraries; a strong faith position does not mean one cannot work with people who function with differing perspectives. Bonhoeffer manifested an earlier understanding of Sissela Bok's insights recorded in *Common Values.* A Christocentric worldview must reach multiple and diverse audiences at what Sissela Bok terms a level of "minimalist value" agreement, not necessarily a "maximalist value" agreement (9, 76) where she differentiated "maximal" and "minimal" values; the first requires complete narrative agreement, and the latter requires partial temporal agreement on specific values in specific situations. Bonhoeffer suggests a similar insight to maximal and minimal value agreement with his emphasis on the ultimate and the penultimate.

Bonhoeffer called a Christian to embrace the ultimate and the penultimate, the maximal and the minimal, simultaneously. In "On Meditation," Bonhoeffer points to a maximal demand on himself as a Christian. Bonhoeffer offers a textured answer to the question, "Why do I meditate?" "Because I am a Christian [. . .] Because I am a preacher of the Word. [. . .] Because I need a firm discipline of prayer. [. . .] Because I need help against the ungodly haste and unrest which threaten my work as a pastor" (30–31). Such statements announce maximal importance of the faith story, a commitment that drives Bonhoeffer's insights. Bonhoeffer fully embraced a Christocentric faith in a maximal fashion.

Yet, on the other hand, Bgnhoeffer understood the necessity of minimal values, reaching out to a world uncomfortable with his own faith story. In a "world come of age," language that addresses a non-Christian world needs attention. Pharisees worried Bonhoeffer; their legalism hurts the creative application of the faith in the particulars of life's demands. Bonhoeffer understood the autonomy of "earthly institutions" (*Ethics* 362). In a "world come of age," the faith story is of great importance, as is the recognition of the autonomy of persons and institutions (*Ethics* 50–51). In a postmodern world of diversity, the Christocentric worldview no longer occupies undisputed "good story" status; in a "world come of age" one invites minimalist value agreement to bring people together around basic issues, not *all* the particulars of a given story. From a minimalist perspective, one can agree on the importance of given segments of a moral story without agreeing on all the particulars central to a given moral story.

In order for a non-Christocentric reader to encounter Bonhoeffer, one must meet him on the ground of the "penultimate," a "minimalist value." A minimal value for engaging Bonhoeffer's work might be responsibility to and for others and an admiration for his courage or a profound interest in how a person of conviction can embrace a world of diversity, a "world come of age." Bonhoeffer addresses the "penultimate" within a "world come of age," calling for honest engagement with a historical moment of diversity and change.

A "maximalist laden value" (Bok 21) reading of Bonhoeffer's work requires accepting a Christocentric worldview. A minimalist reading in a "world come of age" looks for ways in which a person of conviction can meet diversity. Additionally, Bonhoeffer's emphasis on "religionless Christianity" brings the faith story to a world without "maximal" agreement on religious language and specifics.

Bonhoeffer's work suggests how a communicator can work on a "minimalist" level with effectiveness, conviction, and a willingness to meet and learn from difference in five ways. First, Bonhoeffer points to the importance of a guiding public story, a "petite narrative" (Lyotard 60). Second, he reveals the importance of knowing one's own bias in interpretation and the need to caution one's own conviction. Third, Bonhoeffer outlines the necessity of attending to and responding to the historical moment. Fourth, he directs us to the transcendent as a glimpse of insight beyond the self that keeps creativity alive. Finally, Bonhoeffer suggests the importance of faithfulness in response to the historical situation, avoiding responses nourished solely by self-protection.

Bonhoeffer frames a rhetoric of responsibility, not avoidance of the demands of the historical moment. A minimalist reading of Bonhoeffer offers a philosophical and pragmatic model of engagement with a world of difference, not out of arrogance of what one thinks is or deems to exist, or refusal to take a stand, but from moral ground. A minimalist reading of Bonhoeffer permits one to discern the face of the Other. To understand Bonhoeffer, one must engage a "world come of age," recognizing more than a home for Christians. Bonhoeffer offers a way to engage a world of difference from a position of conviction that is not provincial. Bonhoeffer points to interpretation situated in conviction, tempered by caution, and responsive to a sense of the common in a "world come of age."

The Common in a "World Come of Age"

Bonhoeffer understood Dilthey's linking of dialogue and hermeneutics within the interplay of the familiar (interests) and the alien (difference) (Bonhoeffer, *Act and Being* 43). To understand the interpretation of another there needs to be minimal common ground, a place of familiarity, a ground that makes sense to communicative partners. Minimal common agreement permits communicative partners to see difference without the bewilderment of utter chaos.

Bonhoeffer's interpretive framework of a Christocentric bias addresses a "world come of age." He understands that a person of conviction must communicate with those outside one's own narrative assumptions. In a "world come of age," one must connect with those different from oneself, not expecting the same language or the same narrative structure to guide interaction. A "world come of age" is a place of responsibility, responsibility to engage difference without falling prey to the temptation of relativism.

Yet, as one meets a "world come of age," some agreement on interpretation must guide interpretation. Ricoeur reminds us of "concordance" and "disconcordance" (*Time and Narrative* 1: 70–73) in interpretation. The latter is possible because of the memory of the former. Even in disconcordance, there is an implicit or tacit sense of the notion of the "common," making interpretation, not necessarily agreement, possible. A temporal communicative common space permits a common focus of attention that guides communicative interaction. Without some common focus of attention and a willingness to respond to an Otherness that takes us beyond ourselves, we hear only noise or our own self-reflection, resulting in communication grounded in ideologies unresponsive to the historical situation and the Other.

The "common" is the concrete context within which people find themselves at a given time. Bonhoeffer does not situate the notion of the common within a realm of the pure, but within the everyday realm of human interaction; "only statements of pure language can be completely understood [. . .] [T]he more that linguistic expressions remain linked to a concrete life context, the more important is their role in a specific dialogic relation" (Buber, *The Knowledge of Man* 164). In a "world come of age," a willingness to engage another in dialogue in the concrete moment may be the only commonplace possible between persons. A common focus of attention becomes a minimal agreement, permitting one to engage the transcendent through the radical alterity of the Other.

Levinas frames this view of transcendence in his phenomenology of ethics, suggesting that meeting of Otherness offers transcendental glimpses of insight beyond oneself. Bonhoeffer engages the Other with the possibility of transcendence—seeing the world differently through the eyes of the Other and, at times, glimpsing an unclear image of Christ, offering temporal transcendent insight. Bonhoeffer looked for a common focus of attention that permitted the transcendent to emerge during the meeting of difference in "a world come of age." Additionally, he penned "religionless Christianity," not to destroy the transcendent, but to permit the transcendent to break in occasionally from attentiveness to the concrete historical situation. In the interplay of the common and the different, Christ breaks through. The historical situation and the alterity of the Other connect the transcendent with learning, encountering the unknown or unexpected. Bonhoeffer points to the need for minimal common space, minimal agreement, minimal compatibility of presuppositions in a "world come of age" in order to meet the different, the transcendent. The dialectic of his work remains at the forefront of the unity of the common and the particularities of a world come of age. Such dialectic guidance permitted Bonhoeffer to discern the face of the Other, without imposing his image upon the Other. Transcendence fails in the seeing of one's own face, the hearing of one's own voice.

Discerning the Face

Bonhoeffer warned of engagement with difference that begins with inappropriate confidence that assumes God sides only with our opinions and our desires. Bonhoeffer would applaud the insight of a longshoreman, Eric Hoffer, who questioned the crusade mentality of a "true believer" (87). True belief for Bonhoeffer was dialectical, not singular in certainty. Christ is "pro me" (Bonhoeffer, *Christ the Center* 43), as long as we admit difficulty in discerning who Christ is in a given situation. Caution, not conviction, guides the question of "who Christ really is, for us today" (Bonhoeffer qtd. in Bethge, *Dietrich Bonhoeffer* 767). God is not a partisan politician, but the Lord of all. Putting a spin on the language of Hoffer within Bonhoeffer's tradition, a genuine true believer works dialectically, not single-mindedly.

Bonhoeffer's commitment to Christ embraces the dialectic of conviction and humility. Bonhoeffer's appreciation of the Old Testament made him wary of undue confidence related to Christ; he understood the inherent danger of striving to see the face of Christ. We cannot possess the image of Christ; Bonhoeffer's dialectic of true belief rests in a glimpse accompanied by even more lack of clarity. It is this dialectic of conviction and humility that permits Bonhoeffer's Christocentric story to reach beyond a provincial gathering of what Hoffer called "true believers." As stated above, a person interested in moral questions need not agree with Bonhoeffer's premises at a "maximal" level. Bonhoeffer's story at a "minimal" level points to courage in the face of Nazi tyranny, courage in resisting the temptation to possess the face of God, courage to avoid manipulating a tale about God that mirrors one's own desires.

The task of this project is to learn from Bonhoeffer while not excluding the nonreligious reader interested in other persons of courage, persons who addressed the existential demands of their historic moment from a narrative standpoint. For instance, there are dramatic differences, yet fundamental similarities, between Bonhoeffer and Albert Camus. Bonhoeffer lived within the narrative of the faith. Albert Camus lived a story of existential courage in the midst of the absurd—both fought Hitler and the Third Reich with conviction and integrity. Both men are worthy of attention from readers committed to meeting oppression with courage.

Bonhoeffer gave his life in opposition to Hitler and the terror of Nazi power. Bonhoeffer's kinship with Camus, who was critical of the Church, is that both questioned escape through "other-worldliness or pious inwardness" (Dumas 263). Both men met life on its own terms; they met the needs of the historic moment, not within abstract ideals, but guided by commitments to action. The metaphor of "stranger" not only adorns the cover of one of his existential novels, *L'Etranger,* but fits Camus' solitary effort to make sense of a confusing world. Bonhoeffer had similar concerns, but he turned to notions of "discipleship" and "costly grace." Both men recognized and responded to a call for responsibility, not expecting rescue from any outside power.

Camus would counter Bonhoeffer's theology, but he would applaud his spirit and courage capable of opposing the Nazis. Camus, as a journalist, writer, and member of the French underground, and Bonhoeffer, as a professor, pastor, and participant in an assassination attempt on Hitler, met a world of moral cgmplexity that required decisions and actions without guarantee.

Bonhoeffer understood that a glimpse of Christ in the marketplace might rest more in the face of Camus than in the formal Church. For this work to honor Bonhoeffer, it must render honor to persons such as Camus. To make overt space in this project for persons like Camus, persons with different moral positions who engage the historical situation with courage and the hope of assisting the Other, rests within the spirit and horizon of Bonhoeffer's understanding of how a Christian must function in a "world come of age." Exclusion would violate the invitational nature of Bonhoeffer's courage and his caution about feeling that one knows or possesses the face of Christ.

The suggestion of this work is that Bonhoeffer and Camus together remind us of minimal common space: resistance of evil requires courage that emerges in the resistance. Bonhoeffer would add one additional ingredient—confession. As he worked with conviction and courage, he confessed out of fear of conviction without question and with constant reminders of first principles. This minimalist understanding of values engaged with persons of difference helps connect the notion of the common, difference, and confession in an era of narrative and virtue dispute. Bonhoeffer frames confession as central for the person, providing a temporal common space between persons in the meeting of difference.

Confession as the Common

The interpretive importance of the "common" frames the practical value of confession as a minimalist temporal communicative space between persons in a "world come of age." The act of confession permits a minimal common space, minimal common knowledge, and minimal admission of bias to make public entrance into the conversation. Confession invites dialogic minimal common ground in a postmodern era of narrative and virtue contention. The act of confession is the common space where communicative partners acknowledge the importance of sharing "interests" that guide their communication. Confession acts as a communicative "penultimate" in a postmodern culture, offering minimal common ground between persons.

The notion of dialectic underscores Bonhoeffer's framing of confession; Bonhoeffer understands the person as a sinning saint, another reason he cannot take his own religiosity too seriously, which is why his project cannot discount the power and significance of a Camus. This dialectical understanding of the person makes confession a pragmatic necessity, a temporal place of admission, and a reminder to reconnect to the faith story. To deny sin "ends in idolatry" (Bonhoeffer, *Creation and Fall* 124). Confession makes use of sin, pointing a person back to the story, finding gratitude in the midst of temptation—"no temptation is more terrible than to be without temptation" (Bonhoeffer, *Creation and Fall* 126). Experiencing no temptation invites idolatry about one's own goodness. In a complex world, it is difficult to act without doing harm; confession keeps us aware of sin, the limits of human goodness.

Confession is a dialectical concept unifying contraries that advance humanness within a Christian perspective; we live with the possibility of good, evil, constructive action, and human sin. Confession articulates a wrong action that violates the story of the faith, providing a necessary and pragmatic way to reconnect persons to the faith narrative and one another. Confession uses "wrongs" to make "good" visible. As a pastor and theologian, Bonhoeffer understood confession within the narrative of a Christocentric faith. Violation of social practices encouraged by a faith narrative invites sin, calling for confession that reconnects one to the faith story and to others. The desire to eliminate all sin results in an irony—the lessening need for confession, which in turn lessens opportunity to reconnect to the story of the faith.

Acknowledged sin permits confession to turn error into reminder and reconnection. Confession works within the penultimate, recognizing that seeking the "pure" eclipses opportunity to see ways to reconnect to the faith story and to others. Confession lives within the metaphors of the good, the broken, and the hurt, not within the glory of a life with all the answers. Buber recognized that the call of life rests in the inevitability of walking in the mud of everyday life and human relationships. Buber said:

> [T]he human creature! That creature means a mixture. Books are pure, men are mixed; books are spirit and word, pure spirit and purified word; men are

> made up of prattle and silence, and their silence is not that of animals but of men. Out of the human silence behind the prattle, the spirit whispers to you. [. . .] I do, indeed, close my door at times and surrender myself to a book, but only because I can open the door again and see a human begin looking at me. ("Books and Men" 61)

Bonhoeffer suggests a similar walk in the knowledge of sin, avoiding "hardening and obduracy of the heart in sin" that results in "hypocritical piety" (*Creation and Fall* 124). Confession walks in the mud of everyday humanness of a people of faith willing to work for the good, offering up to God alone the task of the pure.

Confession corrects action contrary to the story of the faith, providing a deep sense of irony: temptation and sin provide a reason for reconnection to the faith story. Sin makes confession possible and confession makes guidance by a faith story possible. Temptation and sin permit confession, which takes an unknowing or taken-for-granted faith into the act of confession, permitting the discovery of story-laden clarity once again.

Bonhoeffer's confession moves one to reconnection and change, not to simple recognition of error; he rejected routine use of psychological language and recognized the danger and the sin of melancholy. Bonhoeffer understood unconfessed sin as the nurturing source of melancholy. Unconfessed sin is not the only cause of melancholy, but Bonhoeffer understood nonconfession as one major reason for the emergence of melancholy. Each of us knows someone hiding a particular secret or pain, unable to fight the trap of melancholy. Genuine confession reminds a person of virtues within a narrative system, gpening the opportunity for relief, change, and reconnection to a guiding narrative.

Melancholy finds its way into a life when one ignores the dialectical nature of working with others—trying to be "pure" without admission of sin that reconnects one to the narrative of the faith. Melancholy fosters failure to admit the sin of "wrong" social practices, which would move us from sin to narrative reminder, permitting reconnection, redirection, and the potential for change. Without sin, the metaphor of the "self" makes more sense as a final arbiter of meaning. With limits and sin, human beings require good stories to guide action. The ongoing communicative task requires discerning good stories for new historical moments and the appropriate form of implementation of such stories in a given historical situation.

We cannot be perfect even if we devote all attention to such a task. Philosophically and practically, there is a problem with the goal of perfection. First, our focus of attention is on ourselves. We invite narcissism. Second, we miss opportunities for growth and insight, which often come from mistakes and failure. Indeed, being wherein "But no perfection is so absolute, / That some impurity doth not pollute" (Shakespeare, *Luc* 853–54) is possible and such a goal is not laudable. Goodness is only possible as a by-product of following a narrative structure, making mistakes that move one off course, and then reconnecting to the narrative with greater insight and depth. Confession rehabilitates sin, taking acts of violation and recasting them as reminders of a narrative life. Bonhoeffer understood the dialectic of the inevitability of sin and permitting sin "to come to light under all circumstances" (*Spiritual Care* 55).

Sin is problematic, yet necessary, prompting confession that promotes a story-laden reminder. Sin understood within a faith story finds correction from guidelines, not inflexible rules. A faith story guides without dictating. Such guidance has ambiguity and room for error, mistake, and sin. This understanding of faith story, sin, and confession is akin to Buber's description of the "narrow ridge" (*The Knowledge of Man* 110). The only way to "right" oneself on the narrow ridge is to admit falling off, learn from the event, and enact correction. The metaphor of the narrow ridge assumes falling. The goal is not safety of never falling, but having something to get back on, having a direction. Confession, for Bonhoeffer, rests in a dialectical recognition that sin violates the story of the faith, but without sin, the story of the faith can go unattended. The act of sin is both problematic and essential for keeping the story of the faith known, understood, and vital in the marketplace of everyday decisions. Bonhoeffer worked to distinguish genuine acts of confession from false posturing.

Confession and Learning

Parents often state to young children the importance of honesty, calling their children to confess mistakes. A parental admonition is for the child to have the courage to confess errors and for the parent to model how to correct mistakes. Bonhoeffer understood this simple wisdom and modeled the practice. He adds texture and complexity to the importance of confession. Confession keeps alive a guiding story responsive to the historical situation. Bonhoeffer understood confession as a "breaking through to certainty" (*Life Together* 115). In faith terms, one breaks through the certainty of sin, re-engaging the certainty of the faith story. In "a world come of age," confession breaks through to the awareness of capacity for mistakes, sin, and evil by re-engaging a constructive story-laden alternative. For Bonhoeffer, confession "is the final breakthrough to fellowship" (*Life Together* 110). Confession moves us from pretension to contact with one another within a story-laden framework.

Bonhoeffer situates certainty within a dialectic—the certainty of the faith and the uncertainty of one's knowledge of the faith. Appearance of piety, seeming correctness under all circumstances, masks the power of confession, protecting a false image of righteousness. Confession keeps attention on learning, not desired appearance. Confession calls us to learning and change, not to idealized self-constructions. Confession seeks to right communicative action when behavior is not congruent with stated ideas and beliefs. Confession reminds and informs self and other of one's own position, beginning a chain of reframing action when words and behavior cease to conform to a given story and the demands of the historical moment.

Bonhoeffer's notion of confession permits one to learn from failed social practices as we discern appropriate virtue structures for a complex and diverse world. Confession opens the door to discerning and admitting error that permits negotiation of unknown territory, correcting inappropriate social practices. In a world without an agreed-upon virtue structure, confession assists our learning from the other and our own clarity of position as we meet and serve in a "world come of age." Confession understood in "a world come of age" offers a three-fold pragmatic set of opportunities for learning. First, hearing one's own confession as one tells another permits one to understand one's own stance, increasing self-knowledge and inviting learning. This form of learning guides much of "talk therapy." Hearing one's own position permits one to get it on the table for consideration, moving from unreflective practice. Second, hearing another's confessiof invites learning from the Other. Third, attending to confessed mistakes made by self and Other invites reconnection to the faith narrative and responsiveness to a given unique moment.

A postmodern age, defined by a lack of virtue agreement, inadvertently undercuts one's knowledge of oneself, the Other, and social practices, unless one can keep such knowledge alive in discourse (confession) that redirects action. Confession is a rhetorical key to meeting a world of confusion—lessening uncertainty about self, Other, and social practices, which are key to virtue structures. Confession connects one to the historical situation, to ongoing efforts at learning, to a Christocentric prayer life, and permits one to meet a world come of age from a story of faithful conviction tempered with humility of application.

Beyond Self and Provinciality

Confession moves a person beyond self-focus, reconnecting the person to a faith story, to the historical moment, and to others, pushing the communicator beyond provinciality. Bonhoeffer's dialectic of a Christocentric position and his desire to address a "world come of age" offers theological and secular extension beyond the self. The faith story moves Bonhoeffer to meet a secular world with language attentive to a world outside of religious presuppositions. Bonhoeffer confesses knowledge of a "world come of age" that calls for engagement beyond "my kind," those in agreement with one's own religious presuppositions. Bonhoeffer suggests that

> The world that has come of age is more godless, and perhaps for that very reason nearer to God, than the world before its coming of age. Forgive me for still putting it all so terribly clumsily and badly, as I really feel I am. But perhaps you will help me again to make things clearer and simpler, even if only by my being able to talk about them with you and to hear, so to speak, keep asking and answering. (*Letters and Papers from Prison* 362)

Bonhoeffer's commitment to a faith background permitted him to engage foreground change within the dialectic of conviction and humility. Bonhoeffer had such a certainty of faith permitting him to embrace the uncertainty of a changing world, and he understood that the faith must address this changing world, a "world come of age." Bonhoeffer understood his Christian responsibility to meet and attend to this historical moment.

Confession in a "world come of age" does not suggest purity or even the right answer, just a chance to engage another, to make sense out of difference in a moment of temporal agreement. Confession is the communicative act situated in the good, not the pure. Purity does not require confession. Caution about the pitfalls of feigned purity in expression of the faith permitted Bonhoeffer to ward off a major temptation, the dark side of persons of conviction—forcing others to believe as "I" do. Communication that lives as imposed conviction is antithetical to Bonhoeffer's invitational spirit: "I felt that it was wrong to force religion down his throat just then. Incidentally, Jesus didn't try to convert the two thieves on the cross; one of them turned to him" (*Letters and Papers from Prison* 199). Confession in a "world come of age" takes us beyond provinciality, beyond a crusading mentality, reminding us of the importance of engagement with God's world on terms before us, not the terms we demand.

Bonhoeffer's discussion of the ultimate and the penultimate provides a way to discuss first principles—the sufficient (focus on Christ)—and related principles—the necessary (confession) (*Ethics* 133). In postmodern communication, the act of confession may be the only commonplace between persons from quite different standpoints. It is not the content of confession, but the act itself that becomes a communicative penultimate commonplace.

Confession understood in a postmodern world becomes a communicative penultimate working within the dialectic of faith commitment coupled with knowledge that provinciality of the faith is insufficient in meeting a "world come of age." In the dialectical spirit of Bonhoeffer, reaching out to a world of difference does not diminish one's own commitment to a Christocentric story; one seeks to meet God's world, not one's own wish demand. Bonhoeffer did not ask God's entire world to conform to his wishes. Bonhoeffer understands the danger and evil of a "wish dream" (*Life Together* 26). We cannot wish ourselves into a perfect sense of community. Bonhoeffer's call to confession speaks to a Buddhist colleague, a Marxist friend, and an atheist interlocutor. As a Christocentric religious communicator reaches out to another, he or she need not lose a Christocentric conviction but must additionally attend to a "world come of age" that takes us beyond self and provinciality.

Beyond Self-Disclosure and the Taken-for-Granted

As one connects confession to a "world come of age," the temptation is to equate confession with self-disclosure. To do so misses the vital connection of confession with a world outside the self, beyond provinciality. Perhaps this is one of the reasons Bonhoeffer was so wary of psychological language. "There is the limit for psychology [. . .] for the personal being of the other is a moral reality which cannot be grasped by psychology" (*The Communion of Saints* 35). Moral reality lives not in the self, but within a story-laden framework. Disclosure shares the self. Confession, on the other hand, discloses a story-laden standpoint. Confession works with story-laden content, assuming the power of ideas, the content of a story. Self-disclosure opens the self; confession offers story guidelines that shape a sense of identity knowable to communicative partners.

Confession does not offer answers in "a world come of age"; the act of confession permits a common beginning for communicative discernment. Confession assists clarity—in one's own ideas and in understanding the Other. The confessional act provides clarity for self and Other; contrary to self-therapy, it connects the person to a story, finding guidelines beyond the construct of the self.

In an era of constant change, in a "world come of age," one cannot predict all possibilities; the Other, the historical situation, and even one's own actions, at times, lack identifiable pattern and consistency. Confession permits reconnection with a story that provides a flexible pattern or guideline from which to make sense of ongoing change. Take, for instance, a common occurrence within the life of a first-year undergraduate college student—who as a high school student communicated easily with known friends in a school system in which all worked and played together in elementary, junior high, and high school. Yet, in the first weeks of college, miscommunication occurs. Those that adapt to the new college environment learn to think before they speak—trying to understand the Other, the new situation, and how their own family story offers navigational advice in the new situation. The successful student tenders thoughtful messages considerate of the standpoint of the listener and a new context. If the student is unable or unwilling to deliberate before speaking, the student must search for people just like the "old" friends, missing college as a time of social learning. Without careful communication, a new college student quickly discovers self-disclosed information used as a weapon by someone without the same commitment to loyalty or privacy assumed with high school friends. The newness, the strangeness, of a novel communicative setting needs to engage a simple confession: I have much to learn in a "world come of age," in a community of contrasting expectations and differing communicative standpoints.

The unknown or different makes taken-for-granted communication patterns problematic. A communicator in an age of diversity of standpoints and ideas begins with four basic assumptions that work as confession in action, moving unreflective self-disclosure and taken-for-granted commonality to knowing engagement with a "world come of age." First, the Other does not necessarily work from the same communicative standpoint. Second, communicators need to understand differing communicative standpoints, even positions anathema to their own. Third, errors, mistakes, and problems emerge when communicators encounter unknown standpoints with unreflective taken-for-granted assumptions. Fourth, one needs private and public criteria for evaluation of diverse standpoints. One needs to encounter difference on a public level and at the same time keep one's private guiding story. We learn from the different, not from the taken-for-granted.

Bonhoeffer's struggle with the Nazis adds a complex texture to our understanding of confession. He understood the necessity of being "wise as serpents and innocent as doves" (*New Oxford Annotated Bible,* Matt. 10.16). Confession is not simply a technique, an act of self-disclosure, an act of self-therapy, or unreflective expression that falsely takes commonality for granted. Confession is a minimalist communicative keystone that reconnects action to a faith-centered story, the Other, and the historical demands before one in an age of diversity, difference, and change. Confession is not self-disclosure, but story-centered disclosure of a "community of memory" (Bellah et al. 152–58, 333) that responds to a broken narrative, permitting the act of confession to walk into the breach, offering healing, redirection, and reconnection. Standpoints matter, and confessed standpoints remind persons of narratives that situate our lives.

4
THE PERSON AS STORY-FORMED

Paul Ricoeur on persons:

> By placing its main emphasis not on the *who* of the one speaking but on the *what* of the particulars about which one speaks, including person, the entire analysis of the person as a basic particular is placed on the public level of locating things in relation to the spatiotemporal schema that contains it. (*Oneself as Another* 32)

Dietrich Bonhoeffer on the person:

> [W]e must maintain that the centre of the Christian concept of the person lies elsewhere than in idealism. The attempt of the former to reach the concrete reality of the other was bound to fail, for we have to do with two spheres which are qualitatively different. On the idealist path, from the idea of the universal we come at best to the possibility of the other. The other is a postulate, just as the entire conception of the historical element in Christianity is a postulate for idealism (Christology). On the epistemological and metaphysical path one never reaches the reality of the other. Reality cannot be derived, it is simply given, to be acknowledged, to be rejected, but never to be established by proofs, and it is given only to the moral persona as a whole. The Christian concept of the person rightly sees itself as a view of the whole person. Every idealist construct uses the concept of the mind in order to cut through the living entirety of the person. The Christian concept affirms the whole concrete person, body and soul, in its difference from all other beings in its moral relevance. (*The Communion of Saints* 35)

Ricoeur and Bonhoeffer suggest the difference between an individual and a person. The former is the "who," and the latter, the notion of person, is "what," the story-laden content that shapes and gives identity. It is the "what" of a story that moves a human being from individual encounter with life to situated, story-laden meeting of life as a person, guided by story-laden content, "what." The individual is a "who"; a person, however, lives from a story that gives interpretive power, a sense of "what," story-laden content, to communicative life. Bonhoeffer pointed to an important distinction between the notion of the individual and the construct of the person. The person has a home within a story. An individual works independently. A person finds identity within the story of faith. Confession performs the role of situating a person within a story, continually reconnecting and reminding the person of an ongoing story that shapes the identity. The individual is a free agent. The person is an embedded agent—an agent that must navigate freedom and story-laden restraint.

The previous chapter cited connections and differences between the work of Bonhoeffer and Camus, calling for engagement with each author. Their differences illuminate the distinction between individual and person. Camus' existential writing points to the loneliness and the responsibility of the individual in meeting the absurd. Bonhoeffer's life and writing points to the meaningfulness of a Christian story within which an individual becomes a person, guided in acts of responsibility. Neither writer lessens the demands of life on the human being, but they engage those demands differently—with Camus calling for individual courage in the midst of absurdity and Bonhoeffer situating the person within an interpretive faith story that offers meaning in the midst of loneliness and the demands of life. Bonhoeffer does not begin with the individual, but with the story of the faith, which invites one into Christian personhood. A person is an embedded agent—embedded within a story that offers guidance and degrees of freedom. The story functions as a horizon of significance, offering personhood status as one remains within the expansive, not totally definable boundaries of a given horizon. Once one walks outside those boundaries, one moves to the status of individual, losing a sense of personhood, embracing Camus' individual struggle with the absurd.

Personhood

Bonhoeffer's story-laden framework moves an individual to the status of person. He, like Martin Luther King Jr., called individuals to personhood. King used an American story, the story of the American Dream—of individual success and concern for community (Tocqueville 69–70)—to move one from being an American individual to an American person. Persons in an American Dream understand the story of life, liberty, and the pursuit of happiness for the community, not just for their own success. The individual takes care of the self, confusing "improved means" with "improved ends" (King 211). Persons, on the other hand, rest within a story that propels action, inviting others into the ongoing story. Individuals take care of themselves; persons take care of the story that guides them—a story that gives them meaning and direction.

The notion of person meets otherness, in the form of story, historical moment, and communicative partners. The movement from individual to person presupposes a commitment to an understanding of otherness akin to that of Levinas. Levinas embraced the necessity of radical alterity—the uniqueness of the Other (*Totality and Infinity* 192). The notion of person as both responsive to and situated in a given story and historical situation and responsive to the Other suggests that the notion of person cannot become reified into a static concept. The person responds to otherness, adding texture and change to an ongoing guiding story. An individual accumulates experiences that offer guidance. A person interprets experiences in accordance with an ongoing story, which provides guidance and evaluation. The person responds to life with bias (a story laden-framework) and in the process potentially adjusts the story from that person's own participation. An individual attempts to stand above story guidance; a person lives embedded within the ongoing story of a people. The notion of the Other, radical alterity, represents difference of ideas and insight, keeping a story ever expansive and free from ideological closure.

The movement from being an individual to becoming a person makes sense in everyday life when one joins an organization. If one becomes part of the ongoing story of the organization, then movement to a sense of personhood in the organization is possible. If, however, a person is unresponsive to the alterity of the story, the historical situation, and the Other, one falls into ideological assurance, knowing an answer prior to meeting a unique question.

The notion of person as a story-laden phenomenon emerges in Tolkein's *The Fellowship of the Ring.* The main character, Frodo Baggins, becomes a person within the story of the "fellowship of the ring." Baggins finds himself situated within a story with a plot, events, actions, and main characters. His personhood identity emerges as a by-product of story line. A person finds identity within a story. An individual finds a sense of identity within the notion of self.

Bonhoeffer invites us into two stories that offer a sense of personhood—a Christocentric story and a story of a "world come of age" (*Letters and Papers from Prison* 326–29), which shape personhood within a world of change and narrative contention. Christian personhood is primary in Bonhoeffer's story with a secondary story that addresses the historical moment of change before him.

For communication, the distinction between individual and person is key in how we assist the Other. Moving from individual to person means moving from focus upon self to embedded agency within a story. The gaining of personhood identity does not assume that each story is constructive. The warnings of discussion about personhood are akin to that about story—choose a story with care; stories shape our sense of personhood.

In *The Communion of Saints,* Bonhoeffer frames his understanding of person. He differentiates the notion of person from "atomism" (17) and "individualism" (17–18). He critiques the notion of isolated "I-centres" (17), rejecting this view of the person. Bonhoeffer takes to task a social philosophy that understands persons as guided by a central kernel of consistency that must meet and engage changing social circumstances; such a view moves into ideological status. Bonhoeffer's argument is not that common social philosophy misses the issue of change; his concern is that such philosophy misses the impact of such change on a person: a person is not a stable kernel of consistency, but a responsive story-shaped agent. Additionally, Bonhoeffer offers a critique of a modern sense of the self, pointing to the importance of fragmentation in discussion of the person. Bonhoeffer is closer to a postmodern than a modern view of the self. Calvin Schrag describes a postmodern self in accordance with Bonhoeffer's insights.

> The self in community is a self situated in a space of communicative praxis, historically embedded, existing with others, inclusive of predecessors, contemporaries, and successors. Never an island entire of itself, the self remains rooted in history but is suffocated by the influx of historical forms and forces. The communalized self is *in* history but not *of* history. It has the resources for transcending the historically specific without arrogating to itself an unconditioned and decontextualized vision of the world. (*The Self after Postmodernity* 109)

Schrag, like Bonhoeffer, points to a notion of person becoming real only in social relations with others responsive to a concrete situation, not in isolation. Bonhoeffer ties person to the Other, shaped in the image of God, the ultimate radical alterity. Within a faith perspective, personhood is a social activity transformed by the spiritual. Throughout *The Communion of Saints,* Bonhoeffer suggests, "My real relation to the other man is oriented on my relation to God" (37). The textured view of "person" offered by Bonhoeffer transforms an individual into a person situated within the story of faith, responsive to the uniqueness or "unique face" of the Other and the historical moment. The person does not seek to overpower the Other or the historical moment, but to meet both within a basic presupposition of a Christocentric faith story. Bonhoeffer begins with Christ as "person," then frames his view of person in interpersonal discourse between persons.

Bonhoeffer understands Christ as a person affecting everyday life. The way in which Bonhoeffer sees the person of Christ is through service and responsibility, not in "personality, power, [and] value" (*Christ the Center* 44). The person of Christ lives in action that lives in story, in embedded agents of the faith within the community.

Bonhoeffer does not forget the Christ/God and Christ/Man dialectic of a Christocentric theology. It is, however, Christ as person working at being responsible for others that Christ is pro others, or from our perspective, "pro me" (Bonhoeffer, *Christ the Center* 47).

> "He is able because he is both God and Man" [. . .] His being Christ is his being for me, *pro me.* The being *pro me* is not to be understood as an effect emanating from him, nor as an accident; but it is to be understood as the essence, the being of the person himself. The core of the person himself is the *pro me.* That Christ is *pro me* is not an historical, nor an ontic statement, but an ontological one. Christ can never be thought of as being for himself, but only in relation to me. (47)

The person of Christ personifies responsibility for the Other, offering the saving act of Christ and a Christocentric story. Works alone do not make a Christian, but an embodied faith lived out in responsibility for the Other gives us temporal glimpses of Christ's presence.

Christ as person works on our behalf—this thesis is the key story line of Bonhoeffer's Christocentric theology. The person of Christ makes a difference, pointing to a story of a life of "discipleship," "deputyship," and "costly grace." The story of the faith rests within the actions and the charge of the person of Christ—being for the Other. The concrete story of Christ as person comes in the form of the Holy Spirit into the church, transforming relationships with one another.

> The fact that my claim is fulfilled for me by the other I who loves me—which means, in fact, by Christ—humbles me, frees me from the bonds of my I and lets me love the other—once again, indeed, in virtue of faith in Christ—lets me give and reveal myself entirely to him. (Bonhoeffer, *Communion of Saints* 119)

Accepting the person of Christ as a guiding story transforms the human person and then our relationships with one another. For Bonhoeffer, Christ is the bearer of the Word, the reminder of the story. "He is the Word as the Son" (*Christ the Center* 51). The person of Christ carries the Word, the story of the faith, ever responsive to changing contexts and times between peoples.

Story-Formed Person

The story of the person of Christ is the guiding story for understanding the human person. Acceptance of the person of Christ as responsible for the Other moves the human person into an active sense of mimesis (Ricoeur, *Time and Narrative* 1: 70–71), an appropriate sense of imitation, in that the call of caring for the Other guides the shaping of Christian personhood through a story-laden existence.

Ricoeur describes three ways in which mimesis works within a narrative. First, there is the connection between "doing" and the temporal demands of the historical moment. Second, mimesis permits understanding discordance or deformity as it violates a given plot. Finally, mimesis requires application, a configuring, a prolonging, and then a bringing to an end (*Time and Narrative* 1: 52–90). Using mimesis to explain the connection between the person of Christ and the person within the faith requires action (doing) that imitates the plot of the faith story, appropriately connected to the historical moment, aware of deviation from the plot, and applied in the shaping, developing, and eventual death of a person of faith. Mimesis is a necessary ingredient in an individual's becoming a person of the faith.

In the case of Bonhoeffer's story, the act of mimesis is essential in that the "I" becomes a person connected to the Thou of the Other and the eternal Thou that calls one into the story of responsibility.

> No man can of himself make the other into an I, into a moral person conscious of responsibility. God, or the Holy Spirit, comes to the concrete Thou, only by his action does the other become a Thou for me, from which my I arises. In other words, every human Thou is an image of the divine Thou. (Bonhoeffer, *Communion of Saints* 36)

The story of the faith, based upon responsibility for the Other, moves one from individual to person. From a faith perspective, a human being invites movement from being an individual to becoming a person as one enters a story of the faith by choice, not coercion. The shaping of the person is by the grace of God resting with the story of the faith, not the nobleness of the agent of the faith.

The person works with the constant temptation of life enclosed within individualism. There is no "overleaping the limits of the I" (Bonhoeffer, *The*

Communion of Saints 80). Limits between persons and the power of the "I" permit separateness from others, working to deny the importance of relation for its own sake. The person of faith seeks relation with others with full knowledge of the necessity of distance, the power of sin, and the temptation to fall back upon the "I" alone as a "one-sidedly individualistic" (80) understanding of communicative life. A person of the faith invites an I-Thou relation with the Other, in which distance permits one to understand and engage the Other in the Other's uniqueness, forgoing a distance that simply celebrates the telling "I" of the self. Bonhoeffer points to the importance of restraint of a human nature that begins with the "I" and misses the phenomenological beginnings of life with the Other.

Bonhoeffer offers a picture of a person situated within the story of the faith using dialectic to provide a thoughtful sense of caution to faith conviction. Bonhoeffer's understanding of the person embraces the goal of imitating Christ in the story of the faith with full knowledge of human limits, of sin, and of the importance of living life with others while maintaining distance. After Bonhoeffer emphasizes the connection to Christ, he moves attention to respect for sinfulness that adds caution to the self-assured assumption that we are actually following the story of Christ. He sought to lessen the impulse to offer attributions that seek to disclose another's motivations, feigning knowledge of the other's motivations. Having questions about one's own ability to understand the faith should moderate one's ability to attribute motives to another.

Imitation with Knowing Limits

The story of Christ guided Bonhoeffer's understanding of the faith. He questioned his ability to know the thoughts and wishes of God. Human sin gets in the way of engaging any effort perfectly; the road to hell paved by good intentions forgets limits and sin. Bonhoeffer never forgot the limits a person brings to a given task.

Bonhoeffer understands that persons arise within the community of the Church, reminding us that a church lives with sin and is constituted by members not unfamiliar with sin. It is the dialectic of sin and hope that shapes a person and the ongoing life of the church.

> It is therefore impossible to present the concept of the church without placing it in this inner dialectical history. It is of its essence that it still bears within itself the community of sin and is real only by the constant overcoming of this community of sin. (Bonhoeffer, *The Communion of Saints* 38–39)

The Christian person works with the constant blessing of the story of the faith and awareness of its individual and corporate limitations. Bonhoeffer warns the person and the Church that confession of sins and request for forgiveness reconnect one to the faith story, opening one to the "will of God from Christ anew" (*Christ the Center* 113). Bonhoeffer points to a hermeneutic circle of faith: 1) we begin in faith; 2) we live in sin that generates a need for reconnection to the faith story; 3) we engage confession as the link between sin and reconnection.

We attempt imitation of Christ, but sin leads to less than perfect results, keeping confession as essential to communicative life within the faith. The hermeneutic circle of the faith works with the engagement of persons in a similar fashion: 1) the faith story calls us to meet the Other; 2) the Other calls us to a temptation, a life without the story of the faith; 3) confession of sin of self and Other keeps distance in the equation of the person; 4) such awareness of limits through confession keeps the person situated within the faith story.

The story of the faith differentiates a "person" from the notion of an "individual" and unrestrained freedom. Freedom for the person of the faith lives within constraints of the story of the faith, constraints that form identity and shape action. Bonhoeffer cautions us against a docetic Christology that minimizes the humanness of Jesus, only attending to the "ideas, values, and doctrines" of the faith (*Christ the Center* 80). Just as Christ is real for Bonhoeffer, so is the Christian person. Bonhoeffer does not permit idealization of the Christian person to eclipse awareness of temptation, sin, and self-delusion in the name of the faith. Bonhoeffer's concrete commitment to the person moves him to embrace necessity of distance, recognizing the humanness of the person—both saint and sinner.

The Necessity of Distance

Bonhoeffer assumes the importance of social life in the construction of the person. Bonhoeffer's interest in sociology propelled his contribution to understanding the social nature of the person. He understood sociality as fundamental to the faith: "that it is not good for man to be alone, to the meaning of the creation of woman, that is, of life in sociality" (*The Communion of Saints* 43). Bonhoeffer assumes a phenomenological perspective whereby self-consciousness arises from the presence of the Other. The phenomenological recognition of the importance of the Other for the existence of the "I" requires differentiation and distance between Thou and I. The necessity of the Other for the existence of the "I" makes separateness essential. The Other shapes us, just as the story of the faith given to us by others shapes us.

The notion of person dialectically countered by an emphasis on distance between persons permits Bonhoeffer to address the reality of sin and to understand a person further by attending to the uniqueness of the Other. Without distance, there is no sense of Thou. Without distance, we try to move the Other into our own sphere, engaging in attribution of the Other's motives based upon our own assessments.

Bonhoeffer would consider relational connections without limits a mask for getting our own way. Relational bullying is subtler than schoolyard bullying, but often more determined. Distance lessens the impulse to turn the Other into one's own image. It is this relational bullying that gives power to the phrase "intimacy is a tyranny" (Sennett, *The Fall of Public Man* 338). Christian persons live within the image of God, not of one another. Bonhoeffer calls for us to build relationships "upon the uniqueness and separateness of persons" (*The Communion of Saints* 37). Bonhoeffer, Buber, and Levinas all point in a similar direction of healthy relationships permitting distance. Stopping the Other's ability to offer a sense of difference moves the person into one's own image, halting responsiveness to the alterity of the Other.

The distance Bonhoeffer affords another rests within two basic convictions: this is God's world, and "I" sin. Bonhoeffer, as a pastor, heard the questions: "What kind of people do you want in your Church? To whom do you want to minister?" His answer reminds us whose world we occupy. He simply stated, "We thank God for giving us brethren who live by His call, by His forgiveness, and His promise. We do not complain of what God does not give us; we rather thank God for what He does give us daily" (*Life Together* 28). In *Life Together,* Bonhoeffer stated:

> This applies in a special way to the complaints often heard from pastors and zealous members about their congregations. A pastor should not complain about his congregation, certainly never to other people, but also not to God. A congregation has not been entrusted to him in order that he should become its accuser before God and men. (29)

When we sense a call to distance, we forgo the temptation to make Others like "me." We must meet God's world responsively, never forgetting sin carried by each person, including ourselves. When asking another to live within our relational shadow, we invite danger, the manifestation of sin, and the idolatry of "self."

Distance does not suggest ignoring the Other, but the contrary, responding to the uniqueness of the Other. Without distance, we risk the temptation of seeing the Other as our own image. The importance of distance manifests itself in questions of church growth. Often one hears a small church complain about its inability to grow. The church begins a campaign to lessen distance between persons, to be friendlier. However, the friendliness seldom results in more membership. The friendliness assumes the expectation of particular interpersonal conventions; those not fitting those conventions find themselves unable to fit the implicit interpersonal model. Instead of growing, the church continues at its current size, becoming increasingly homogeneous in interpersonal actions. The church brings in some, but loses others, depending upon adherence to a given, yet unstated, set of interpersonal expectations.

Diminishing distance does not invite diversity; it invites more uniform communicative social practices. If a church wants to grow in an age of diversity, distance that permits us to see and respond to another, not to our own image, needs to guide interaction and growth. There is wisdom in Martin Buber's adage from *Between Man and Man* that real meeting begins in distance; the Thou needs respect, not expectations for social practice conformity. Reinhold Niebuhr was correct about the power of irony (*The Irony of American History* 153). The irony of meeting the Other is that sustained distance permits respect and clarification from awareness of the uniqueness of the Other. Displaced distance with the interpersonal hope of increasing intimacy and increased church membership fails when the church tries to meet the goals of individuals with communicative social practices centered more upon the self than the faith story. Distrust of distance in interpersonal contact finds implementation in the impulse to psychologize the motives of another's communicative actions, a temptation about which Bonhoeffer offered repeated warning. Also, such distrust of distance invites what Martin Buber called "overrunning reality" (Buber qtd. in Friedman, *The Hidden Human Image* 301). Distance permits meeting and understanding another over time, permitting appreciation of uniqueness of the Other.

Psychologism

Distance keeps psychologism at arm's length. The impulse to assume we know the motives of another was a major communicative misstep of the twentieth century. Without distance in communicative relationships, we invite the full force of psychologism. Psychologism assumes that one has the ability to interpret the motives of another more accurately than the person doing the action. Psychologism lives by attribution. Attributing motives to another in an act of psychologism displaces distance and assumes transparent passage into discernment of another's reasons for a given action.

Bonhoeffer states:

> There is also a parallel isolation among the clergy, in what one might call the "clerical" sniffing-around-after-people's-sins in order to catch them out. It's as if you couldn't know a fine house till you had found a cobweb in the furthest cellar, or as if you couldn't adequately appreciate a good play till you had seen how the actors behave off-stage. It's the same kind of thing that you find in the novels of the last fifty years, which do not think they have depicted their character properly till they have described them in their [. . .] impurity. A basic antisocial attitude of mistrust and suspicion. (*Letters and Papers from Prison* 345)

Psychologism is a secular sniffing for sin, the sin of an individually disapproved-of motive assumed by the interpreter.

Psychologism lives where distance loses to the impulse to attribute motives to another's actions, assuming the other is transparent. Distance lessens the impulse of psychologism, resting within a basic assumption—the judge is not without sin, warning against the everyday impulse to attribute motives to another. The sin of the interpreter offers caution and a respect for distance in engaging the Other without being innocent about the nature of the self or the Other.

On Human Nature

Bonhoeffer reminds us of the universality of sin and the limitations of oneself and the Other. As one avoids the impulse for psychologism, caution guides communicative life. Caution about oneself and the Other, not mistrust, typifies Bonhoeffer's response to the nature of the human.

The Word of God gives messengers an unerring insight into their own human nature: "Beware of me."

> The disciples are not expected to show fear of men, nor malice, nor mistrust, still less a sour misanthropy, nor that gullible credulity which believes that there is good in every man; they are expected rather to display an unerring insight into the mutual relations of the Word and man. If they are content not to pitch their hopes too high, they will not be perturbed when Jesus warns them that their way among men will be one of suffering. But there is a miraculous power latent in this suffering. (Bonhoeffer, *Cost of Discipleship* 238)

Bonhoeffer takes us from the person of Christ to a human person offering distance to the Other so that the image of God, not our image, finds its way into interaction. He cautions us that respect for the person in the image of God requires constant awareness that the human being is not without sin.

Bonhoeffer commented on theology unwilling to take the notion of sin seriously. His view of the person rests within the dialectic of the image of God and the limitations of the human, the inevitability of sin. This dialectic claims the action of a Christian person—calling for respect without losing understanding that one must go into the "vulgar crowd" (Bonhoeffer, *The Cost of Discipleship* 223). This vulgar crowd includes us, you and me.

Just as one thinks Bonhoeffer has settled on a position, he adds another dialectical caution. No matter where one starts in one's reading of Bonhoeffer, one finds a counter suggestion. As he reminds us of the "vulgar crowd," he also suggests that a Christian person needs to love enemies. Becoming a person of the faith calls for struggle against ordinary human nature armed only by a story of the faith within which we live, not an ideology within which we fend off difference by ignoring the unpleasant and the evil.

Bonhoeffer reminds us of the limits of human nature and the equal importance of the faith repositioning the person to attempt the seemingly impossible—to love one's enemies. "To the natural man, the very notion of loving his enemies is an intolerable offence, and quite beyond this capacity; it cuts right across his ideas of good and evil" (*The Cost of Discipleship* 163). To become a Christian person is not to assume naiveté, but knowingly to embrace a calling that stands against an ongoing culture that seeks to protect the self at all costs. Such a person, in the words of Bonhoeffer, takes on the "peculiar," the "extraordinary," walking against the "sphere of natural possibilities" (*The Cost of Discipleship* 169).

The Christian person works within the dialectic of the extraordinary with full knowledge of personal limits of sin. The Christian person finds identity and direction in the life of the faith engaged with others with full knowledge of one's own limits. Bonhoeffer calls the Christian person to a life of "ethical solidarity" (*The Communion of Saints* 80). Bonhoeffer counters the natural human nature of individualism with an understanding of the person situated within the story of the faith tempered by knowledge of limits and the need for constraints on action.

Restraint as Communicative Beginning

The importance of relational distance privileges communication with restraint. Not only does one count upon the restraint of the Other to protect one's own freedom, one must restrain one's own desire to make the Other into "me." Bonhoeffer respects the importance of restraint. Restraint averts "the final plunge into the void" (*Ethics* 108). "[T]he 'restrainer' is the force which takes effect within history through God's governance of the world, and which sets due limits to evil" (108). Communication without restraint, like any human activity, ends in corruption. Such is the reason that scholars of free speech, like Richard Johannesen, connect freedom and responsibility of speech (6–9); restraint guides communicative freedom.

Distance permits freedom, offering necessary restraint from which closer connection naturally emerges. Communication understood within such a perspective permits the "I" of the Other to emerge in its unique fashion, restraining the impulse of one's own "I" to attempt to shape the other falsely. Such an approach to communication is wary of the "managed smile" (Arnett, *Dialogic Education* 114). Distance begins not with a smile, but with respect for the uniqueness of the other.

Bonhoeffer tempered a sense of communicative importance; communication was not a panacea for Bonhoeffer. Communication cannot offer easy answers. Communication serves as a verb, not a noun, in Bonhoeffer's project. Communication carries a worldview, a perspective, and a virtue structure responsive to the Other. Bonhoeffer frames communication as essential, but not sufficient. Communication as a verb transports communicative good or evil into action. What restrains communication also shapes its content, its ultimate impact on God's world. Communication is both form and substance.

Bonhoeffer's understanding of communication assumes a Christocentric worldview responsive to the Other and the historical moment. Using the example of building a log home, communication is the mortar that holds the structure together. Communication is the glue of human communities; it is the mortar connecting ideas, people, and communities.

What restrains communication are story-framed ideas that shape communicative life together. Communicative life does not begin in expression, for Bonhoeffer, but in story-laden ideas, presuppositions of the faith. Repeatedly, he points to the first principle of his view of communication; communication connects the basic first principle of Christ as the center with the needs of the historical moment and the Other. The first principle of the faith finds structure in communicative mortar, suggested by the following:

> So the First Commandment calls us to the sole, true God, to the omnipotent, righteous, and merciful One, who saves us from falling into nothingness and sustains us in this congregation [. . .]
>
> "Hear, O Israel: The Lord is our God, the Lord alone; You shall love the Lord your God with all your heart, and with your soul, and with all your might" (Deut. 6.4). To this our God we pray with complete confidence, as Jesus Christ has taught us, "Our Father, who art in heaven." (Bonhoeffer, "The First Table of the Ten Commandments" qtd. in Godsey 57, 59)

Bonhoeffer's first principle that restrains and shapes communication is Christocentric. Bonhoeffer frames religious communication with open acknowledgment of bias of Christ that begins before the human "I."

Bonhoeffer differentiates communication and talking. The latter rests with expressivism and the "I" driven by personal expression alone. The former begins with content, connecting with the historical situation and the Other. Communication, differentiated from talking, begins with content, knowledge of a given standpoint. Bonhoeffer is less likely to equate communication with the notion of process than with the metaphor of carrier: communication is a carrier of ideas and content. Communication carries ideas and content into the field of interpretation and action.

Bonhoeffer's textured understanding of communication is akin to the vast expanse of ice under the surface view of an iceberg; communication is not only a carrier, but also a phenomenon of depth. Communicative depth invites learning based upon ideas/content. Bonhoeffer communicates a faith story that begins with content and is open to learning in the meeting of the historical moment and the Other.

Bonhoeffer's communicative depth begins with content of faith conviction (standpoint that frames direction) based upon Christ the Center (the ultimate focus of attention) and attentiveness to persons (embedded agents) and to the historical situation, which gives rise to revelation (ideas and insights that transcend the taken-for-granted). The goal of such communication is to temper individual confidence insensitive to the demands of story-laden content, persons, the historical situation, and new insight of revelation.

Bonhoeffer's religious communicator embedded within the story of the faith, tempered by insight and responsive to the historical situation, moves the religious communicator from individualism to a person situated within a story—situated personhood; story-laden content moves from talking and expression to listening, response, and learning from the historical situation and the Other. "It will be well to hold fast to the New Testament, otherwise we shall scarcely avoid the greatest danger, that namely of arguing for the humanitarian standpoint, with its fatal confusion of *eros* and *agape*" (Bonhoeffer, *The Communion of Saints* 120). The New Testament, for Bonhoeffer and this project, offers a story-reminder of the beginning of Christocentric communication.

Bonhoeffer underscores the conventional difference between *eros* and *agape,* with the former suggesting self-fulfillment and the latter suggesting a sense of service. Communication works within constraints of story-laden content and responsiveness to historicity and the Other. Additionally, Bonhoeffer contends that religious communication restrains the impulse of individualism more commonly associated with a conventional view of *eros.*

Tempering Individualism and Information Control

To encourage a sense of personhood requires restraining a human nature that moves in increasingly individualistic directions. Such a view of communication contends with Schleiermacher's "idea of the individual's need to communicate" (Bonhoeffer, *The Communion of Saints* 96). Bonhoeffer reworks Schleiermacher's position, suggesting that the assumption that human beings need to communicate is individualistic, missing a textured understanding of communication that rests within content of a story and a desire to learn. Bonhoeffer moves us from the need to communicate to the need to communicate something—in his case a Christocentric story of the faith. The key for Bonhoeffer is not ultimately the need to communicate, but the content of the communication. Bonhoeffer's communicative corrective moves communication from a position of individualistic expression to a stance of situated meaning, meaning situated within the story of the faith.

It is the region of the "among us," what Martin Buber called the "between" (*Between Man and Man* 202–3), that moves one beyond individualism. What happens between persons, between the historical moment and persons, between the faith story and learning permits a person to live within an ongoing story that continues to find life, texture, and definition.

The dialectical movement of content and learning frames communicative praxis in the "between" of freedom and restraint; Buber offers freedom responsive to concrete life, freedom and restraint of the plot line of a faith story. Such a view of communication on the run with guiding restraint embraces learning and responsiveness to the historical situation and the

Other with attentiveness to a given story-formed standpoint. Bonhoeffer points to communication akin to the creative concrete action of a musician with exceptional background upon which he draws, who is then responsive to the historical context and the listeners. Creativity emerges from preparation and a responsive heart. Bonhoeffer loved music that united content and responsiveness.

Failure to unite content and responsiveness places false confidence in information accuracy, causing one to miss a glimpse of the communicative moment, and to mistake clarity for communication. Accuracy of information is not the same as communication—ask any parent. Parents know that, at times, accuracy can put a relationship at risk. As children mature and move from one stage to another, parents must also move; accurate information is not the same as an accurate sense of when and how to say what about another life.

Bonhoeffer pointed to the difference between information accuracy and communication in *Life Together* as he discussed the danger of preaching at another (information accuracy), calling instead for pastoral responsibilities of listening and meeting the Other (communication). He warned against "an impatient, inattentive listening, that despises the brother and is only waiting for a chance to speak [informational truth]" (98). Being correct is not necessarily communication; correctness in the guise of information unresponsive to the person and the historical situation misses the communicative mark. A good parent, a good friend, a good communicator must learn the danger of confusing information accuracy with helpfulness of communicative engagement.

There is communicative temperance in Bonhoeffer that does not settle for easy answers. Bonhoeffer bypasses the extremes of expressivism and information accuracy for a more demanding communicative texture. It is the faith story, the Other, and an ongoing commitment to learning (openness to revelation emergent in the historical situation) that frame communicative engagement with another.

One needs an understanding of Bonhoeffer's communicative texture in order to bring hermeneutic insight that permits one to see the implications of some of Bonhoeffer's stark statements, such as: "Nothing can be more compassionate than the severe rebuke that calls a brother back from the path of sin" (*Life Together* 107). Understood as expressivism, this statement violates Bonhoeffer's commitment to humility. Understood as information accuracy, this statement violates Bonhoeffer's commitment to the historical moment and context. The above statement understood outside of expressivism and information accuracy rests within a faith story of conviction called out by a historical moment, responsive to the Other, committed to ongoing learning supported by the pragmatic necessity of confession before, during, and after communicative engagement. Such a seemingly blunt, yet generally appropriate, communicative gesture requires understanding of the hermeneutic sophistication of Bonhoeffer's project: commitment (Christocentric content) shaped by humility through confession and learning, which tempers individualism.

> The "among us," the "now" and "here" is therefore the region of our decisions and encounters. This region undoubtedly varies very greatly in extent according to the individual, and it might consequently be supposed that these definitions could in the end be interpreted so widely and vaguely as to make room for unrestrained individualism. What prevents this is the fact that by our history we are set objectively in a definite nexus of experiences, responsibilities and decisions from which we cannot free ourselves again except by an abstraction. [. . .] this nexus is characterized in a quite peculiar manner by the fact that until our own days its consciously affirmed and recognized underlying basis has been the form of Christ. (Bonhoeffer, *Ethics* 88)

Bonhoeffer lamented the narrowing of education in music, the arts, and the sciences. The nineteenth century witnessed educational "innovation" that changed education from being an "extensive" to an "intensive" task (Bonhoeffer, *Letters and Papers from Prison* 219), inviting specialists and increasing fragmentation in human life. Music and the arts framed from preparation, responsive to the moment, do not give way to the worlds of technicians and expressivists.

Bonhoeffer pointed to a content-based story within which a person situates a life and commitment that continues to find shape in "communicative praxis" (Schrag, *Communicative Praxis* 17), not a priori answers.

Communicative Praxis

Bonhoeffer's religious communication is responsive; he points to communication as ongoing learning, learning on the move, learning on the run, in the wake of everyday disruption. In Bonhoeffer, one discovers the "concrete" as action and decision making on the move. Bonhoeffer avoids "abstract" logic framed a priori to the context; he rejects unreflective utterances based upon personal preference and a solidified position. Bonhoeffer pointed to content/story ever responsive to the concrete moment, attentive to the revelation of Christ in the concrete moment of human meeting.

Praxis, defined as theory-informed action, is pragmatic communication necessary in times of shifting ethical guidelines and unforeseen change. Praxis requires connecting the "why" of action with communicative practice. Praxis rejects unreflective communicative practices, embracing reflective communicative engagement. A communicative shift from unreflective communicative action to reflection before action privileges knowing "why" before acting. When an agreed-upon narrative background guides communicative action, unreflective practices go unchallenged; reflection is pragmatically not necessary before action in such a setting. Such a communicative environment rich in unreflective tradition finds little need for theory. However, in an era of postmodern narrative dispute, we must reflect on assumptions before we engage another. We cannot assume the Other shares "our" assumptions. Theory sorts out assumptions for the speaker and provides a context for the listener. Theory, understood loosely as reflective awareness of communicative assumptions that shape action, gives currency to philosophy, theology, and reflection before acting. Praxis also requires bringing a knowing "why" into creative conversation with the historical moment. Praxis is theory-informed action addressing a genuine need in the historical moment. Theory gives distance and insight into a given event, forgoing the impulse to assume that one works within an agreed-upon universal narrative structure. Action tempers theory with historical engagement, and theory moves action away from unreflective presuppositions about the world as we would want it or pretend it to be.

Praxis connected to communicative action suggests textured background knowledge played out in action. Calvin Schrag, in 1986, introduced "communicative praxis" (*Communicative Praxis* 17–111) as a way to describe the "texture" of complexity, uncertainty, and the multiplicity of communicative options. Communicative *praxis* becomes a metaphor for doing communication on the run, on the move—connecting well with Bonhoeffer's story-centered movement. Schrag frames communicative praxis within the prepositions "about, by, and for whom" (*Communicative Praxis* 32–47). Communication is about something, by someone, and for someone. Schrag's understanding of "by someone" assumes a decentered agent or subject. The subject discovers communicative praxis in "discourse but also action" (Schrag, *Communicative Praxis* 11). Schrag additionally uses the term "texture" to underscore the interplay of text, perception, and action, to offer primacy to no one element. Communicative texture shapes the "I."

> The "I" in concrete speech transactions [lives] embedded within a tradition of the already spoken, the already written, and the already accomplished social practices; self-consciousness breaks forth as a dialogic event with embodied and decentered subjectivity. (Schrag, *Communicative Praxis* 172)

The decentered subject lives within a multiplicity of social practices, traditions, and stories characterizing a postmodern era. Communicative *praxis* describes how we negotiate such a moment.

Both Bonhoeffer and Schrag reject attempts to "know" the "appropriate" response to the historical moment before meeting it. Theory and response to the historical moment drive action, not simple a priori answers to complex, textured settings. Each of us has met a person who offers quick, flat reads of situations that require understanding of subtle nuances before discerning a temporal answer. A person known for quick readings of a text or situation provides an immediate response without respect for the complexity of the issue at hand, displaying the danger of "communicative provinciality" that propels communicative responses void of *texture.* Provinciality is a trained incapacity, a practiced inability, to examine issues and events differently. The acquired habit of examining life *with* texture lessens our natural inclination toward what we already know (text), lessens our desire for the familiar (perception through communicative provinciality), and lessens reliance upon agent-centered action. Schrag's prepositions take on currency beyond everyday understanding. In communicative praxis, the "about" includes a textured combination of texts—content, social practices, and traditions. The notion of "by" includes an embedded agent within content, social practices, and traditions. The preposition of "for whom" suggests an embedded audience within content, social practices, and traditions. The communicative act of communicative provinciality misses the ongoing texture of communicative exchange. The habit of examination, doing a "textured" reading, is essential in a time of narrative disruption and virtue contention. Theory and action in dialectical unity restrain the excess of one element without the other and restrain the impulse of an unreflective "I." A story in action becomes a lived humanities-based form of theory in action in communicative life.

Story-Construction in Action

Bonhoeffer's commitment to conviction (his deep Christocentric perspective) and his pragmatic "humility" (*Letters and Papers from Prison* 383) point to a story-formed communicative praxis attentive to the historical moment. He brought responsiveness to the texture of communicative life, forgoing a priori answers to complex and changing historical events. Such responsiveness explains the communicative texture that permitted Bonhoeffer to pen *The Cost of Discipleship,* considered one of the purest books on pacifism written in the twentieth century, and then participate in an attempt to assassinate Adolph Hitler. Responsiveness to the changing texture of communicative life is not for those desiring purity of action or constant stability; communicative texture requires taking a theory/story into thoughtful engagement with persons and the historical moment. Attending to and responding to the textured changes of communicative life require story-guided confidence and the humility to change as one addresses and learns from particular situations, persons, and calls to service.

While in prison awaiting his fate, Bonhoeffer wrote about his unwillingness to disregard the complexity, the difficulty, the "texture" of life, in order to secure comfort.

> The idea that we could have avoided many of life's difficulties if we had taken things more cautiously is too foolish to be entertained for a moment. As I look back on your past I am so convinced that what has happened hitherto has been right, that I feel that what is happening now is right too. To renounce a full life and its real joys in order to avoid pain is neither Christian nor human. (*Letters and Papers from Prison* 192)

Real living (Buber, *Between Man and Man* 202–3) requires openness to life's texture; not all of life comes neatly organized before it happens. The story of the faith gives guidance, not "the" answer; the story of the faith is not a crystal ball but a map with limited detail, a call to be responsible, and a reminder to pray.

Bonhoeffer's commitment to the texture of communicative life situates him within theory and particular application as a communication engineer. A communication engineer, as opposed to a communication technician (Arnett, "Technicians of Goodness" 353–55), brings theory into contact with the unique and particular situation. In contrast, a communication technician follows known paths, imitating ideas and actions that worked in previous situations and settings. A communication technician follows plans outlined by another, designed in the abstract, provided for a "similar" situation. A communication engineer knows the theory, the story, and then applies and alters that knowledge appropriately in response to each unique setting.

Bonhoeffer, as a communication engineer, met each historical situation with religious rhetoric tempered by dialectical questioning and the possibility of dialogue. A communication engineer engages a theory or story-framed communicative praxis responsive to a given historical situation. Bonhoeffer, as a communication engineer, embraced a thoughtful understanding of communicative construction. He constructed one communicative building, bridge, or structure at a time, ascertaining the requirements for each given setting and situation. Bonhoeffer understood that communication, like a well-constructed bridge, makes a difference in people's lives, enhancing their quality and safety, when constructed for a unique situation. An engineer builds one bridge, one communication event, at a time, each requiring preparation, listening, and respect for the uniqueness of the requirements of a given setting and historical moment. He offered a communicative praxis that keeps a guiding story from atrophying into a rigid ideology, providing a story on the move, a responsive story ever shaping the person, the embedded agent of religious discourse.

5

STORY-CENTERED TRUST

Confession "Between" Persons

Maurice Friedman on mistrust:

> [T]he mistrust of existence itself would enter as a corroding force into every relationship making impossible full acceptance of the present and going out to meet it with our whole being. Then the present would indeed become nothing but a vanishing moment in which the future is forever going over into the past. Ultimate trust—trust in existence itself—is trust in the present and future at once. ("The Bases of Buber's Ethics" 195)

Dietrich Bonhoeffer on mistrust:

> No wonder if mistrust, suspicion and censoriousness crept into the Church. And no wonder if every brother who falls into sin incurred the uncharitable criticism of his brethren, now that Jesus has said this. All this distrust would ruin the Church but for the word of Jesus which assures us that the bad tree will bring forth bad fruit. It is bound to give itself away sooner or later. There is not need to go about prying into the hearts of others. All we need do is to wait until the tree bears fruit, and we shall not have to wait long. This is not to say that we must draw a distinction between the words of the prophet and his deeds; the real distinction is that between appearance and reality. Jesus tells us that men cannot keep up appearances for long. The time of vintage is sure to come, and then we shall be able to sift the good from the bad. Sooner or later we shall find out where a man stands. (*The Cost of Discipleship* 213)

Buber and Bonhoeffer outline the danger of mistrust, a mistrust in existence, the very ground of existence. They point to trust as a form of interpersonal sustenance or basic nutrient that moves life from survival to meaning. Bonhoeffer's dialogue, his engagement with others, witnesses to the necessity of veracity/congruence of word and deed that embraces a contextual and textured/dialectical understanding of "truthful" communicative meaning—a truthfulness that invites confidence and clarity of meaning. Bonhoeffer's congruence of word and deed unites the "ultimate" and the "penultimate" (*Ethics* 120–87) with a complexity that understands the necessity of understanding truth within the particular, not the abstract. This textured reading of truthfulness permitted lying to the Nazis, understood as a "penultimate" form of congruence that addresses evil with appropriate veracity, guided by an "ultimate" story of the faith. Congruence of word and deed requires the "ultimate" governing criteria—a Christocentric understanding that frames the "why" for assisting God's people—with flexible implementation in the "penultimate."

Penultimate connection between word and deed permits a textured sense of congruence (not a legalistic understanding of congruence) under demanding circumstances. Bonhoeffer made penultimate judgments guided by the ultimate power of the faith story. The ultimate provides direction; the penultimate calls for courage to live responsibly in the ambiguity of the given historical moment. Bonhoeffer points to a life of conviction that demands responsible action discerned in the moment, responsible action unavailable in a priori answers. Conviction, understood by Bonhoeffer, forsakes abstract assurance for responsibility to meet and discern action in the existential moment. Bonhoeffer's trust is in the "ultimate," God's world; it is an existential trust of God's world in the midst of confusion and human error.

Bonhoeffer affirmed trustworthiness of God's project as he met narrative and virtue contention in a "world come of age" (*Letters and Papers from Prison* 326–29). In a "world come of age," responsibility for decision making about penultimate congruence between word and deed accompanies a religious life. A penultimate responsible life leaves behind the assurance of "pure" or "righteous" a priori answers, requiring thoughtfulness, attentiveness, and interpretive skill that shape decision making in the midst of a given moment. Decision making within the realm of discerned "good," not an abstract sense of the "pure" or the "perfect," requires confession as a public check and as a way of discerning realignment of word and deed.

Bonhoeffer lived within a family that understood the consequences of penultimate decision making, a family that understood leadership willing to engage existential decisions in a complex world. The following words from Karl Bonhoeffer, Dietrich's father, suggest knowledge of the penultimate as the sphere of leadership.

> I hear you know that we have suffered greatly and lost two sons and two sons-in-law through the Gestapo. As you can imagine, this has taken its toll on us old folk. For years, we endured the tension, the anxiety about those arrested

> and those who were not yet arrested but in danger. But since we all agreed about the necessity of action, and my sons were also fully aware of what they could expect if the plot miscarried, and had resolved if necessary to lay down their lives, we are sad, but also proud of their straight and narrow attitude. We have fine memories of both sons from prison . . . that move both of us and their friends greatly. (Bethge, *Dietrich Bonhoeffer* 933)

Bonhoeffer's family provided an intellectual and morally responsive setting from which to understand the cost of conviction taken into the realm of the penultimate. Bonhoeffer knew theory and an ultimate story of the faith and had a courage that forsook the safety of theory and proclamation alone, taking him into the realm of existential action, penultimate decision making.

Such trust in the ultimate and in engagement with the penultimate permits one to take the risk of action with conviction that when one discovers error in one's direction, the act of confession works to reconnect one to the faith story. Confession is a communicative reminder of the ultimate that guides without dictating a given penultimate action. A communicator making decisions within the penultimate finds guidance within an ultimate story with confession functioning as a communicative reminder of the horizon of decision-making.

Trust in God's world permits confession to function without a priori dictates or wishes of the individual self. Confession finds answers outside of dictate and personal preference, separating confession from self-disclosure. Additionally, Bonhoeffer's confession is contrary to the impulse to unburden the self or blindly to follow abstract moral teaching. Bonhoeffer's confession seeks a third path, realigning a guiding ultimate story of the faith with implementation in everyday penultimate decision making. Confession works not for "me," but for the story of the faith. Confession reunifies word and deed—reconnecting penultimate existential decisions and an ultimate Christocentric commitment to the faith. Confession is a penultimate first principle of communicative action that begins with trust in God's world supported by an ultimate guiding Christocentric story of service that engages a world come of age.

Bonhoeffer's trust in God's world underwrites a contextual perspective, a perspective alien to absolutes. No one with a modest knowledge of Bonhoeffer would confuse his perspective with a stereotypical absolutist religious position. Bonhoeffer's work with an absolute position becomes contextual with his dialectical commitments. He was so committed to a contextual perspective (Arnett, "Dialogic Civility as Pragmatic Ethical *Praxis*" 331–36) that one must take care to separate his work from subjectivism. With his insights far afield from objectivism, he outlined their difference from subjective decision making. Distinguishing confession from self-disclosure was central to his understanding of confession as an alternative to subjective expression. Bonhoeffer's commitment to a Christocentric story and his engagement in the historical moment of a world come of age drive his life and work. It is neither Bonhoeffer's personal insights (subjectivity) nor an ideology of the faith (objectivity), but the dialectic of the narrative of the faith and the historical moment that informs the communicative agent.

It is not experience of life but experience of the cross that makes one a worthy hearer of confessions. The most experienced psychologist or observer of human nature knows infinitely less of the human heart than the simplest Christians who live beneath the cross of Jesus (Bonhoeffer, *Life Together* 118–19). Confession bears the weight of a moral communicative ultimate-connection to the faith story. Self-disclosure bears the weight of the agent alone. Confession bears the weight of the call upon the agent to meet the demands of a given historical moment from the insights of an ultimate story of the faith—a trust that affirms the world as God's, even as this same world matures to a "world come of age." The trust calls for our responsibility, not for our request for direct intervention from God.

Word and Deed

An ultimate sense of trust in God's world, in God's word, permits one to work for a penultimate effort at trust in service of the faith-connecting word and deed. Such an effort at connection is naturally flawed and limited, requiring confession that acknowledges incongruence of word and deed, underscoring confession as a practical check on incongruence of statement and action. In a world come of age, in a time of responsibility for decision making amidst confusion, in an era when conviction is suspect, the person of the faith must connect word and deed with openness to correction. Ambiguity and lack of a priori assurance about *the* correct action requires a conviction checked by constant review—the task of confession. When one strays too far from the ground of the faith or misses the historical moment, confession permits one to make amends, reconnecting word and deed.

From this standpoint in history, Bonhoeffer's commitment to a faith story seems out of step with a postmodern age, yet upon further consideration, his insights provide a person with a faith commitment in this era a model for navigating narrative contention. Postmodernity is a moment of acknowledged diversity, not an era without conviction. It is a time of contending convictions attempting to navigate differences.

For a postmodern world, Bonhoeffer demonstrates that a person of moral conviction can meet a world of narrative and virtue contention with integrity, humility, a willingness to learn, and courage to decide and act without complete assurance. Bonhoeffer's dialectic of conviction and humility/openness guides engagement with difference. Bonhoeffer stood upon ground of conviction without falling prey to unreflective ideological assurance or confusing self-disclosure with proclamation. Bonhoeffer understood that in a time of narrative and virtue contention the test of discourse is action driven by the demands of the historical moment within the horizon of the faith story. The faith story has elasticity, but also limits. Viewing the test of conviction in action, not in abstract theory or self-appointed righteousness, requires recognition of the complexity of "communicative praxis" (Schrag, *Communicative Praxis* 17–111) that unites discourse and action. The complexity of conviction in a moment of narrative disruption offers entrance into Hans Gadamer's understanding of word and deed in the Platonic dialogue *Lysis.* Gadamer contends that Plato wanted to provide a legacy for Socrates—a legacy that differentiated his life from that of a Sophist.

The first essay in Gadamer's book *Dialogue and Dialectic* is entitled "*Logos* and *Ergon* in Plato's *Lysis,*" suggesting that the center of Plato's differentiation of Socrates from the Sophists is the "Doric harmony of *logos* and *ergon*" (20), word and deed. The harmony of word and deed made Socrates' taking the cup of poison inevitable. Gadamer suggests that the Doric harmony of word and deed drives Plato's utopian philosophy—"although again only in words" (20). The story of Socrates (Plato 116d–118) turns on differentiating him from the Sophists; he died for what he believed. Distinction from sophism requires willingness to test ideas, accepting the burden for the testing of ideas.

Confession corrects and transforms incongruence between *logos* and *ergon* (Gadamer, "Logos and Ergon" 6), realigning word and deed in communicative action. Confession of a position, such as Christocentric ground taken into a world of difference, a "world come of age," offers admission and insight to the Other and oneself. Bonhoeffer illustrated how a person of conviction, a person situated on firm ground, could meet a world of difference in a time of competing assumptions contrary to one's own position when guided by a commitment to an ultimate Christocentric story and responsiveness to the historical moment.

A common critique of sophists recognizes absence of accompanying or supporting actions. In a time of disputed narrative and virtue structures, connecting word and deed provides veracity of communicator congruence between word (commitment) and deed (implementation). Confession moves communicators from the danger of sophism, reconnecting communicators to a narrative structure, an ultimate ground tested in penultimate implementation.

Confessing ground, commitment, position, standpoint in communicative action moves words to acts of responsibility in decision making in the ongoing existential moment. Linkage of word and deed in the test of action lessens the sophistic impulse to confuse words alone with a life of faith. Conviction must stand the test of action. The popular critique of sophists is two-fold: 1) critics questioned their ground or conviction; and 2) people questioned their willingness to test ideas in everyday life. Bonhoeffer points to the importance of conviction tested and then through confession modified, shifted, and changed. Rhetorically, words connect to an audience and to changing contexts.

Bonhoeffer's dialectical thinking approximates the complexity of response necessary in meeting the demands of the concrete moment. Complexity of application and testing in the arena of action go unheeded in sophistic speech. Sophists offer words without support, foregoing the step of veracity, the test of ground in action. The sophist hopes that an audience will limit critique to style and abstract logic of ideas, forgetting questions about connection between words and action in a given setting.

The irony of Plato is that he saw the need for harmony of word and action, but framed his work within theory, not action. Unlike Plato, the words of Bonhoeffer live in harmony of word and action, offering the reader assurance of a "life of dialogue" (Friedman, *Martin Buber* 300), a life in which ideas manifest themselves in action-laden concern for the Other. Linking word and deed requires a "life of dialogue" "between" (Buber, *Between Man and Man* 202–3) the call of the ultimate and the necessity of the penultimate. Unlike the sophist, Bonhoeffer addresses the historical moment within the horizon of the story of the faith out of deep conviction and trust in the veracity of an ultimate story that engages a "world come of age."

"Between Word and Deed"

Bonhoeffer's union of word and deed comes with no technique for proper implementation. Confession guides a sense of self-monitoring based upon a given story of conviction (ultimate) and the ongoing historical situation (penultimate decision making). Answers live within the "between," a land of guided conviction, ever responsive to correction.

The metaphor of the "between" points additionally to dialectical ground, such as conviction and a pragmatic humility, ultimate and penultimate, lasting and temporal application. Embracing a Christocentric position that is application-driven acknowledges the difficulty of aligning word and deed. Confession discerns answers sensitive to temporal demands. Confession opens the door of conviction to questioning "between" God, the faith story, and the demands of a given situation. Confession is the temporal evaluator of conviction in action, functioning as the "between" link of faith story and demands of the historical moment.

Confession lives "between" (Buber, *Between Man and Man* 202–3) ultimate and penultimate ground, linking one to God, to the historical situation, and to a life beyond solitary interaction. Penultimate sharing of confession with one another keeps one from falling into arrogance of conviction or, after discovering error, falling into the isolated abyss of self-despair. In *Life Together,* Bonhoeffer stated: "He who is alone with his sin is utterly alone" (110). Bonhoeffer understood the dialogic importance of confession in linking one another, the ultimate (the story of the faith), and the penultimate (temporality of interpretation of the faith and responsiveness to the historical moment).

Bonhoeffer wrote as a twentieth-century Isocrates; his words and deeds lived within a standard, a narrative standard for a polis languishing in confusion. As John Poulakos suggests, Isocrates had

> a general conception of rhetoric as speech leading to concerted action for the benefit of the polis; for it is this conception of rhetoric that informed Isocrates's teaching of the art and that distinguished him from other rhetoricians. He advanced rhetoric as the art of speaking for the polis.

Isocrates sought to reconnect word and deed of the people of the polis. Bonhoeffer did the same for the Christian community. He called for a community of commitment guided by an ultimate story of the faith. Bonhoeffer, unlike Plato, would not so readily reject the intellectual insights of all sophists, at least one of whom understood the necessary interplay of context and ideas.

Both Isocrates and Bonhoeffer understood the importance of connecting word and deed within the demands and reality of a given community; otherwise, one's voice goes, appropriately, unheeded. Bonhoeffer sought a

Christian vocabulary that met the community and took the ultimate into the penultimate, "a world come of age." Bonhoeffer connected words with the community of his time, situating vocabulary, permitting engagement of the Other in a given historical moment. The community, like the historical moment, is a penultimate that finds itself informed by the ultimate, the Christocentric story of the faith.

Bonhoeffer lived in a moment of corruption within the German polis. He understood the story of the faith as a counter story, offering a check on corruption. Hitler attempted to co-opt the possibility of a competing story by installing a unified German Church, which Bonhoeffer rejected (Bethge, *Dietrich Bonhoeffer* 392–96). Bonhoeffer's rejection of Hitler lived not within the realm of the ultimate, but within the penultimate. He understood the impossibility of an ultimate, pure story defeating Nazi tyranny. Bonhoeffer's penultimate commitments permitted him to feign allying with the Nazis in an effort to stop them. Bonhoeffer did not lose conviction of the ultimate Word, a Christocentric story. He took that story into a penultimate world in which faith and concern for the community must bear the test of action.

Bonhoeffer countered the German polis with adherence to an ultimate evaluative standard, the story of the faith. Bonhoeffer pointed to confession that integrated the rhetoric of conviction with attentiveness to application in the concrete moment, ever guided by an ultimate standard that evaluates word and deed, at times in opposition to actions of the polis, the accepted life of the community. Ultimately, it was neither the community nor the Christocentric story of the faith that propelled Bonhoeffer; it was the dialectic interplay of the community, the historical moment, *and* the story of the faith that guided Bonhoeffer's rhetoric of responsibility. The penultimate and the ultimate together provide necessary ground for communicative meaning and action. The dialectical ground of the ultimate and the penultimate requires attentiveness to implementation and a "good" congruence between word and deed, not "pure," perfect, or isomorphic linkage of word and deed.

Without an understanding of the good, the necessity of confession and correction, Bonhoeffer's positive appraisal of temptation would not be possible. Bonhoeffer considers temptation to rest at the heart of the faith—at the heart of the question of Doric harmony. Bonhoeffer quotes both James and Luke with a reminder of the necessity of temptation: "Blessed is the man that endureth temptations, for when he hath been approved, he shall receive the crown of life, which the Lord promised to them that love him" (Jas. 1.12 qtd. in Bonhoeffer, *Temptation* 128). The promise of Jesus Christ proclaims: "Ye are they which have continued with me in my temptations, and I appoint unto you a kingdom" (Luke 22.8 qtd. in Bonhoeffer, *Temptation* 128). The notion of the good, not the pure, frames the horizon of a faith of temporally responsive action. Bonhoeffer trusted in God's word and God's world, permitting an understanding of human life framed within the "good," not the perfect. It is trust in the perfection of God that allows the person to correct and redirect action in accordance with the story of the faith. Trust rests in the story of the faith, not in the individual.

Seeking the Horizon of the Faith

Bonhoeffer's ideas rest uneasily with a "technicians of goodness" mentality (Arnett, "Technicians of Goodness" 353–55), which wants to implement perfection based upon imitation of an idea that worked in one place at one time. Bonhoeffer did not expect or want imitation; he understood the importance of working within the horizon of the faith, not offering specific answers. Bonhoeffer met a "world come of age" without losing his Christocentric standpoint; he adapted, compromised, and altered, never losing sight of the horizon of a given story of conviction. In Bonhoeffer's work and life, one witnesses an ongoing line of demarcation outside the horizon of possibilities that he would not cross. The horizon of possibilities for Bonhoeffer permitted multiple "correct" responses with recognition that a "wrong" response outside the story of the faith keeps humility and confession ever part of religious communicative life.

Bonhoeffer worked with limits within the horizon of the story of the faith. He understood the danger of Nazi intrusion into the Church and signed the Barmen Declaration (Bethge, *Dietrich Bonhoeffer* 371). He returned to Germany from America to fight for Germany, putting his own life at risk. He participated in an attempt to assassinate Hitler, knowing well that he walked on the far side of the horizon of the faith with such participation. Bonhoeffer understood that penultimate action could not violate the horizon of the faith story but responded creatively to the guiding story. Bonhoeffer understood the power of Reinhold Niebuhr's words: "Man is constantly tempted to the sin of idolatry and constantly succumbs to it because in contemplating the power and dignity of his freedom he forgets the degree of his limitations" (*The Nature and Destiny of Man* 1: 166). A horizon presupposes a multiplicity of correct answers responsive to a given historical situation without ignoring the reality of the limits of a given horizon.

Congruence of word and deed understood within a vocabulary of philosophical hermeneutics, specifically the notion of horizon informed by the insight of Hans Gadamer, suggests an interpretive set of possibilities within an interpretive horizon. For instance, a pastor may find many ways to care for a congregation. At times one may listen, at other times offer advice, and on rare occasions ignore the horizon of care responsive to particular people at particular times. However, once one leaves concern for the Other's welfare situated within the realm of the faith, one does something other than pastoral work. The line of demarcation of a horizon permits many "right" interpretations, with the chance of being "wrong," outside the horizon of the event, an ongoing risk.

Specific words and actions do not offer insight into congruence with a given deed; instead, the horizon of the words and actions, an expansive set of possibilities responsive to the historical moment, offers evaluative space for understanding specific deeds. Working for congruence "between" the horizon of the words and a given deed requires a "horizon of consciousness [. . .] out of which only particulars are truly given as experiences" (Gadamer, *Truth and Method* 215). The notion of horizon connects to Husserl's phenomenological work, permitting one to understand the particulars of a given phenomenon within a horizon. For instance, a rectangular two-inch-thick board that is 8' by 4' within the horizon of dining might become a table, but within the horizon of a cold winter with limited heating materials, it might become firewood. The horizon within which one lives alters the encounter with the particulars; one meets one empirical substance and discovers multiple phenomena. A horizon is not a rigid frontier, but something that shifts with a phenomenological focus of attention. A "horizon of intentionality [. . .] constitutes the unity of the flow of experience. [. . .] For everything that is given as existent is given in terms of the world and hence brings the world horizon with it" (Gadamer, *Truth and Method* 217). It is within a given horizon that words and actions make sense. Bonhoeffer understood the necessity of a horizon in evaluation of the coherence and congruence of words and actions.

Confession is a warning that announces one's, horizon, not just discrete individual words and actions. Working within the horizon of an ultimate narrative structure requires attentiveness to the historical situation and a willingness to address and adapt and, when necessary, act from conviction that places one's own being at risk. As Rainer Mayer suggests, Bonhoeffer read with God at the center, not institutions or the self, which then challenged institutions and the reader (180–81).

> [C]ontemporary Christian theologians who proclaim the death of the biblical God cannot gain any support from Bonhoeffer. Bonhoeffer distinguishes between true transcendence and metaphysics, between faith and religion. The fading away of the reality of a supreme being in a world beyond does not affect the reality of the biblical God! [. . .] He emphasizes: "God is the supramundane reality transcending consciousness, the lord and creator. This postulate is the unconditional requirement of Christian theology." (Mayer 181)

Bonhoeffer did not confuse institutional loyalty or even loyalty to the self with the narrative commitment of the faith; the latter trumps, offering a check on institutional and individual action.

The life of the community checks the story of the faith, keeping one from ignoring the importance of application and contact with others, while the story of the faith checks penultimate actions within a given community. Bonhoeffer's dialectic of word and deed, ultimate and penultimate, community and faith story offers textured checks and balances in the search for a "good" sense of congruence in the action of the faith. Bonhoeffer calls for a religious communicator to manifest trust in the horizon of the story of the faith. He offers an alternative to relativism and absolutism with the horizon of a story requiring interpretation in accordance with given circumstances.

Trust Beyond Self-Disclosure

Discerning a "good" connection between word and deed does not suggest openly telling another all that comes to mind. I witnessed a person telling one "disclosure victim" after another his story. The result of numerous exchanges was similar—the person imposed upon afterward worked to avoid the disclosing storyteller. Like an innocent hoping for magic of change from the act of telling a story, my "disclosing colleague" moved from person to person imposing the same message with the same results—"disclosure victims," who then fled from his conversational proximity. Inappropriate disclosure avoids listening and renders the Other an object in one's "telling project."

Appropriate self-disclosure assists listening therapies and binds relationships between friends; there is a constructive place for self-disclosure, permitting the Other to know and understand a given position. The act of self-disclosure assists discernment. Confession actually works in a similar fashion with one major difference—the point of reference that guides the evaluation. The point of reference for self-disclosure is the self. The point of reference for confession is an ultimate, the story of the faith. It is the story, not the person that we trust. Constructive use of self-disclosure and confession permit discernment of answers to confusing and ambiguous situations with different standards of reference.

Confession requires timing, attentiveness to persons, the sharing of information, and an ongoing commitment to change—realigning word and deed within a narrative commitment. Confession tested in dialogue includes an initial judgment about *what* (content), to *whom* one should speak (communicative partner), responsiveness to *where* (historical situation), and the narrative standard that frames a communicative *why* (the story of the faith) that guides the interaction. The Biblical adage, to "be wise as serpents and innocent as doves" (*The New Oxford Annotated Bible,* Matt. 10.16), suggests the importance of discernment before one speaks. Asking questions about *what, who, where,* and *why* places narrative commitment responsibility upon the communicative agent, who listens before speaking—confession presupposes listening and discernment connecting a narrative standard to the Other and to the historical situation. Trust rests not in self-disclosure, but in a story from which one discerns guidance.

Discernment guided Paulo Freire's commitment to a story of literacy. He sought to empower persons with the ability to discern through literacy. Freire understood the impossibility of dialogue between oppressors and the oppressed working from mutually hostile narrative structures. Freire rejected dialogue as a technique that could stop abrasive response from a person of power. Dialogue cannot happen in all settings; however, discernment is necessary in all settings, even if only to determine that dialogue is not possible in a given setting. Discernment requires, at a base level, a commitment to a story of literacy. Literacy permits one to read and encounter information beyond pronouncements from another and beyond one's own personal preference, or "emotivism" (MacIntyre, *After Virtue* 11–14, 16–35). Phenomenologically, confession requires literacy to "read" or "understand" the story of the faith taken into responsive engagement with the Other and the historical situation.

Neither Freire nor Bonhoeffer used the standard of those in power or personal judgment as the key for discernment; both worked from story-informed centers of guidance outside an individual agent or institution. For Bonhoeffer, literacy required a story of faith that supersedes governmental power and self-prejudice. To engage another in conversation requires lessening reliance on both institutional structures and self-insight; instead, one attends to the narrative of the faith in a given historical situation. For

Bonhoeffer, the narrative guide is the faith story. For Freire, the guide is a story of literacy and liberation (Arnett, "Paulo Freire's Revolutionary Pedagogy" 489–97). Each understands that one must discern answers within the limits of a story calling for commitment.

Bonhoeffer placed trust "between" faith story and the historical moment, in thoughtful engagement, using dialectical thinking to temper misplaced confidence in institutions or the self; congruence of word and deed in action takes the story to the world before us. Bonhoeffer's dialectical impulse emerges repeatedly in an effort to locate the "right" linkage of word and deed in a given situation. Bonhoeffer, known as the community theologian of the twentieth century, also stated: "Where his truth enjoins me to dissolve a fellowship for love's sake there I will dissolve it, despite all the protests of my human love" (*Life Together* 35). Bonhoeffer, the emerging bright scholar, left academic life to join the pastorate (Bethge, *Dietrich Bonhoeffer* 221), living a hermeneutic of dialectical tension that revealed engagement with word and deed in a time of narrative disruption and lack of clarity. Bonhoeffer's trust in the story of the faith meeting historical demands and the uniqueness of the Other dialectically tempers undue conviction. Such trust makes possible the meeting of communicative uncertainty. The uncertainty lives within a trusted story horizon of the faith. One may err, but in confession, the story itself calls one back to the story of the faith.

Bonhoeffer and Communicative Uncertainty

Honest engagement typifies Bonhoeffer's meeting of communicative uncertainty. Trust in an ongoing faith story permits Bonhoeffer to ask consistently, "Are we still of any use?" (*Letters and Papers from Prison* 16). He did not take self-importance for granted. For Bonhoeffer, being of use required following the story of the faith in a time of communicative and moral uncertainty. Bonhoeffer revealed a commitment to the "unity of contraries" (Buber, *The Knowledge of Man* 111), linking conviction and uncertainty, the call to make a difference with self-doubt, and the necessity of responsibility with caution. He met uncertainty with tempered conviction, offering a model for us today as we negotiate a postmodern world of narrative and virtue contention.

Bonhoeffer was executed by Hitler more than a half century ago; yet we turn to him to understand a postmodern recognition of metanarrative decline, a moment of narrative and virtue contention. Postmodernity presupposes agency embedded within narrative structures, a world no longer guided by one agreed-upon metanarrative structure. Postmodernity is not an era without narratives, but an era with multiple and competing narratives. A recognition that persons are unable to stand above history, but are embedded within narrative structures and therefore bereft of a transcendental glimpse at truth, defines communicative life in postmodernity. The human being has no assurance that a given action is "correct" or "right." Recognition of the demanding nature of discerning appropriate action does not invalidate a transcendental faith perspective. A transcendental faith perspective in postmodernity is but one of many competing narrative structures; there is no one universally accepted position.

For Bonhoeffer, a faith perspective presupposes a belief in the transcendental without expecting such a belief to provide "the" answers to problems of daily life. As Bonhoeffer stated, God is not *"Deus ex machina"* (*Letters and Papers from Prison* 282), who comes down from the heavens to assist when beckoned. Life, understood by Bonhoeffer, unlike a Greek drama that regularly used such devices, requires the person to make responsible decisions in the midst of embeddedness within the historical moment. For Bonhoeffer, decisions that propel actions rest in conviction without complete assurance of accuracy. Immersion in narrative life, inability to stand above the fray of historicity and make proclamations of truth, defines human existence. Transcendence happens in glimpses, guided by the story of the faith, carrying with it a sense of caution and wariness about conclusions. One is never one hundred percent sure of a transcendental glimpse; all too often our own subjectivity substitutes for what we want to call a transcendent glimpse. Such is the Old Testament caution that we cannot look directly into the face of God; only indirect glimpses are possible.

In spite of uncertainty that accompanies embedded action, we must evaluate and act. Bonhoeffer understood that responsible action situated in uncertainty of knowing has a constant companion—guilt. Not knowing "the" answer, being aware of one's own limits, positions decision making within a sphere of flaws, uncertainty, and ongoing questioning of conviction. When more than one action looms as possible, any choice presupposes error and lack of assurance of knowing "the" required action. Morally reflective persons sense guilt as the companion to a chosen action absent complete confirmation of its truth-value. In the middle of a communicative action, one hears a quiet voice of guilt or one's conscience, or what George Herbert Mead called the "me" (173–78, 192–200). The voice of the "me" asks of us: "Are other options possible that are, perhaps, even more viable? Is this, your selected option, really 'right,' the 'correct' decision?" Guilt in religious communication works with a conviction that there is a faith story worthy of our trust.

Acting within knowledge of limits, our embeddedness, is a postmodern reality. It is a mistake to assume that such knowledge and action present a new reality. Anyone caught in a demanding moment of decision, unable to stand above the historical moment, left with incomplete knowledge, makes a decision understanding the existential reality of embeddedness of human existence. A parent deciding on an operation for a child that might lengthen life or end it abruptly knows such reality. A spouse deciding what to do for a loved one on life support knows such reality. All those who converse with the seemingly impossible demands of life, knowing that the wisdom of Solomon is not upon one's own house, understands the deeply embedded and uncertain nature of human decision making. All we can do is trust the story that guides us, not the answer. The answer is a temporal penultimate, the best we can do at a given moment.

Bonhoeffer offers insight into decision making in a time of uncertainty, framing tempered conviction as the heart of communicative wisdom. While in prison, Bonhoeffer wrote a brief drama *(Drama)* and a short novel *(Novel)*. In the drama, the main character, Christopher, has a disease that will claim his life in a year, which in fictional form suggests the nature of Bonhoeffer's own fate. The drama examines the struggle between aristocratic impulses and concerns for the common person—Bonhoeffer's own challenge generated from his privileged background. Even in the final stages of Bonhoeffer's life, conviction and questioning are central to his work. Questioning does not diminish Bonhoeffer's faith but keeps alive his conviction without a blind, unreflective commitment to narrative adherence.

In the drama, questions about what virtuous actions are provide the subject of discussion between the main characters. They sense the breakdown of metanarrative agreement and witness the growing power of Nazi ideology. Such questioning of foundations continues in this historical moment. The constructive result of a foundational breakdown is threefold: 1) the breakdown of foundations makes us more aware of our embeddedness in narrative limits; 2) multiple foundations permit/require choice; and 3) choices require us to acknowledge the ground under our feet, in this case, the story that guides us. In essence, conviction rests in the form of ground with knowing limits, experiencing doubt, and recognizing one major assumption; ground under our feet requires narrative background that shapes understanding, interpretation, and response to God's world.

Bonhoeffer understood that ground under one's feet is necessary as one meets difference. Bonhoeffer would not romanticize an era of narrative contention. However, neither would he lament such a moment. Narrative confusion makes a person of conviction figure out why a given ground is worth standing upon.

Bonhoeffer writes in his drama:

> HEINRICH. And if, then, death sits in your breast in the shape of a piece of shrapnel, grinning at you every day—and you don't know for what purpose you are alive and for what purpose you are dying—yes, then it's a miracle if you don't go mad with the urge to live and with despair, with hatred of all that lives, and with craving for wild pleasure. Give me ground under my feet, give me the Archimedean point to stand on—and all would be different.
>
> CHRISTOPHER. Ground under your feet—I have never understood it like that. I believe you are right. I understand—ground under your feet, to be able to live and to die. (*Drama* 46–47)

Bonhoeffer points to dialectic in his religious communication: we meet uncertainty with ground under our feet—examined and questioned ground—ground assumed with Kierkegaard's understanding of *Fear and Trembling.* Bonhoeffer calls us to trust a faith story that permits us to meet uncertainty, not with assurance of outcome, but with conviction that narrative guidance can and will assist. Trust in the ultimate guides the penultimate, never forsaking the danger of an uncertain world.

Grounded Conviction

Grounded conviction gives one a commonplace to turn to for guidance. As one listens, interprets, and responds to others, ideas, and the historical moment, one brings a grounded sense of conviction. Bonhoeffer pointed to the importance of knowing and acknowledging one's own position, one's own set of interests, and one's own bias that must be questioned, tempered, and enriched in the test of everyday life.

The ground of conviction embraced the model of Christ, a call to discipleship, and a moral mandate of service to Others. This sense of ground is the overriding message of Bonhoeffer's faith story. Bonhoeffer discussed the notion of the "fixed" (*Creation and Fall* 28–32) as "fixed" things that light the "things" or goods of creation. The ground of conviction from which Bonhoeffer worked was never to forget the story of faith behind the "fixed." [W]e believe in God *beyond* this created world" (*Creation and Fall* 31). Bonhoeffer reminds us of the concreteness of trust, the power of the *beyond* of God.

> The old rationalistic question still remains about the creation of light on the first day and of the sun on the fourth day. Herder has spoken eloquently of how the biblical author may have had in mind a break of day in which the light breaks forth before the sun. Perhaps he was right. But it must be said that light makes the sun what it is and not the sun the light. [. . .] The light *per se* of the creation, the light which lay formless over the formless darkness, bound to form, to law, to the fixed, to number; but it remains in God, it remains God's creation, and never itself becomes calculable number. (Bonhoeffer, *Creation and Fall* 31–32)

Bonhoeffer never forgot who is both the ground and the light. Bonhoeffer's insight into the penultimate nature of the fixed reminds us of a trust that gives insight into the ultimate importance of ground, permitting us to meet uncertainty. The story of the faith does not rest on fixed ground, but on ground capable of meeting uncertainty.

The ground of conviction for Bonhoeffer—not fixed, but situated within a life of responsibility without the security of knowing the outcome in advance—requires the ongoing interplay of beginning knowledge, more learning, the test of service and the ongoing repetition of a life of service based upon responsible action and learning. Bonhoeffer entered a communicative setting with the story of the faith, a willingness to learn from Others and the historical moment, and confidence to test ideas in service to Others.

A Ground for Learning

This historical moment goes by a number of different linguistically awkward descriptors: postmodernism (Lyotard 81), postindustrial (Bell 14), the era of the parenthesis (Naisbitt 252). These awkward sounding terms suggest transition and change with this particular era, postmodernity, resting between modernity and some yet to be understood or named era. Argument and resistance over odd sounding terms such as *postmodernity* continue; we may not agree on the appropriate term for this moment, but many do agree that we live in a time of significant change. Agreement on definitions may not be possible, but agreement on the horror of terrorism, the reality of war, dramatic swings in the stock market, and ecological concerns make us ever concerned about this particular moment. The assurance of progress underlying modernity is no longer a universal given. Our changing ground, our changing moment, and our time of responsibility live within this juncture of change.

This historical situation understood as an era of transition labeled with awkward sounding terms that symbolize change without a clear direction challenges the presupposition of an agreed-upon metanarrative foundation capable of carrying universal understanding. One can accept the decline of a metanarrative without lament or assuming that this moment of transition is historically novel. To accept this moment as an era of transition, change, and narrative contention does not suggest that we are the first, or will be the last, to encounter transitional moments that shake foundations, giving way to communicative uncertainty.

Transition and narrative contention should surprise no one. We no longer live in an Athenian polis where agreed-upon public virtues frame social practices that shape an agreed-upon narrative structure known by a people. Today's competing narrative structures contrast with the Athenians' privileged voice of agreed-upon narrative within the polis, which excluded women and slaves, people outside the participatory ranks of citizens. Even in Athens, there was no agreement among all; privileged voices reigned in democratic participation.

Taking Athens as an ideal leaves us with discerning agreement about "common" virtues and "common" social practices within a small band of people. Today's global society brings together a diverse array of persons and ideas vying for acceptance in the public arena.

Within the last century, the United States experienced rapid change from small groupings in farm and small towns to large, diverse associations of people in urban centers. The United States entered World War II with the majority of its people living in rural and small-town America. Changing opportunities for employment resulted in people migrating from rural settings and small towns into urban centers. Urban life embraced diversity out of a pragmatic need to employ persons in the machinery of the Industrial Revolution.

The Industrial Revolution gave people from diverse parts of the United States and the world reason to enter urban centers, propelled by a sense of hope attached to this new and often bewildering place called the city, resulting in displacement from rural settings. To assist one's family through gainful employment, people moved to centers of industry, emerging places of commerce, accepting change and transition in order to survive economically.

Today, we once again meet transition and change. Perhaps our response to change and transition rests upon two assumptions. First, new demands disrupt lives; the pain of disruption is real and demands recognition. Second, recognition of the normality of transition and change moderates our sense of the uniqueness of this moment—transition is commonplace in human history. To assume that this moment of change is more demanding than life depicted in the move from agrarian to industrial life invites "bad faith" (Sartre 86–116). Upton Sinclair's *The Jungle,* Charles Dickens's *Hard Times,* and the writings of Marx—illustrated by *Capital: A Critique of Political Economy*—and Engels's, *The Condition of the Working Class in England in 1844* announce the darker side of the transition from agrarian to industrial life. Should we expect transitions to be seamless and without discomfort when such moments have affected others in demanding and all too often adverse ways?

How did the blacksmith feel about the advent of the automobile? How about the printer in the move from set to movable type? Even optimism about innovation and new economies, followed by economic collapse from overexpansion, is not novel. In less than a decade we witnessed "dot.com" companies build great wealth, only to lose financial backing and in many instances the business itself. Rapid development of companies in a "new economy," followed by premature death of many new players, is the ground upon which change and innovation take root. Not all new ideas or companies prosper in times of transition, and not all change is for the better, but whatever the eventual evaluation of a new idea or system, the connection of the word "novelty" with change generates a historical oxymoron. Change is often painful, but not historically novel.

This moment of technological revolution is real, just not as unique as we might wish to believe. Transitions permit us to work out specifics of change, with all the vicissitudes of undue optimism and extreme pessimism. The "worked out" specifics influence financial and social aspects of human living. During transitions, the ground beneath our feet shifts. Shifting foundations are not novel to human history. Carl Rogers was correct: what we consider most personally unique is generally quite common. Transitional change understood in historical perspective requires awareness of the inevitability of significant change and foundational disruption. Only historical ignorance and inadvertent narcissism permit us to assume that transitions and change define this moment alone; we have much in common with those that have come before us.

This thesis of change without romanticism or fear shapes Neil Postman's 1999 work, *Building a Bridge to the Eighteenth Century: How the Past Can Improve Our Future.* Postman states that history is the metasubject needed in a good education.

> There is no escaping ourselves. The human dilemma is as it always has been, and it is a delusion to believe that the future will render irrelevant what we know and have long known about ourselves but find it convenient to forget. (11)

Postman reminds us that even in a world come of age, knowledge that others met change keeps our moments of sorrow and joy from transition in perspective.

Recognition of the long arm of historical change offers a commonplace, a narrative of sorts—a narrative composed of persons engaging, meeting, and at times lamenting change. Acknowledgment of change links us to many who walked on this earth long before our consciousness of this particular transition and change. Many met the demands of change by fighting, accommodating, and, at times, seizing opportunity from social and economic transitions.

The diversity of response to change rests in reaction to many extreme moments in human history. For instance, the French Revolution altered France and, arguably, Western culture. Victor Hugo, Alexis de Tocqueville, Edmund Burke, and Thomas Paine offered differing accounts of the consequences of this historic change; those authors agreed on only one issue—the French Revolution was a moment of profound transition. Our era is hardly more demanding or confusing than that of the French Revolution or the movement from an agrarian to an industrial age. Even to suggest that we live in a narrativeless moment (Arnett, "Existential Homelessness" 229–45) that renders us homeless fails to secure the uniqueness of our own moment. The words of the historic Black spiritual, "Sometimes I feel like a motherless child a long, long way from home," reveal that homelessness is not novel or recent.

To privilege our status or position is an unproductive comparison, requiring us, on the one hand, to judge the other without "being there" and, on the other hand, to give ourselves too much credit for novelty of the challenge before us. Narrative confusion is not unique; it accompanies any historical moment that no longer has narrative agreement on what constitutes a "good life" or what constitutes agreed-upon social practices essential to "success" within a stable era or narrative structure.

In this moment of transition, the notion of the "good life," no longer backed by the power of social consensus, indicates another moment of transition upon us. This reality calls for acceptance, not romanticizing the uniqueness of this historical moment. Acceptance without lament permits us to learn from difference: from others, from the historical moment, from changing social practices. Communicative uncertainty is not alien or strange to the human community when one recognizes that many have already and many will yet encounter moments of change. Taming communicative uncertainty begins by placing the notions of transition and change within historical perspective. The religious communicator works with a tradition, a faith perspective that connects the person to those who have and must later endure transition and change. Bonhoeffer understood that even in transition a faith perspective calls for the hallowing of the everyday. Even transition and change open the door to the narrative of the faith, reminding one to hallow the given rather than engage in routine lament for what is missing.

Bonhoeffer met change with a basic trust. He was confident that the story of the faith would endure no matter what the challenge before us. No matter what the change before us:

> Jesus Christ, incarnate, crucified and glorified, has entered my life and taken charge. "To me to live is Christ" (Phil. 1.21). And where Christ lives, there the Father also lives, and both Father and Son through the Holy Ghost. The Holy Trinity himself has made his dwelling in the Christian heart, filling his whole being, and transforming him into the divine image. (*The Cost of Discipleship* 343)

There is trust in the story of the faith of the Father, Son, and Holy Ghost living incarnate in a world of change, no matter what the change, in a world come of age. With a trusted story, the test of a religious communicator is not stability, but challenge of changing ground.

The Ground of Narrative Testing

Bonhoeffer met shifting secular life with the ground of the faith. He did not permit change to invite distrust of life or propel distrust within the Church. While one meets change, the pain and the distrust of shifting ground, Bonhoeffer calls one back to a basic conviction, a basic trust—the faith. Dramatic change provides a test of the ground of faith and permits one to reorder one's convictions: What constitutes the center of one's life? What is the ground that ultimately shapes conviction?

For Bonhoeffer, one must reject distrust of life by rejecting suspicion of the Other's motivations and the demand for the world to conform to our wishes. Bonhoeffer sought change through responsibility while affirming God's world, which often moved contrary to his own wishes. Bonhoeffer trusted this world to God; he did not limit the power of God only to those within the Christian faith tradition.

In prison on July 1944, Bonhoeffer wrote:

> God goes to every man when sore bestead,
> Feeds body and spirit with his bread;

For Christians, pagans alike he hangs dead,
And both alike forgiving.

("Christians and Pagans" 26)

Bonhoeffer offered conviction without privilege. He met life with responsibility and conviction. Bonhoeffer trusted the story of the faith to call him to responsibility, ever reminding him to avoid feelings of complete assurance. The world can use such trust today—a trust willing to meet the testing of everyday life, with actions forever garbed in the humility of the question of one's own ground and one's own righteousness. "Who am I? They mock me, these lonely questions of mine. Whoever I am, thou knowest, O God, I am thine" (Bonhoeffer, "Who Am I?" 18). So much trust permits uncertainty and responsiveness to the Other and the historical situation to guide communicative life. Confession for Bonhoeffer begins with trust, an existential trust in God's world, meeting the historical moment, limiting lament, foregoing life in a dream world. Bonhoeffer lived firmly in God's earthly home, in a "world come of age."

6

A FRAGILE ABSOLUTE

The Faith Story in the Marketplace

Alasdair MacIntyre on "moral crisis":

> Do not however suppose that the conclusion to be drawn will turn out to be one of despair. *Angst* is an intermittently fashionable emotion and the misreading of some existentialist texts has turned despair itself into a kind of psychological nostrum. But if we are indeed in as bad a state as I take us to be, pessimism will turn out to be one more cultural luxury that we shall have to dispense with in order to survive in these hard times. (*After Virtue* 5)

Dietrich Bonhoeffer's comments on the "how" and "why" to hallow the everyday:

> When the spirit touches
> man's heart and brow
> with thoughts that are lofty, bold, serene,
> so that with clear eyes he will face the world
> . . . .
> when then the spirit gives
> . . . .
> content and meaning—
> . . . .
> [. . .] the spirit that grasps and befriends him,
> . . . .
> steeling himself in the hour of fatigue—
> . . . .
> wherein he finds refuge and comfort and strengthening [. . .]
> ("The Friend" 30)

This historical moment defined as a time of moral crisis is not novel; moral crises accompany every significant historical transition. However, this era uses language that calls attention to this "moral crisis" propelled by incompatible narratives and incommensurable virtue structures. MacIntyre suggests that agreed-upon narrative background makes agreement possible in a given historical situation, and such agreement is no longer in place (*After Virtue* 6–22). Narrative disagreement makes conversation about "right" and "wrong" increasingly demanding. Bonhoeffer reminds a person of faith of the location of strength and courage for engaging such a moment—a world come of age without agreement on a common virtue structure.

Bonhoeffer framed a "world come of age" (*Letters and Papers from Prison* 326–29) around three major assumptions: 1) God as deus ex machina willing to save us at our demand is an unworkable position; 2) the world of difference (contrary virtue structures) needs recognition; and 3) we have responsibility to assist God's world; the responsibility rests with us, not divine intervention. Bonhoeffer and MacIntyre point to the importance of meeting a moral crisis in a world come of age. Bonhoeffer penned the beginning of such a moment in 1944, and more recently, MacIntyre in such works as *Dependent Rational Animals: Why Human Beings Need the Virtues* articulates the demands upon us in such a moment of narrative contention. Bonhoeffer understood the fragility of agreement in a changing world, while simultaneously affirming a commitment to a Christocentric worldview.

A major key to Bonhoeffer's interpretive project is the ability to read the demands of the historical moment, a sense of historicity literacy. It is not just what one knows, but the ability to take what one knows and match it to the needs of the moment, that defines the art securing the success of rhetoric. To interpret any text with depth of insight requires one to be well read and philosophically attentive. Bonhoeffer sensed that a world come of age, what we now call a postmodern culture, requires the ability to read and understand the philosophical-pragmatic differences in competing narratives. This ability is a survival skill in a world of change and contention.

Ideas destined for appropriate action address the questions of a given historical moment. Such ideas drive praxis, theory-informed action; they do not arise from a social vacuum. Such ideas answer the concerns of a given historical moment. Bonhoeffer's ideas not only meet the demands of the rise of the Third Reich but illuminate our historical situation of postmodern virtue contention and difference. Both moments are examples of narrative disruption with agreement on virtue structures no longer present; Bonhoeffer's era and this one have historical connection in that answering a call with responsiveness to narrative contention unites the two moments.

Without the confidence of deus ex machina, a God that solves all problems, Bonhoeffer walks with a faith story that engages the historical moment that presents itself. He does not know all answers before he meets the demands of a given situation. Bonhoeffer walks with a "fragile absolute" as his guide. Bonhoeffer's story meets a changing world, finding texture and insight from the meeting and from engaging new ideas.

> Of necessity, that can go on only till people can by their own strength push these boundaries somewhat further out, so that God becomes superfluous as a *deus ex machina.* [. . .] The church stands, not at the boundaries where human powers give out, but in the middle of the village. (Bonhoeffer, *Letters and Papers from Prison* 282)

The church only stands in the middle when it is a learning community, not merely a "telling" community. Engagement with the historical moment acknowledges the necessity of application, pointing to the fragility of an assurance ever-uniquely applied. Application of ideas to the historical situation becomes an act of bringing the fragile (the temporal) into contact with an absolute that we glimpse with only temporal sight—such is the notion of revelation.

The physical voice of Dietrich Bonhoeffer left us in the middle of the twentieth century. Yet his voice rings as a contemporary companion, communicating the importance of the unity of the fragile and the absolute in trembling unity. Seeking ground upon which to stand in a temporal place of shifting sand of narrative contention invites a perception of moral crisis. Times of contentiousness about moral ground are not novel—witness the Israelites in captivity, the civil rights movements in the United States and South Africa, liberation movements throughout the world, and ongoing contention in the international community. Each situation suggests narrative disagreement, a moral crisis of guiding principles. Moral crises arise when contention over first principles becomes part of our normative communication structures.

A Moral Crisis

MacIntyre's contemporary understanding of "moral crisis" is revealed in the title of his book, *After Virtue.* "After virtue" implies that we live in a postmodern era lacking a unifying narrative standard announcing agreed-upon social practices that we consider virtuous. Without one narrative standard, we are unable to agree upon interpretation of whether or not a given action is virtuous. For instance, I asked students the following question: "What is the reaction of friends if you defend someone wrongly accused?" The students volunteered that reactions varied from disinterest to fear to amusement and from affirmation and support to disgust. Even among "friends," common agreement on social practices central to a given virtue system is lacking—there is no uniformity of interpretation. MacIntyre stresses that our "moral crisis" lacks a sense of "why" without a sufficient moral vocabulary held in public agreement. Moral language is in "grave disorder" with "emotivism," decision by personal preference (MacIntyre, *After Virtue* 2, 11–14, 16–35), guiding much of contemporary decision making. The moral standard of emotivism becomes "me"; the self becomes "criterionless" in a public sense, relying only upon personal preferences as the anchors for "right" and "wrong."

> [The] key characteristic of the emotivist self [is] its lack of any ultimate criteria. When I characterize it thus I am referring back to what we have already noticed, that whatever criteria or principles or evaluative allegiances the emotivist self may profess, they are to be construed as expressions of attitudes, preferences and choices which are themselves not governed by criterion, principle or value, since they underlie and are prior to all allegiance to criterion, principle or value. [. . .] [T]he emotivist self is as having suffered a deprivation, a stripping away of qualities that were once believed to belong to the self. The self is now thought of as lacking any necessary social identity, because the kind of social identity that it once enjoyed is no longer available; the self is now thought of as criterionless, because the kind of *telos* in terms of which it once judged and acted is no longer thought to be credible. (MacIntyre, *After Virtue* 33)

The moral crisis of which MacIntyre speaks comes from contention of narrative and virtue structures. Such a moment is, indeed, upon us, but not new, as suggested above. However, those living through such times cannot ignore moments of narrative disruption; pain may have historical companions, but it is still personal. Bonhoeffer's insights inform us and offer confidence in the possibility of meeting disruption with conviction—the conviction of a guiding moral story. In the movie *The Majestic,* the main character loses his memory in an accident, finding himself welcomed into a town as a long-lost war hero. Months later, his memory returns as he is forced to defend himself before the committee on un-American activities. This person of little moral conviction finds courage situated within a story of the life of a fallen hero, Luke, the real deceased war hero with whom the town had confused him. Before going to the committee meeting, he is offered by a friend a gift—a small volume of the U.S. Constitution. In the memory of Luke and within the pages of the U.S. Constitution, the main character in the film begins to understand for the first time the conviction and courage necessary to contend with the committee on un-American activities. Two good stories—one of sacrifice by a genuine war hero and another contained within a document protecting our ability to assemble and to think freely—situate his courage. Our unlikely hero moves from amnesia to knowledge of stories that call forth courage, a reason to live and to die. Bonhoeffer, in the agony of prison, offered a picture of such courage; he lived a good story, revealing the power of a story of conviction in a moment of narrative and virtue disruption and confusion. A faith story meeting the difficulties and crises of contention becomes a rhetorical fragile absolute, working to persuade the agent with a call to courage without the zeal of an ideologue.

A moral crisis over what constitutes a first narrative, first social practices, first principles, a first philosophy brings one to ask on what one can depend. For Emmanuel Levinas, the answer lies in the face of the Other, attending to the Other as first philosophy—"I am my brother's keeper" (Cohen xii). In the face of the Other one finds a call to responsibility—what Bonhoeffer engaged as a first philosophy conviction of "deputyship" (*Ethics* 224–27). Like MacIntyre today, Bonhoeffer and Levinas understood that meeting a moral crisis from a stance of deputyship or responsibility for the Other requires a deep commitment to language situated within a moral story capable of providing a narrative alternative—a ground of conviction of first principles.

As is typical of his work, Bonhoeffer connected a moral story—the language of the faith within a dialectical commitment—to conviction and testing in the human community. The preface to Bonhoeffer's first major work, his doctoral dissertation, *The Communion of Saints: A Dogmatic Inquiry into the Sociology of the Church,* connects theology and social context. Bonhoeffer's words of July 1930 frame the preface to this work and announce the driving force of his religious scholarship.

> Ideas such as "person," "primal state," "sin," and "revelation" are fully understandable only in relation to sociality. The fact that every genuinely theological concept can be correctly comprehended only when set within and supplemented by its special social sphere is proof of the specifically theological nature of any inquiry into the sociology of the church. (13)

A moral crisis of first principles propelled Bonhoeffer's walking of theology into the social context of his time. He wanted theology to answer questions of the historical moment before him, not questions situated in the abstract ideal of academic logic.

When first principles are at risk, narratives are at risk. In such a moment, one cannot look to narratives for answers; instead, one finds social practices that assist a given historical moment, and, from such action, new narrative engagement and formation emerges. Enduring narratives guide social practices and, in addition, when narratives are confused, remnant social practices offer partial guidance. In the interpretive language of Paul Ricoeur, narrative and social practices function as "whole" and "part." Narrative and social practices offer interpretive insight into each other, providing a richer understanding of communicative life. However, when narrative life is unclear, social practices become the foundation for narrative renewal.

The test of communicative life, for Bonhoeffer, was in the marketplace. He looked for communicative social practices of discipleship and service: "The church is the church only when it exists for others" (*Letters and Papers from Prison* 382). The test of the communicative social practices of the faith occurs outside the Church, the institution charged with narrative protection. It is the marketplace, a place of contention and difference, that tests a faith story of service taken into communicative action.

Into the Marketplace

Bonhoeffer took the story of the faith into the marketplace—a place of difference, a place of exchange, a place where "buyer beware" lives in action. This metaphor of exchange represents the nonutopian nature of Bonhoeffer's story. Bonhoeffer's social practices of attending to the Other took him into a marketplace of diversity of ideas and persons where difference vies for acceptance in the public arena. Bonhoeffer did not walk away from the marketplace but understood it as the place of testing—testing of the faith story.

The marketplace makes a livelihood possible as one leaves the confines of self-sufficiency. A by-product of participation in the marketplace is discovery and testing of ideas. The following Hasidic tale suggests the value of the metaphor of the marketplace as a place for learning. This tale was offered to contend with a colleague's objection to the use of the term marketplace, resting within the perspective of Bonhoeffer's engagement of a "world come of age." Bonhoeffer understood that at times the marketplace is the only place where answers can be located.

Members of a congregation came to the rabbi and asked, "Rabbi, what can we do to lessen our pain and confusion?" The rabbi responded, "Pray." Two weeks later, the people returned and stated, "Rabbi, we have prayed, but the pain and confusion remain. What are we to do now?" The rabbi answered, "You must go home and study." The people returned home to study, only to discover no relief from their pain and their confusion. The people returned two weeks later with continuing sorrow. They cried, "Rabbi, we prayed and we studied. There is no lessening of our pain, no lessening of our confusion. What are we to do now?" The rabbi paused and asked his people to wait for him as he found his cloak. The rabbi returned and said, "When prayer and study cannot help, we must walk together into the marketplace; the marketplace offers insight when nothing else assists." In times of confusion, we walk together hoping to find answers in the mix of people and ideas in the marketplace.

The above story does not minimize prayer or suggest that study is unimportant. Prayer and study prepare one for the marketplace, the place of testing of learning and insight gained from prayer and study. Applying prayer and study in the marketplace of diversity requires leaving the safety of utopian prayer and study, engaging God's world with all the insights that prayer and study offer. The principles taken into the marketplace make all the difference; such is the reason Bonhoeffer begins with God as first principle and service or discipleship as penultimate implementation principles. The place is secondary to what one takes into a given place of exchange. The marketplace is important to Bonhoeffer as a concrete place of a living faith. The marketplace offers no principles, only a place for the faith to meet the test of everyday life. A good story acts in the marketplace, tested by veracity between action and story and fidelity between story and historical moment.

A "good story" judged by short-term success or failure in the marketplace alone misses the importance of long-term impact on the marketplace of ideas. Only in 1996 was Bonhoeffer exonerated from the status of traitor by the German government for his opposition to Hitler and the Third Reich—years after his participation in the assassination attempt on Adolph Hitler (*Christian Century* 929).

Engagement in and with the world emerges from a story-guided communication framework, a moral story capable of providing ground under one's feet as one meets a diverse and contentious marketplace of ideas and persons. Bonhoeffer's life and work announce the importance of a moral story that meets the historical moment in the test of everyday action. Bonhoeffer clearly takes a Christocentric story of faith-driven service into the marketplace of difference. The manner in which he made this move fits with his commitment to dialectical tempering.

Human Institutions

Bonhoeffer's story of the faith rests within the dialectic of a Christocentric worldview and recognition of the autonomy of human institutions. The marketplace is a place for testing and influence, not a place of purity, not a heaven on earth, not a shelter within which to wait for constant intervention of a father figure—"*deus ex machina*" (Bonhoeffer, *Letters and Papers from Prison* 341). It is the marketplace that tempers an abstract faith; Bonhoeffer engages a world come of age in the dialectic of the faith story and the meeting of the marketplace.

> [The Church] is not concerned with the Christianizing of the secular institutions or with subordinating them to the Church, that is to say, with abolishing their "relative" autonomy; it is concerned rather with their true worldliness or "naturalness" in obedience to God's word. It is, therefore, precisely in their genuine worldliness that the secular institutions are subject to the dominion of Christ. (Bonhoeffer, *Ethics* 325–26)

Bonhoeffer's dialectical tempering and testing of a faith story in the marketplace disappoints those wanting God's explicit reign in every decision and simultaneously disheartens those wanting to ignore a story of the faith. Bonhoeffer's dialectic acknowledges the influence of the faith and the autonomy of secular institutions. The marketplace is the meeting place of Bonhoeffer's dialectical engagement with the faith.

Bonhoeffer's story of the faith works dialectically and rhetorically. He openly attempts to persuade secular institutions without forgetting their autonomy. Such a story of the faith of conviction lives without naiveté; there is no presupposition that the world conforms to one story or that all others will applaud one's chosen story in the marketplace.

Bonhoeffer recognized the difference and the autonomy of the story of the faith and the marketplace. He understood the interplay of four major dimensions: Church, family, culture, and government (*Ethics* 286). The rhetorical nature of the faith story requires constant effort to influence all dimensions of life without losing respect for their individual autonomy.

The tandem effort of respect for autonomy and call to influence took Bonhoeffer into the marketplace, framing a "world come of age" with a faith story capable of meeting a diverse population with conviction, tempered by a willingness to learn and propelled by an effort to persuade void of the illusion that the secular world would naturally affirm a faith story. As Larry Rasmussen and Renate Bethge suggest, Bonhoeffer rejected an apocalyptic eschatology of a religious utopianism. Instead, he claimed a theology of the cross, situated within a "permanent eschatology" (Rasmussen and Bethge 83). Bonhoeffer understood the call of persons of faith into a marketplace that tests a faith story with inevitable suffering, without constant participation in God's glory. Permanent eschatology knows no end; it embraces the ongoing life of God's story and God's people, offering direction without a conclusion. A concluding moment rests in God's hands, not in the predictions of his people. A permanent eschatology requires one to work in the marketplace with the guidance of the story of the faith and without illusion.

The colleague who pleaded with me not to use the term "marketplace" in this work was concerned that "marketplace" frames Bonhoeffer as interested in commerce. My colleague's worry was both correct and in error. Bonhoeffer, of course, considered God, not commerce, as the first principle. However, Bonhoeffer was unwilling to ignore reality before him; commerce is central in the maintenance of life outside an agrarian family structure. Commerce replaces a self-sufficient lifestyle with a marketplace of exchange—the good and bad of difference and encounters with the unknown.

The marketplace traditionally provided a place for people to gather: trade brought different people and different goods together (Jefferson 76). Encounter with difference through the meeting of diverse people and cultures provided opportunity for exchange and learning. The marketplace is not a pure place; it introduces foreign or alien people and ideas in the act of learning. Those unwilling to encounter the marketplace desire a world of Eden in which the tree of knowledge and difference was never touched. The utopian life of Eden is counter to the dialectical story of the faith that guided Bonhoeffer.

The "tree of knowledge" of good and evil moves human beings to actions of sin against one another. The tale of Cain killing his brother powerfully renders the message that we walk in the presence of evil. The coming of Christ permits the metaphor of the "tree" to enter the story of the faith once again. The tree transformed into a wooden cross offers a message of redemption; the person of faith enters the marketplace, guided by service, knowledge of the faith story, and the recognition of the demands of the cross. "What a strange tree of life, this tree on which God himself must suffer and die" (Bonhoeffer, *The Cost of Discipleship* 94). The end of the story of Eden is sacrifice and suffering—"costly grace."

The call of the cross offers suffering and service, giving direction as one enters the marketplace. One does not walk alone as one meets Cain in the marketplace. The story of the faith permits one to forgo utopian visions of life, warning against the temptation of "false security" (Bonhoeffer, *Temptation* 115). The marketplace is a place without constant familiarity, a place disruptive of our security. The marketplace is the place of difference in ideas and persons, a place where both Cain and Abel dwell.

The metaphor of the marketplace reminds us of a flawed, but informative, place where differing people, ideas, and goods gather. Bonhoeffer understood the faith task as living in permanent eschatology in everyday life. The story of God's suffering and service lives permanently in the marketplace of difference of ideas, goods, and persons.

The marketplace of ideas and diversity of persons inevitably results in disagreement and contention. The familiar conviction that the best ideas rise to the surface through debate reminds us of marketplace consequences in political life. The metaphor of marketplace suggests public disagreement, the trading of goods and ideas. It is a "tough minded" (James 13) place.

A Marketplace of Evil

There is no guarantee that a marketplace will be good or even neutral. At times, an entire market seems to succumb to evil. Bonhoeffer understood God's message as a guide through all life, but a "world come of age" of idea exchange, commerce, industry, and culture requires "relative autonomy" (*Ethics* 362). The marketplace is not a heaven on earth; it is no utopia. It often becomes a place of evil when only one product or idea guides communicative life together; when one has limited or no access to the marketplace, less influence in the public sphere results, permitting hegemonic control of public life.

The marketplace is far from holy ground; it is a place of good and evil. Any dialectic has the possibility of falling into excess on one issue and deficiency on another. Aristotle's practical insight (II.viii–ix) manifested itself in the excess of evil in the Nazi marketplace. A fundamental social justice question for Bonhoeffer's Germany was: "How can we regain open access to participation in the marketplace?" Keeping people in their "place" requires lessening opportunities of "certain" persons to influence the marketplace, limiting the flow of new ideas and commerce into the marketplace. Jews were restricted from participation in commerce by the 1938 "*Reichsgesetzblatt,*" part 1, page 1580, signed by Goering, and they were restricted from idea exchange and university teaching by part 4 of *"Das Programm"* (Shirer 242–51). Bonhoeffer's authorization to teach on the faculty at the University of Berlin was withdrawn August 5, 1936. Bonhoeffer, banned from university instruction, was later banned from the marketplace of ideas in September 1940, by a Gestapo order forbidding him to speak in public and later in 1941, forbidding him to print or publish any of his work.

The first steps of oppression against the Jewish people excluded them from a world of commerce. The second step limited idea exchange. Then the Nazis limited religious ideas in the marketplace. The Nazis imposed a national church, the "Reich Church," which the Reichstag formally recognized on July 14, 1933 (Shirer 237). Ludwig Müller, a fervent Nazi and friend of the *Führer,* was elected "Reich Bishop" in September 1933 at the synod held in Wittenberg (Shirer 237). Rebellion against this decision permitted the birth of the Confessing Church. Finally, the destruction of family life and death of agreed upon public conventions of protection became the norm with the construction of concentration camps beginning at Dachau on September 22, 1933 (Shirer 212). At this point, all Bonhoeffer's constituent parts of the public domain—church, culture, government, and commerce—disallowed participation by the Jews.

To stop someone from participation in the marketplace limits the possibilities of a life, as witnessed by Bonhoeffer's twin sister, Sabine, in the following story. In 1929, Sabine married Gerhard Leibholz, whose father was Jewish. Gerhard was a Protestant. The family heritage and culture made concerns for Jewish life vital. The Nazis stated that "A Jew is a person descended from at least three grandparents who are full Jews by race. [. . .] 2) A Mischling who is a subject of the state is also considered a Jew if he is descended from two full Jewish grandparents" (First Regulation to the Reich Citizenship Law, November 14, 1935). This definition made "inferiority" of blood, not the "inferiority" of one's goods or one's character, key to exclusion from the marketplace.

Sabine recounted a "nasty incident in the marketplace of Stralsund" (qtd. in Robertson, *The Shame of Sacrifice* 62). In a car with her father-in-law, they drove through the marketplace guided by their chauffeur. Crowds dressed in SA uniforms insolently pressed up against the windows of the car, making it clear that the Leibholzes (Jews) were not welcome in the marketplace. The Nazi-controlled marketplace took on limits tied to bloodline, unrelated to what one could make or purchase. The livelihood of persons was at risk as the marketplace increasingly excluded those without Aryan blood when on July 6, 1938, the "Nazis prohibited Jews from trading and providing a variety of specified commercial services" ("The History Place Holocaust Timeline").

In spite of the evil that dominates the marketplace, the marketplace cannot be avoided; exchange of goods and ideas offers opportunity to engage the world with responsible action, propelled by the story of the faith. Bonhoeffer understood the marketplace as a place where a faith "calling" meets the demands of everyday life (*Ethics* 254). The call of Christ comes to life in the marketplace of diversity of ideas and persons making a living, engaging the world. Bonhoeffer did not equate a sense of call with seclusion; he situated "calling" in the everyday demands of the marketplace of ideas and commerce.

Ernest Feil writes:

> [. . .] Bonhoeffer tried to think historically to an ever-increasing extent; this was a countermove to "idealism" on his part. He was extremely interested in properly understanding the concretion of faith in the world: "Reality is the sacrament of the commandment." For the sake of this reality, Bonhoeffer was open to the world. The world was to be an integral part of faith because in Jesus Christ the world is really the world accepted by God. On this basis Bonhoeffer could unreservedly accept Dilthey's interpretation of modern times, only to use this interpretation to protest against Dilthey's thesis of an inward, universal, unecclesiastical Christianity. (250)

Engagement with reality, not idealism or utopianism, drove Bonhoeffer's project—it drove him into the marketplace.

Bonhoeffer rejected a free-market fundamentalism; he saw no earthly utopias. To engage the marketplace unromantically, pragmatically accepting its possibilities and pitfalls, is the action that calls for discipleship in the demands of the concrete historical moment—walking the faith story of service into a marketplace, a place of difference.

Engaging the Marketplace Within a Faith Story

Bonhoeffer engaged the marketplace, but never alone. He met the marketplace within the story of the faith. Bonhoeffer's story begins with a first principle, God, specifically Christ. He met the marketplace with his feet firmly on the ground of a Christocentric faith story–laden position. A Christocentric worldview is Bonhoeffer's first confession, shaping his life and scholarship, situating him to meet the world from a clear bias, a religious position; his worldview rests on the dialectic of religious assurance that permits him to engage doubt and testing within the rigors of engagement in the marketplace.

Bonhoeffer began with a Christocentric assumption: Christ is "pro me" (*Christ the Center* 43). Christ died for our sins, revealing a stance that is pro person, supportive of human life. This service premise of Christ is the foundation of a faith story taken into the marketplace. Bonhoeffer was Christocentric, accepting the story of service for others. A Christocentric position finds Christ alive "as Word, as sacrament, and as community" (Bonhoeffer, *Christ the Center* 48). Christ begins the story of faith for Bonhoeffer, a story shaped by the Word, by sacrament, and by community. The Word, the sacrament, and the community provide one with the support and courage to meet the marketplace.

Obscured Discernment

Word, sacrament, and community are three elements of the faith story that carry the face of Christ. Discernment requires attending to the face of Christ in each setting. A person of faith, however, must be wary of the temptation to give Christ a face that meets our personal or political demands. In the marketplace, one might glimpse the face of Christ, discerning how to engage another in a manner consistent with the faith.

Discernment of the face of God in a particular situation requires entering the marketplace with a twofold action. First, one enters with Christ as companion, and second, one recognizes the difficulty of discerning Christ's face in a given setting. One asks "who Christ really is, for us today" (Bonhoeffer qtd. in Bethge, *Dietrich Bonhoeffer* 767). One searches for direction in a given historical moment. Christ lives in Word, sacrament, and community. However, Christ's visibility depends upon one's attention to the demands of today, this historical moment, which guides discernment of "Who Christ is for us today."

Bonhoeffer engaged the marketplace asking "who Christ really is, for us today" (qtd. in Bethge, *Dietrich Bonhoeffer* 767). He sought the will of Christ in a given situation, providing a model that keeps before us the importance of reaction and implementation within the spirit of the faith. Asking, "Who is Christ today?" in a given situation emphasizes discernment and direction seeking taken into an ambiguous and demanding environment—the marketplace.

Once again, Bonhoeffer used dialectic; he understood Christ as the center, but a Christ with a face obscured from total view or comprehension. Complete certainty in discerning Christ's face in the marketplace escapes us. In the marketplace, Christ can be the person of business, the proletariat calling capitalism to task, or even Dostoyevsky's idiot. To assume that one "knows" the face of God without any doubt too easily leads to "idolatry"

(Bonhoeffer, *Temptation* 124). Christ is not an idol nor an effigy created in our own desired image. Discerning the outline of Christ in a given setting recognizes the ambiguity and difficulty of the task of "seeing" God.

Christ walks into the marketplace with us as we remember the difficulty of seeing his face. We discern Christ's role in a given historical moment, not foisting upon him a role, a face, in accordance with our ideological demands. The moment we claim to "know" Christ in one role or as one person, the face of Christ is lost. Christ walks into the marketplace as the center of the story and the historical situation, within ambiguity and a call for caution.

The Old Testament warns of the danger of seeing the face of Yahweh (*The New Oxford Annotated Bible,* Judg. 13.22). Bonhoeffer took the Old Testament seriously, warning us not to assume knowledge of the face of God. "In man God creates his own image on earth" (*Temptation* 37). To reverse the act of creation, man creating the image of God, obscures the face of Christ, confusing us with false bravado. We do not see the face of God with clarity; we never know completely whether the face we see might be that of another, or our own reflection, or a glimpse of God. Such a view suggests that we cannot know the will of God with complete assurance. When we demand undue visibility and clarity, we walk with dangerous conviction and assurance into the marketplace. In ambiguity, we discern answers and risk action, even as we live in partial recognition of the face of Christ. A religious communicator lives in both assurance and knowledge of error.

When we evade the error of complete assurance, we reject a theology unwilling to meet ambiguous and unclear moral situations. Not totally comprehending or knowing the face of Christ in a given situation keeps us from "complete hardening and obduracy of the heart in sin, in fearlessness and security before God, hypocritical piety" (Bonhoeffer, *Temptation* 124). The obscured face of Christ tempers conviction and certainty of our perceived discernment.

A Marketplace of Difference

A reader working from a faith story contrary to Bonhoeffer's Christocentric commitment can experience minimal engagement of Bonhoeffer's dialectical standpoint by attending to his union of story coherence and intentional ambiguity of application. The first phase of Bonhoeffer's dialectical effort requires knowing the story, which in Bonhoeffer's case is a Christocentric faith of service and discipleship. The second phase questions one's own discernment skills, living with only partial glimpses of the face of Christ. Story knowledge and admitted ambiguity permit one to try to answer "who Christ really is, for us today" (Bonhoeffer qtd. in Bethge, *Dietrich Bonhoeffer* 767) in a given historical setting and situation, but not with complete confidence. Reassessment of story, ambiguity, and historical appropriateness ever guides a story-laden view of communication; in Bonhoeffer's language, confession works as a communicative link between story coherence and ambiguity of application, offering a way to live within the horizon of the faith.

Bonhoeffer's work suggests a "minimal" and a "maximal" set of values (Bok 67–81) for engaging difference. First, the story frames a position mixed with caution permitting engagement with the historical situation, framing a "minimal" set of guidelines for engaging a world of difference from a position of conviction, unwilling to assume that one has the only answer. Bonhoeffer points to a dialectic of conviction and humility. From a "maximal" position, Bonhoeffer frames a Christocentric position that works from a knowing position maximally concerned and cautious about one's own self-righteousness.

Bonhoeffer united a "maximalist value system" (Bok 21) with a "minimalist value system" (13–19), permitting him to address a much larger audience. He let his public standpoint be known while leaving no doubt about the necessity of working with and understanding those with differing viewpoints.

Bonhoeffer lived within a pragmatic conviction that one must find hope where hope lies unnoticed—hope not within the confines of a person, but within good stories that can guide human beings in the struggle against stories of oppression and pain. Jacques Ellul in *Perspectives on Our Age* suggests such a view of hope.

> [. . .] Christians should be bearers of Hope *(esperance)* in a society like ours—hope for people plunged in anguish and plagued by neurosis. [. . .] Christian Hope does not [. . .] believe in humanity. It is precisely the contrary. Christian Hope means being convinced that we will not go along completely on our own. It is an affirmation of the love of God. [. . .] Christian Hope, the Hope so fundamental to the Biblical texts, has a reason for being, a place, only where there is no more human hope. Human hope *(espoi)* is the feeling that tomorrow will be better. One may be in the throes of an economic crisis today, but one may have grounds for hoping that the crisis will be over in one or two years. So long as human hope of this sort exists, there is no reason for Hope *(esperance)*. [. . .] Hope has no *raison d'etre* unless there is no more reason for human hope. This is the Hope against hope. Hope will then simply be the fact that because God is God, because God is love, there is always a future. (108)

Hope framed in the story of the faith sustains encounter with a marketplace of difference. Hope centered in the story of God, based upon self-restraint of self-confidence, frames a God-centered theology situated within human caution, not easy answers.

This work begins with a story understood and lived by Dietrich Bonhoeffer—the story of the faith lived with a hope beyond hope, a hope beyond the individual and institutions. Hope propelled by freedom and restrained by caution about false enthusiasm for the individual or institutions rejects privileging either the metaphor of the self or the metaphor of institution. Bonhoeffer rejects the institution of the church as the center of life as quickly as he does the self. He suggests a third alternative between the limits of the self and blind loyalty to institutional structures. Bonhoeffer offers a communicative picture for people of faith without the "I" or the collective "us," the institution, taking center stage—a responsive faith of service. From the story of the faith one meets the historical needs of the moment in service, propelled neither by the strength of self nor by institutional loyalty.

Bonhoeffer points to a story of faith that rejects an "ethical atomism" (too much focus on the individual) and "natural forms of community" (too much focus on collective life) (*The Communion of Saints* 72); both miss the importance of life shaped by God. The metaphor of self becomes a "moral cul-de-sac" (Arnett, "Therapeutic Communication" 149–160), a frozen ideology. Alasdair MacIntyre contends that we are in a moral crisis unlike any other; human history has taught us the evil and destructive power of totalitarian environments propelled by unyielding narrative structures, against which Bonhoeffer contended. One must be ever wary of the unthinking confidence of a follower within the security of a narrow and blind worldview. Bonhoeffer's writing and his life reveal his opposition to totalitarian evil, whether collective or solitary.

A person of faith must engage the marketplace, placing discernment of the faith in a more privileged position than self or institution, keeping caution and reassessment as constant companions. Bonhoeffer points to a dialectical unity of absolute certainty and the fragility of human insight, calling us to watch whom we actually follow—God, or a god created in our own image, according to our own needs.

As Bonhoeffer warns us about institutions and the self, he places responsibility within our hands—a responsive responsibility. In *Letters and Papers from Prison,* one finds the elementary beginnings of another Bonhoeffer book. He wrote:

> *Chapter 1* to deal with:
>
> (a) The coming of age of mankind [. . .]. The safeguarding of life against "accidents" and "blows of fate"; even if these cannot be eliminated, the danger can be reduced. Insurance (which, although it lives on "accidents," seeks to mitigate their effects) as a western phenomenon. The aim: to be independent of nature. Nature was formerly conquered by spiritual means, with us by technical organization of all kinds. Our immediate environment is not nature, as formerly, but organization. But with this protection from nature's menace there arises a new one—through organization itself.
>
> But the spiritual force is lacking. The question is: What protects us against the menace of organization? Man is again thrown back on himself. He has managed to deal with everything, only not with himself. He can insure against everything, only not against man. In the last resort it all turns on man. [. . .] Our relation to God is not a "religious" relationship to the highest, most powerful, and best Being imaginable—that is not authentic transcendence—but our relation to God is a new life in "existence for others," through participation in the being of Jesus. The transcendence is not infinite and unattainable, but the neighbour who is within reach in any given situation. (380–81)

Bonhoeffer, in dialectical fashion, warns us about too much self-reliance, then warns us about blind commitment to an organization, including the Church itself, and then says, "In the last resort it all turns on man." A responsive faith finds strength within the story of the faith, recognizing that one's own responsibility rests with response to the breath of God. God breathes into us, calling us to a responsive faith of service in the marketplace. Bonhoeffer engaged prayer and study; such contemplation brought him to the marketplace, the place of testing.

Bonhoeffer understood that the marketplace was a godless place, a place of opportunity for some and suffering for many. The marketplace is shaped by opinion and popularity. It is a place where leaders are tempted to "wash their hands" of demanding decisions. The actions of a "leader" disowning an action in order to placate a people has deep Biblical roots, not only as a major moment in the last days of Jesus's life, but as a metaphor for evil steeped in the seduction of popularity.

Larry Rasmussen states this position well, using Bonhoeffer's words and his own interpretive insights.

> The letter of 18 July states that "man is summoned to share in God's sufferings at the hands of a godless world," so "he must therefore really live in the godless world, without attempting to gloss over or explain its ungodliness in some religious way or other. He must live a "secular" life, and *thereby* share in God's

> sufferings." By a "secular" life Bonhoeffer means one of intense "this-worldliness." (123)

Bonhoeffer's reflections on the risk, ambiguity, and necessity of participation in the marketplace emerge in blatant form in the section in *Letters and Papers from Prison* that Bethge entitled "After the Failure" (367–407). Marketplace engagement is a call to participation in the "this worldliness of Christianity" (Bonhoeffer, *Letters and Papers from Prison* 369). Bonhoeffer wrote that note to Bethge from Tegel prison on July 21, 1944—one day after the assassination attempt on Hitler.

Bonhoeffer considered in the letter the issue of worldliness, not wanting it confused with secular comfort. Yet, on the other hand, he rejects a life of holiness and saintliness. He states that *The Cost of Discipleship* was his last visit to such a project, which he completed in 1937. He recounts his French pastor friend, Jean Lasserre, a pacifist, wanting to pursue a life of sainthood, and Bonhoeffer reflects that he (Lasserre) was on his way. Yet, even at that juncture, Bonhoeffer was wary of such a Christian vocation. Sainthood was too far afield from Bonhoeffer's emerging view of Christian worldliness, a worldliness defined not by comfort, but by discipleship willing to follow the suffering model of Christ—as a man, not as a God.

> I don't mean the shallow and banal this-worldliness of the enlightened, the busy, the comfortable, or the lascivious, but the profound this worldliness, characterized by discipline and the constant knowledge of death and resurrection. [. . .] I discovered later, and I'm still discovering right up to this moment that is it only by living completely in this world that one learns to have faith. One must completely abandon any attempt to make something of oneself, whether it be a saint, or a converted sinner, or a churchman (a so-called priestly type!), a righteous man or an unrighteous one, a sick man or a healthy one. By this-worldliness I mean living unreservedly in life's duties, problems, successes and failures, experience and perplexities. In so doing we throw ourselves completely in the arms of God, taking seriously, not our own sufferings, but those of God in the world—watching with Christ in Gethsemane. (Bonhoeffer, *Letters and Papers from Prison* 369–70)

Bonhoeffer understood the twofold character of difference in the marketplace: not all agree with a Christian perspective, and a Christian called to responsibility to make a difference in a place of contrasting perspectives embraces a dialectical life of the absolute and tentative, the stable and the fragile—the dialectical call of an engaged faith in a marketplace of difference. This work suggests that Bonhoeffer met the marketplace from a dialectical framework of conviction and doubt, pointing to the pragmatic necessity of understanding religious communicative life as propelled by a dialectical metaphor that began this chapter—a fragile absolute.

A Fragile Absolute

In an era no longer wed to universal principles and absolutes, Bonhoeffer suggests an alternative between groundlessness and absolutes—conviction with humility and caution, a dialectic capable of guiding Christocentric engagement within a marketplace of difference. In a course on communication ethics, I listened to a number of priests uncomfortable with a postmodern critique of universal or absolute positions. I suggested the following: You must maintain your standpoint, your absolute, and function in a postmodern world that contends with your position. Postmodernity does not suggest living without a stance, but acknowledgment that multiple stances or positions exist. Postmodernity makes an absolute position appropriately fragile; we encounter others with the possibility of conversation, the possibility that one or both of us might find another position persuasive enough to foster change. Postmodernity requires a faith willing to engage other positions and to learn from those contrary to one's own position.

Bonhoeffer understood what we now call a postmodern communicative lens as necessitating attention to paradoxical demands: 1) working from a position, a ground—for Bonhoeffer a Christocentric standpoint from which he spoke, and 2) recognizing that a multiplicity of differing views meets us in the marketplace of everyday life. He was responsive to "this worldliness" (Bonhoeffer, *Letters and Papers from Prison* 369); enacting "Religionless Christianity" (280–82) stresses the need for religious life to meet the secular world and for persons of faith to avoid equating faith with institutional commitments.

Bonhoeffer's uniting of what this work calls "the absolute" and "the fragile" embraces a learning model of a faith lived out in service. The faith story meets the historical situation; the absolute of God meets the fragile insight of our knowing the faith and an ability to read appropriately the needs of the historical situation. One then takes an absolute into the fragile interplay of the marketplace with a responsibility to attend to error and correction via guilt, then confession, and then reengagement shaped by learning from difference. The person of faith leaves behind a position of "telling" and forges into the marketplace as a learner.

A postmodern culture requires constant learning; a culture based upon difference rejects absolutes for all and learns only from encountering positions of Others. Learning becomes the key metaphor for a postmodern culture. One must learn the absolute that propels the Other, even if that absolute is the denial of absolutes. At first glance, admission of an absolute appears as a bane or blight on a postmodern culture. However, as a postmodern culture rejects a universal absolute, it must respect individual absolutes that hold particular narrative structures, "humble narratives" (Arnett, "Communication and Community" 44–45), together. In short, the notion of absolute textured in the hands of Bonhoeffer learns from the Other and the historical situation.

A given narrative structure exists alongside a multiplicity of narrative and virtue structures, each with a common center that makes it unique and each propelled by what Slavoj Žižek calls "the fragile absolute." In a postmodern culture, one encounters the fragility of an absolute each day as one meets narrative structures that compete for attention and time.

Žižek outlines the importance of a "fragile absolute" as he looks at Christianity through the eyes of Marxist questioning of the means of production and the dispirited sense of the sacred that emerges in a pure market economy. His "fragile absolute" is a utopian vision of revolution against a capitalist economy, calling for new means of production that offer service and concern for others. He initially worries that in this postmodern moment of virtue contention, religious voices are once again erupting. His first impulse as a Marxist is lament, yet later he suggests that Christianity and Marxism are at their best when preserving a "fragile absolute"—the importance of an Otherness that defines a better world and offers a vision for action that serves and cares for the Other. Clearly, Bonhoeffer and Žižek do not offer the same vision, but in general terms, each is concerned about a "fragile absolute"—a vision of a good life that calls one to service and concern for others. This use of absolute is not universal, but tied to the story that informs communicative action.

Bonhoeffer gave voice to the importance of the "fragile absolute," which works to offer checks on excess. He combined theory (theology and the sociology of community) and practice (as a pastor and ethical leader) situated within a context that both tested and shaped his ideas in practical life. Bonhoeffer's work witnessed to creative checks and balances on the excesses of theory, of action, and of the historical moment.

Dietrich Bonhoeffer, in *The Communion of Saints,* states,

> [. . .] God's judgment extends over both individual and collective persons. [. . .] God recognizes the ultimately recalcitrant will as free; the man who wants only

> himself gets his own way, but simultaneously finds that in asserting it he has brought about his own religious death; for man lives only in communion with other men and with God. (201)

Bonhoeffer finds freedom within checks and balances, within a fragile absolute that unites narrative conviction and the temporality of the historical moment.

Bonhoeffer called the church to meet the marketplace in all its contentiousness and difference with decision making guided by the "good," not the "pure." Bonhoeffer walked faith into the marketplace of decision—exemplifying how a narrative of the faith guides in the complexity and confusion of discerning the concrete good, forgoing the luxury of abstract purity. Ultimately, Bonhoeffer met the marketplace in confession. First, one takes a faith narrative into the marketplace of compromise with a commitment to the good, the penultimate, not expecting the pure or the ultimate in this life. Second, articulation of one's own position provides clarity for self and other. Third, confession keeps one aware of the purer, the more ideal, and how one falls short of the mark, even as one knowingly lives the penultimate, the good.

Confession keeps before us our humanness, calling for renewed clarity, humility, and constant awareness of the difficult task of making human decisions in a complex and virtue-divided world. The fragile absolute of the faith in action guided Bonhoeffer, who, like the wise rabbi, understood that at times we must take prayer and study with our cloak into the marketplace and together find the answers that seem resistant to theory alone. The marketplace tests a fragile absolute, a faith responsive to the unique needs of God's world.

7

A DIALOGIC CRAFTSMAN

Hallowing the Everyday

Seyla Benhabib on constructive dispute:

> [I]t is a dispute about whether modern moral theory since Kant has been an accomplice in the process of disintegration of personality and the fragmentation of value which is said to be our general condition today. My intervention in this debate intend[s] to show that, judged from the confines of moral theory, and without delving into this larger issue about modernity and its discontents, the debate between neo-Aristotelians/neo-Hegelians and discourse theorists is still very much continuing. Although it is too trite to think that all philosophical debates lead to good endings, my own personal sense at this stage is that this confrontation has invigorated rather than weakened contemporary moral theory. (363–65)

Dietrich Bonhoeffer on reconciliation:

> The concretely Christian ethic is beyond formalism and casuistry. Formalism and casuistry set out from the conflict between the good and the real, but the Christian ethic can take for its point of departure the reconciliation, already accomplished, of the world with God and the man Jesus Christ and the acceptance of the real man by God. (*Ethics* 86)

Bonhoeffer and Benhabib point in similar directions. Ethics must contend with what is present before us, not what we demand theoretically or abstractly. To deny what is present before us moves us into abstract speculation, away from concrete life. A stance that denies the given, rejects the historical moment, and is blind to the events before one is more akin to a philosophical chess game than the encounter of human beings with real living. Bonhoeffer did not trust abstract education that ignores the real. Bonhoeffer understood the oppressive educational world that Herman Hesse described in *Beneath the Wheel* and *The Glass Bead Game: Magister Ludi*. Education unresponsive to the historical situation, resting in the abstract, is too often unhelpful. Ideas need application, hence the metaphor of craftsman (Aristotle 1097b.24–29): "Perhaps only the truly cultured intellectual becomes homesick, and not the intellectual" (Bonhoeffer, *Letters and Papers from Prison* 184). The cultured person crafts a home; an intellectual considers the characteristics of what a home might be. Bonhoeffer knew the responsibility of crafting places for people to live.

The act of real living is a craft engaged within a clouded, unclear, often confusing space. The blurring of vision provides insight propelled by a basic conviction that we have to craft responsibility to care for a home given to us by God. No matter how problematic the real may be, Jesus has brought reconciliation to this home. We cannot run; we cannot ignore the reality before us. Even in the midst of serious disagreement and confrontation, a stance of affirmation, of hallowing the everyday, needs to guide a faith-driven communicator. A religious communicator answers the call of a craftsman—who knows the craft, applies the craft, and cares for the craft itself. The story of the faith applied and cared for in application with the real meets us in daily living without a template and within the reality of unclear vision.

Meeting the Real in Faith

As one seeks to meet the real, hallowing the everyday that Jesus has reconciled, Bonhoeffer warns of the danger of reifying God's creation by refusing to understand and address the evolving nature of human life as transition and change. Specifically, he warns of two temptations that deny the changing face of the real: *securitas* and *desperatio* (*Creation and Fall* 123). Seeking undue security and acting desperately are counter sides of the same temptation, a temptation that diverts us from trust of God's world. Securitas turns faith into mere law and technique, and desperatio ceases to "hallow the everyday," dwelling in self-pity (123). Both false security and despair move attention from the historical moment, missing God's creation. Security encourages looking for answers in a technique, law, authority, or a stable place. Despair keeps the focus upon the self, again missing God's creation. Both temptations remove a communicator from the historical moment of God's creation, placing one's focus of attention on false security—self-manufactured, self-maintained angst.

The religious communicator forgoes the temptations of security and despair and attends to dialogue that confronts both false security and undue focus upon despair about the unknown consequences of change. Bonhoeffer points to communication that engages faith in genuine meeting with the historical moment, whether or not that moment agrees with our personal hopes and wishes. Such communication places confidence not in the historical moment alone or solely in some abstract version of the faith, but rather in a dialogue between faith and historical moment. Dialogic confrontation of the fear of change permits one to bypass the ever-present temptation of undue concern for security and the counter side of the same coin of temptation—feelings of utter despair.

The religious communicator takes the faith into the historical moment, whether the situation is a time of stability or narrative contention and virtue disagreement. A historical moment of faltering familiar foundations requires discerning the what, the why, and the how of a given faith story. Challenged familiarity makes us focus on the concrete situation in dialogue with a faith story—requiring us to take neither the faith nor the historical moment for granted.

Moments of transition require discernment about what is important; deviation from the familiar invites communication beyond unreflective routine. Sorting through previously taken-for-granted assumptions permits us to determine the helpful and the historically appropriate, requiring us to discard, support vigorously, and champion as appropriate a particular response in a given moment of transition.

Preparing for the Meeting

Bonhoeffer's life and work offer evidence of the importance of bringing depth of learning and study to the dialogue of faith and the historical moment. His commitment to learning provides a blueprint for a religious communicator seeking constructive engagement with the historical moment. Bonhoeffer's keys to learning were twofold. First, he was an avid learner and reader. Second, he understood the necessity of learning from dialectical comparison. His academic learning met the demands of life-threatening decisions. He engaged ideas from multiple disciplines, from theology to philosophy to literature to sociology to music. His broad knowledge base permitted thoughtful engagement with the historical moment. In philosophical terms, the text of everyday life opened richly as he brought interpretive resources to understanding and action. Bonhoeffer did philosophical hermeneutics in everyday life. He engaged philosophy in everyday communicative interpretation. Bonhoeffer did not just engage life; he discerned life with philosophical thoughtfulness.

Bonhoeffer attended to the unique characteristics of the historical moment without forsaking the story of the faith, permitting a practical religious communicative stance to emerge from the union of historical moment and faith story. In the afterword of Bonhoeffer's *Meditating on the Word,* John Vannorsdall offers a picture of Bonhoeffer taking the faith into action. It is the faith story first, then action, that defines Bonhoeffer. His faith guides action and interpretation of the world before him. Bonhoeffer was not a professional activist; his faith story and the story of his family equipped him with the energy and conviction necessary to face the Nazis. He offered a counter interpretive voice. Bonhoeffer lived within a family story of originative thinking and response.

> Frau Julie Bonhoeffer at the age of ninety-one walked through a cordon of brownshirts to buy strawberries from a Jewish merchant. Her grandson, Dietrich Bonhoeffer, died for his defiance of the Nazis. [. . .] The aged and the aristocratic have a way of dealing with riff-raff, and Dietrich was not a social activist in the contemporary sense. [. . .] [W]e begin and end with an ear bent to hear the Word of God. We begin with an ultimate devotion the outcome of which is sometimes cordons crossed or prison and death. [. . .]
>
> I would be wary of Bonhoeffer if he emphasized the self rather than the God who meets us, but he does not. I would be wary if he emphasized the self over and against the community of believers, or the written and preached Word over and against the Lord's Supper, or judgment over and against the grace of God in the cross of Jesus Christ, but he does not. I would be wary if meditation led Bonhoeffer away from the world in which we live. But Frau Julie crossed the cordon to purchase strawberries from a Jewish merchant, and Pastor Dietrich crossed the line which Hitler drew. (147, 149)

Additionally, Bonhoeffer's indifference to anything political for much of his life (Bethge, *Dietrich Bonhoeffer* 678) provides a unique dialectic of disinterest and responsibility. Dialectically, Bonhoeffer's initial lack of interest in political life and an aristocratic sense of responsibility provided unique, fertile soil for a faith commitment that is in the world, but not totally driven by the actions of the world. He engaged historicity without being at the mercy of the immediate moment; he brought a faith perspective to the immediate situation.

In preparation for meeting the historical moment from a faith perspective, Bonhoeffer understood differentiation. He did not confuse the historical moment with a faith story brought to the task. Bonhoeffer seems to have understood Levinas's basic phenomenological requirement—not confusing "this" with "that." We do not learn from forced similarity, but from differentiation. Levinas's emphasis on Otherness demands differentiation. Martin Buber followed a similar path, suggesting that all true relation begins in distance in *Between Man and Man.* Bonhoeffer worked from a similar communicative wisdom—distance and difference need to guide encounter with the Other.

Bonhoeffer requires distance in engaging the historical world—distance that permits one to see what "is" and distance that permits one to bring the faith to interpretive insight. The "incognito" (Bonhoeffer, *Christ the Center* 112) of Christ is one major way Bonhoeffer stresses this point. He first articulates that Christ performed miracles; he then suggests that to concentrate on the miracles misses the trace of Christ. Second, not even the empty tomb can provide historical evidence. The historical moment is met with "the decision over faith or unbelief [that] is already taken" (Bonhoeffer, *Christ the Center* 113). A person of faith meets what "is," but such connection to the historical moment comes with a faith commitment made before the encounter. Encountering the now without confirming or questioning a faith commitment offers a "unity of contraries" (Buber, *The Knowledge of Man* 111) central to a dialectical position. The two realms communicate and work together in a "world come of age," but they are not the same two realms. Meeting "this" world does not lessen the importance of a faith commitment grounded in conviction that accepts "that" mystery and "incognito" of Christ.

Difference and distance permit the communicator to learn from what "is" and to keep in place an interpretive center from which one meets reality—for Bonhoeffer, this interpretive base is *Christ the Center.* One learns from difference and one brings a unique standpoint to the encounter. Differentiation requires a dual action of learning from the Other and engaging one's own standpoint. This dialectical encounter of learning and position permitted Bonhoeffer to negotiate uncertainty without turning his faith into a rigid ideology or following the historical moment in a relativistic direction. The necessity of differentiation and distance allowed Bonhoeffer to understand the interrelated but different nature of public and private discourse.

Differentiating Public and Private Discourse

Bonhoeffer's differentiation of public and private discourse has philosophical and pragmatic implications for communicative life. The emphasis on differentiation invites learning and awareness of position without falling prey to sectarianism or relativism. There is autonomy of spheres of life, and simultaneously, Bonhoeffer never forgets that this is God's world. He offers a dialectic of differentiation and privileged importance of the faith, not for all, but for a Christian communicator.

> [T]he solution of the much-discussed problem of the autonomy of the secular institutions [. . .] is good reason for laying stress on the autonomy of, for example, the state in opposition to the heteronomy of an ecclesiastical theocracy; yet before God there is no autonomy, but the law of the God who is revealed in Jesus Christ is the law of all earthly institutions. The limits of all autonomy become evident in the Church's proclamation of the word of God, and the concrete form of the law of God in commerce and industry, the state, etc., must be perceived and discerned by those who work responsibly in these fields. Here, so long as it is not misunderstood, one might speak of a relative autonomy. (*Ethics* 362)

Dialectically, Bonhoeffer reminds us that differentiation and the simultaneous interplay of spheres never permits us to forget that this is God's world. Such differentiation with interconnected influence frames the difference and the mutual influence of public and private communicative spheres.

One way to moderate uncertainty that affects the public domain is to bring a private narrative alternative to the public domain. Such a communicative style permits one dialectically to be in the world, but not of the world. This move of "narrative" and "private" together requires discussion. Normally, the notion of narrative equates to the public domain, not private life. However, in moments in which the public domain finds itself ruptured and without narrative consensus, the notion of public rests more with the word "power" than with the word "agreement" or "consensus." The Nazis imposed a public life upon the people. Bonhoeffer's private narrative position found life outside of emotivism, within knowledge of a competing narrative structure that was not part of Nazi-approved public life. Bonhoeffer brought a private position that actually was a competing narrative, a narrative competing for attention in the public domain. Bonhoeffer maintained distance from public life orchestrated by the Nazis through his rich life of reading, prayer, and meditation. He moderated uncertainty through a rich and thoughtful private domain. Bonhoeffer's private position that contended against the Nazis was affirmed by others who tried to keep alive an alternative narrative vision for Germany. He and others privately held a narrative that subversively competed for attention in the public domain.

Bonhoeffer found assurance in meditation and work with the Scriptures; he connected himself to a counter narrative. Problematic public narratives are fought by counter private stories hoping to contend for attention as public narratives, keeping alive the opportunity to shift narrative consensus in the public domain with alternative insights. Neil Postman, early in his career, wrote *Teaching as Subversive Activity.* Postman assumed that "good" teaching calls into question problematic assumptions. Similarly, Bonhoeffer's commitment to prayer, meditation, and the Scriptures suggests a book Bonhoeffer could have written: *The Faith Story as Subversive Activity.* Bonhoeffer's private devotions permitted him to counter a privileged story in the public domain. He met narrative contention with a privately enriched and supported faith alternative. Bonhoeffer revealed the power and the necessity of differentiating the horizons of public and private discourse.

Bonhoeffer's aristocratic background with a genuine sense of noblesse oblige prepared him to encounter the historical moment, helping him meet the challenge of differentiating private and public life. As Richard Sennett in *The Fall of Public Man* suggests, the world of the aristocracy rests upon observation of difference between the public and private domains. Granted, not many from Bonhoeffer's world of "divine learning" challenged the Third Reich (Bethge, *Dietrich Bonhoeffer* 207–8), but the necessary social practices for understanding private and public domains accompany an aristocratic worldview. Bonhoeffer's private world connected him to an alternative narrative of the faith, permitting him to challenge Nazi atrocity. Again, in the private domain, the remnant of an alternative narrative was present. In his *Letters and Papers from Prison,* Bonhoeffer openly accepts his aristocratic perspective and then dialectically frames a way of understanding this worldview in a "world come of age," based upon virtues independent of class rank.

> Unless we have the courage to fight for a revival of wholesome reserve between man and man, we shall perish in an anarchy of human values. The impudent contempt for such reserve is the mark of the rabble, just as inward uncertainty, haggling and cringing for the favor of insolent people, and lowering oneself to the level of the rabble are the way of becoming no better than the rabble oneself. When we forget what is due to ourselves and to others, when the feeling for human quality and the power to exercise reserve cease to exist, chaos is at the door. [. . .] Anyone who is pliant and uncertain in this matter does not realize what is at stake, and indeed in his case the reproaches may well be justified. We are witnessing the leveling down of all ranks of society, and at the same time the birth of a new sense of nobility, which is binding together a circle of men from all former social classes. Nobility arises from and exists by sacrifice, courage, and a clear sense of duty to oneself and society, by expecting due regard for itself as a matter of course; and it shows an equally natural regard for others,

> whether they are of higher or of lower degree. We need all along the line to recover the lost sense of quality and a social order based on quality. Quality is the greatest enemy of any kind of mass-leveling. Socially it means the renunciation of all place-hunting, a break with the cult of the "star," and open eyes both upwards and downwards, especially in the choice of one's more intimate friends, and pleasure in private life as well as courage to enter public life. Culturally it means a return from the newspaper and the radio to the book, from feverish activity to unhurried leisure, from dispersion to concentration, from sensationalism to reflection, from virtuosity to art, from snobbery to modesty, from extravagance to moderation. Quantities are competitive, qualities are complementary. (12–13)

The above quotation offers a sense of the aristocratic bearing that Bonhoeffer brought to his commitments. It is this perspective that permitted him to differentiate public and private discourse. Yet, in the end, he moved to a point of virtue not dependent upon class that is open to all. Bonhoeffer was unwilling to release the assumption that some ideas and commitments are better than others. Thus, he entered a world come of age from a clear position, a Christocentric and humanities-educated perspective.

Bonhoeffer's aristocratic background permitted him to differentiate public and private life. He was not as vulnerable as some who knew no public standard capable of challenging Nazi expectations. Bonhoeffer's private world—nourished by ideas, the arts, and the story of the faith—accompanied him into engagement with the historical moment. His naturally practiced differentiation of public and private life permitted his private domain to function as a critical benchmark from which he could judge Nazi-approved public action.

Bonhoeffer's aristocratic bearing was accompanied by a Christian commitment to service, a responsibility for Others: his "elitism was modified by a Christian commitment to seeing history 'from below, from the perspective of the outcast, the suspects, the maltreated, the powerless, the oppressed'" (Zerner 143). Bonhoeffer was an aristocrat called to responsibility, educated in the social practice of differentiating private and public worlds.

It is important to pause and reflect on this positive reading of Bonhoeffer's aristocratic life. A positive reading of aristocracy can be problematic, inviting an unhealthy aristocratic sense of self-esteem (Arnett and Arneson 118) based upon bloodline and money more than productivity. Bonhoeffer, on the contrary, had a healthy aristocratic bloodline situated within productive and responsible action. Bonhoeffer reflected the best of an aristocratic culture that took seriously the responsibility of noblesse oblige. Bonhoeffer's cultured family and his understanding of faith called him to responsibility nourished by dialectical observation of social practices responsive to both public and private life. He was prepared to meet a changing public domain with questions enriched by moral conviction supported by a thoughtful and textured private domain. The privileged Nazi position in the public domain could not move his private position; he offered a counter narrative quietly contending against Nazi hegemony. Bonhoeffer was prepared to meet a Nazi effort that collapsed public and private life into coerced social support of the Third Reich. Practiced at differentiating private and public beliefs and actions, Bonhoeffer was able to function by differentiating perspectives offered by the Nazi public domain and his faith-driven private domain. Bonhoeffer's aristocratic bearing and his commitment to service were dialectical keys to his preparation for the task before him. He was unwilling to collapse public and private life into a single sphere. Instead, he permitted each domain of life to coinform and, when necessary, challenge the other.

The importance of differentiating public and private spheres is central to the work of Hannah Arendt in *The Human Condition,* which offers a cogent analysis of the danger of private and public domain collapsed into a single sphere that she called the "social" (38–49). The collapse of private and public domains invites the construction of the "social" world, a world of conformity and image. Arendt, a Jewish scholar, understood the danger of a privileged public domain consuming one's private world. A person must have distance between a privileged public domain and a private domain. Protecting difference between the two domains enhances the richness and depth of both private and public life. Without the integrity of the two spheres, one loses the ability to question and check the action of one of the respective realms.

Bonhoeffer had aristocratic status in Nazi Germany, yet he did not concur with the ongoing Nazi public narrative. His private counter narrative kept him from falling into "lock step" with the ongoing public position of the Third Reich. Such a task was not easy. Bonhoeffer gave his life in opposition. Bonhoeffer's choice differed dramatically from Martin Heidegger's, whose support of the Third Reich continued to follow him, even after his death. When public and private realms become confused, communicative consequences emerge, privileging the "social," undergirding conformity, and resulting ultimately in the loss of one's ability to offer a check and balance on private and public life.

Arendt avoided the "social" as she worked with vocabulary ever sensitive to the differentiation of public and private domains. Without differentiating the public and private realms, one puts at risk the notion of excellence and individual recognition, moving to a realm of the social, a domain of conformity.

> Excellence itself, *arete* as the Greeks, *virtus* as the Romans would have called it, has always been assigned to the public realm where one could excel, could distinguish oneself from all others. Every activity performed in public can attain an excellence never matched in privacy; for excellence, by definition, the presence of others is always required, and this presence needs the formality of the public, constituted by one's peers, it cannot be the casual, familiar presence of one's equals or inferiors. Not even the social realm—though it made excellence anonymous, emphasized the progress of mankind rather than the achievement of men, and changed the content of the public realm beyond recognition—has been able altogether to annihilate the connection between public performance and excellence. While we have become excellent in the laboring we perform in public, our capacity for action and speech has lost much of its former quality since the rise of the social realm banished these into the sphere of the intimate and the private. [. . .] Neither education nor ingenuity nor talent can replace the constituent elements of the public realm, which make it the proper place for human excellence. (Arendt 48–49)

Arendt, like Bonhoeffer, protected difference in order to permit excellence to emerge. Excellence emerges in differentiation, not in leveling. Without a private realm that can question the social, there is often an imposed form of public excellence, which the Nazis used to propel people toward conformity.

Differentiation of public and private domains protects individual excellence, opening up the text of Bonhoeffer's actions and explaining the "why" of existence of Martin Buber's "great character." The "great character" knows the rules and regulations so well that he or she has earned the right to violate them (*Between Man and Man* 116). What permits one to have such insight is a private realm that offers checks and balances on ongoing public life and vice-versa. With the collapse of public and private life into the "social," a form of social conformity limits private intimacy and public excellence, imposing a "sameness" that fits a given setting.

Without differentiation of public and private domains, neither domain can dialectically question the other, resulting in two problematic communicative consequences. First, the collapse of public and private domains unleashes the impulse to unmask the private motives of another, refusing to respect that person's private domain. Second, blurring of public and private domains permits the marketplace to take on social consequences of supposedly fulfilling human lives, when the role of the marketplace is simply to offer financial support for pursing public and private excellence.

At best, the marketplace is a place of opportunity for enhancing both the private and public domains. Bonhoeffer understood the importance of meeting the marketplace, meeting the penultimate. There is no question about the importance of the marketplace; the issue for Bonhoeffer is not the marketplace, but the necessity of engagement with the meeting. He accepted the marketplace but did not permit a marketplace defined solely by the social (the collapse of public and private domains); it is *how* we meet the marketplace that determines whether we assist in temporal protection of the public and private spheres or continue the decline of public/private differentiation, contributing to the rise of conformity and the social.

Bonhoeffer suggested: "There is danger of confusing and mixing the two spheres [. . .] in a purely spiritual fellowship" (*Life Together* 38). Bonhoeffer called for limited activities of spiritual retreat for fear that one could lose the public and the private form of life. For groups that seek to escape the ongoing struggle of public and private life, he cautions against heresy that refuses to "live like the rest of the world, [that] let[s] him model himself on the world's standards in every sphere of life" (*The Cost of Discipleship* 46). The avoidance of public and private dilemmas becomes a form of heresy in Bonhoeffer's engagement with God's world.

Public space permits diversity to meet and discern what course to follow. Consideration of a diversity of ideas requires a public arena, which necessitates differentiation between public and private. Bonhoeffer understood that a healthy culture makes space for both private and public discourse. Attentiveness to and learning from diversity requires reclaiming the difference between private and public space. Both good and problematic issues vie for public space and privilege—only the long hand of history and God know whether we adopt the "right" actions in a given moment. Bonhoeffer's understanding of "right" brings faith and the historical moment into honest meeting. "Right" action rests within the penultimate, in the meeting of everyday life, not in the ethereal of the ultimate. The first penultimate test of ideas for Bonhoeffer is the dialectic between public and private positions. Conversation between public and private domains permits one to question both spheres, learning from the interaction. When the public and private spheres become too intertwined, one loses the first line of checks and balances of a given sphere of life.

The Limits of Unmasking and Lament

The confusion of public/private discourse puts at risk a public domain, which houses the argumentative parameters of a people. When the public domain becomes a "social" construction encouraging conformity, the ability to pursue excellence loses coherence and influence. Without some distinction between the two domains, we invite the "social," a place of conformity without differentiation, without uniqueness, a place where one idea is as good as any other. Unmasking the private motives of another in a public task puts at risk the power of both the private and public domains. Such blurring encourages simple adherence to the marketplace, which situates a communicator within a web of conformity leading to the "social." The social gathers strength as one unmasks the motives of another, trusting in one's own ability to attribute "real" motives to another's behavior. Additionally, routine unreflective use of lament suggests that the public world does not fit one's private demands. Bonhoeffer was slow to unmask the motives of others and slow to lament that God's world did not conform to his wishes. Both the private domain of the Other and the public domain of the world before us require respect—not necessarily agreement, but acknowledgment of a meaningful separate reality, even one with which one does not concur.

Discussion of the dangers of routine unmasking is not new; it is the center of work by Victor Frankl, Martin Buber, and Bonhoeffer. Each witnessed the danger of routinely questioning the motives of another. Discussion of conformity and the notion of the marketplace depend upon the insight of Hannah Arendt. As mentioned earlier, the concept of the marketplace tends to bother many academics. Using Bonhoeffer's dialectical insight, one can read this annoyance in two contrary and equally important ways. First, some simply want to act as if the marketplace as a sphere of influence does not exist. Second, there is wisdom in questioning the notion of the marketplace. The marketplace understood as a place of conformity and the social puts at risk public and private differentiation. Bonhoeffer's life offers a third alternative—entering the marketplace, not as a social sphere, but with the hope of adding to the public and private domains of human life. The marketplace need not level and erase all differentiation. The communicative task for Bonhoeffer, for Arendt, for Buber, and for Frankl is to keep a rich texture of life available—minimizing the power and the significance of the social, even in the marketplace. In essence, one must walk into the marketplace, and, at times, one must question the motives of others without contributing to the blurring of a public and private life—which then puts at risk checks and balances on differing spheres of life.

In essence, the problem is not unmasking, but routine and unreflective unmasking. Additionally, the problem is not the marketplace, but the arena of the social that the marketplace can enhance or minimize.

Unmasking

Bonhoeffer rejected the impulse to unmask the motives of the Other. Unmasking can cut one off from learning, resulting in response to self projections rather than actual events taking place. Understanding the importance of textured discourse lessened Bonhoeffer's impulse to draw rash conclusions about the Other. His discourse was as "innocent as a dove" and as "wise as a serpent." He did not pick apart discrete bits of discourse, but looked for patterns of deeds and actions.

Such a dialogic spirit is not unduly optimistic about the Other but is instead "realistically hopeful." Bonhoeffer's communicative style was akin to Christopher Lasch's (*The True and Only* 80–81) differentiation of optimism and realistic hope, with the latter requiring grit and lack of surprise in engagement with disappointments of life and with Others. Bonhoeffer pointed to a dialogic attitude of realistic hope not taken aback by the limits of human nature, the propensity to sin, the impulse to wrong the Other; he rejected falsity of noble speech. One need not move to routine distrust to live with realistic hope. One needs to discern whether actions are congruent or incongruent with words, while remembering that all human beings, including oneself, live within the good, the penultimate, not the pure, the ultimate. Perfection is not a realistic goal of human life for a person of the faith knowledgeable about the fall, sin, the redemption of Jesus, and the ongoing importance of confession that reaches beyond the fall to the redemption of Christ.

Words framed within undue expectation of purity cloak humanness, seeking to ignore incongruence between deed and the human tongue. Bonhoeffer understood false prophets and met them, not with suspicion, but with patience: patience that looked for the fruits of labor. A false prophet lives by words that cloak and obscure. Bonhoeffer offered interesting insight about false prophets who live by cloaked actions attempting to use the language of the community against the community itself: "[H]e conceals his dark purpose beneath the cloak of Christian piety, hoping that his innocuous disguise will avert detection. He knows that Christians are forbidden to judge, and he will remind them of it at the appropriate time" (*The Cost of Discipleship* 213). "False prophets" or "false teachers" were countered by Bonhoeffer with a dialectical response: 1) do not routinely give into suspicion; 2) patiently watch actions. Bonhoeffer offers a dialogic response that rejects the extremes of routine suspicion and routine false optimism about the Other.

Bonhoeffer questioned routine unmasking of the real; he rejected psychologism, the routine questioning of the other's motives. In *The Cost of Discipleship,* Bonhoeffer called for a disciple to live life in action, not within the realm of questions. Constant posing of questions and problems permits one to bypass one's own responsibilities. "Only the devil has an answer for our moral difficulties, and he says: 'Keep on posing problems, and you will escape the necessity of obedience'" (*The Cost of Discipleship* 80). When one keeps the focus of attention upon another's shortcomings rather than one's own, the call to discipleship and action goes unheeded. Bonhoeffer's dialectical orientation did not preclude reflection but rejected hyper-reflection on issues that take one from the call to obedience and action.

Bonhoeffer attended to action, not the psychological reason behind a given action, citing Mark 2.14: "And as he passed by he saw Levi, the son of Alphaeus, sitting at the place of toll, and he saith unto him, Follow me. And he arose and followed him" (qtd. in Bonhoeffer, *The Cost of Discipleship* 61). Bonhoeffer's following comment is helpful in explaining his position: "It displays not the slightest interest in the psychological reasons for a man's religious decisions" (*The Cost of Discipleship* 61). Bonhoeffer did not attend to motivations; he attended to action. At first blush, Bonhoeffer's actions seem in contrast to those of his father, who was the "leading Berlin psychiatrist and neurologist from 1912 until his death in 1948" (Bethge, *Dietrich Bonhoeffer* 23). Yet, his work is remarkably consistent: Karl Bonhoeffer did not accept a Freudian view of the world but concentrated upon human behavior. Dietrich Bonhoeffer pointed to the danger of projection and undue self-confidence that permit one to critique the motives of another from the standpoint of one's own bias.

A nontraditional "Saturday College" student expressed frustration over an instructor who questioned the motives of adult students for attending college at such a late date. Bonhoeffer would have rejected the comments of the faculty member. Perhaps he would suggest: "It does not matter why you study, only that you study and learn." For Bonhoeffer, an instructor does not have the right to call for a particular motivation to learn. Some learn because parents demand that they do so. Some learn because employers request more credentials. Some learn to model for children. Moreover, some learn because of the love of learning. The task for a teacher is not to discern reasons for learning, but simply to facilitate the learning. Just so, a pastor cannot ask, "Why are you here in church?" The question is not "why?" The question is "How can we learn about the faith together?" The focus is on the learning and on action, not on the motivation for the action.

Witnessing evil all around him, Bonhoeffer did not embrace the temptation to unmask the Other. "Why" another does what he or she does rests in the hands of that person and God. The consequences of an action rest within a community; the community has the right to address the actions, but it does not have the right to speculate upon inner thoughts. The inner life of another is sacred, off limits to speculation. Bonhoeffer refused to embrace "psychologism," motive attribution. He rejected the false confidence of motive attribution for theological reasons of the sacredness of another person, not to protect individual privacy.

In Bonhoeffer's novel, the main character, Christoph, asks Ulrich for advice on this very issue—and receives a theological answer.

> "There must be a point to it," he had said at the time, "that the inner life of another is by nature inaccessible to us, and that no one can see into our inner being. We must obviously be meant to keep it for ourselves and not share it with another."
>
> After reflecting for a long time Ulrich had answered, "Except with God—or with a human being given to us by God, who can keep as silent as God does." (*Fiction from Prison* 92)

Bonhoeffer understood what Buber called the demonic of the twentieth century, "the monstrous, the dreadful phenomenon of psychologism" (Buber, *A Believing Humanism: Gleanings* 151). The sacred inner life of another emerges only in confession to God and to a responsible Other. Confession comes, however, from the agent involved in a given action, not the interpreter of the action.

The importance of Bonhoeffer's rejection of unmasking is twofold. First, he engaged the sacred. Second, the sacred found support within theological concerns. The ecumenical movement of the World Alliance, of which Bonhoeffer was a member and an emerging leader, he criticized. He stated: "There is still no theology of the ecumenical movement" (Bonhoeffer qtd. in Bethge, *Dietrich Bonhoeffer* 247). Bonhoeffer consistently sought theological rationale for actions. He wanted a clear sense of "why" for a given action. A religious sense of "why" minimizes the impulse for unnecessary and inappropriate lament.

Without Lament

All of us know someone eager to complain, to see the wrong, to point out imperfection. Bonhoeffer understood such an impulse and called for discipline necessary to tame the power of routine critique. Bonhoeffer met his time, the historical moment, without ready reliance upon lament. A number of major authors framed by the Nazi experience chose a similar route, such as Arendt, Buber, Frankl, Levinas, and a non-Jewish voice—Bonhoeffer. Each met that moment with conviction and faith, without undue reliance upon lament.

Bonhoeffer was reluctant to routinely engage lament in everyday life. When asked to name the ideal parishioners to whom he would wish to minister, he stated that he would welcome whomever God gave to him; whoever was a member deserved his care and attention (*Life Together* 28–29). Such comments typify his encounter with life from the vantage point of faith and discipleship. There are times for genuine lament, genuine sorrow. Routine lament, however, can register dissatisfaction with the world as it is, a world unable to attain the perfection demanded by "me."

Lament can too quickly come from an ethic embraced in the abstract, not in the concrete, in the give and take of human life. Bonhoeffer cautioned against an abstract ethic; he called us to understand concrete ethical life.

> The attempt to define that which is good once and for all has, in the nature of the case, always ended in failure. Either the proposition was asserted in such general and formal terms that it retained no significance as regards its contents, or else one tried to include in it and elaborate the whole immense range of conceivable contents, and thus to say in advance what would be good in every single conceivable case; this led to a casuistic system so unmanageable that it could satisfy the demands neither of general validity nor of concreteness. The concretely Christian ethic is beyond formalism and casuistry. (*Ethics* 85–86)

The caution against lament keeps one focused upon the historical moment, and such caution keeps one from the clutches of another form of unmasking—not the Other, but existential life itself.

Unnecessary or routine lament does more than violence to the Other, it violates God's creation. Such lament unmasks existential life propelling discussions often heard from colleagues unwilling to admit the passing of modernity, unwilling to admit this moment of virtue contention. One imagines Bonhoeffer offering the following to concerned colleagues: "Modernity and the story of progress were making the faith less and less relevant and necessary. You once again have a chance to bring a faith-centered story to the public conversation. Narrative disputes provide opportunity for theological reflection and reconsideration. I suggest you take this opportunity and cease needless lament." What we call this moment is not the issue. The key historical issue is that narrative contention walks among us. The events of September 11, 2001, that engineered the deaths of many in the twin towers in New York, numerous conflicts, and interminable wars should call for us to examine the dramatic difference in narratives that guide action. We may experience great pain and disgust over these events, but we cannot step away from this historical moment composed of dramatic differences among competing narrative allegiances.

One of the major lessons Bonhoeffer offered was the necessity of meeting the world as it is on its own terms, without giving up one's value-laden perspective. Bonhoeffer walked within a Christocentric narrative position that encountered different and evil narrative presuppositions. Admitting what is does not equate with agreement; however, if one denies the historical moment that shadows the path of today, it is impossible to transform a given situation. Bonhoeffer's credentials, earned in virtue contention with the Nazis, exhibit how a faith-centered story navigates a constructive direction even in the most demanding of times. Bonhoeffer walked within a faith-centered narrative. From this position, he displayed conviction and courage. Yet, it is not the conviction and courage alone that imbue his work with such power. Bonhoeffer's implementation of a faith story within the dual commitments of conviction and humility warrants embracing a paradoxical voice that resists quick, flat, and ideologically driven readings of complex human events. Bonhoeffer was and is a standard bearer of a faith position that meets a world of difference on its own terms with clarity of position or standpoint.

A Reluctant Standard Bearer

Bonhoeffer distinguished between a "person" and an "individual" (*Letters and Papers from Prison* 344), with the former embedded within the story of the faith, engaged in the historical moment, and the latter attempting to stand above the historical situation. A dialogic standard bearer works as a person, not as an individual, in the meeting of existential life. A person works within a story as a storyteller. Bonhoeffer worked within a story of faith, in which a person finds ground upon which to meet the historical moment, engaging a given charge or task.

Bonhoeffer's unity of conviction and humility suggests a religious communication style appropriate for a communicative standard bearer, a recognized carrier of the virtues of a community. A standard bearer is not just a person of good values; values are personal. A standard bearer is a person committed in action to the virtues of a given community. Bonhoeffer embraced the virtues of the faith community with appropriate flexibility. Additionally, the fact that Bonhoeffer was responsive to the concrete and creative manner in which particular virtues were to be carried out in response to the Other and the historical situation frames his life as a dialogic standard bearer. Bonhoeffer's unity of conviction and pragmatic humility models caution against acts of narcissism and undue self-confidence.

The difference between the terms *person* and *individual* implies that only a person can become a standard bearer of a community. A person's formation within the community permits the community to bestow an unofficial title of standard bearer. An individual can never assume such a title alone—the title is unattainable by individual competition. Only a community can connect one intimately and publicly to the story of a people.

Aristotle's Greek Athenian world, from which the notion of standard bearer arises (1113a25), points to Bonhoeffer's standard-bearing actions, with Bonhoeffer's polis being God's people. At the center of Bonhoeffer's communicative life and action is *Christ the Center*. Bonhoeffer is the standard bearer of a Christocentric community seeking to engage the world with conviction, honesty, confession, and necessary realignment and change.

Both Aristotle and Bonhoeffer point to the community as the final arbitrator of excellence, with differing views of the community providing alternative story identities. Aristotle encouraged the pursuit of virtues that might shape a life as a standard bearer of excellence. Bonhoeffer, on the other hand, understood only one standard bearer of excellence as central to his Christocentric theology. For Bonhoeffer, the ultimate standard bearer is Christ. Stated in Aristotle's language, Bonhoeffer wanted to be a craftsman of the faith, leaving no doubt that there is only one standard bearer. This work understands Bonhoeffer as achieving craftsman status as a religious communicator, recognizing that his goal was not to attain the status of standard bearer of thoughtful religious communication. Bonhoeffer is a reluctant standard bearer, finding himself in such a position in spite of his reluctance and distrust of such language. Ironically, a person without the desire to be a standard bearer is more likely to be placed in such status at the behest of a community.

Bonhoeffer, as a communicative standard bearer of the union of seemingly contrary acts, engaged religious communication with texture and wisdom. Aristotle encouraged pursing virtues appropriate for a standard bearer through knowing the craft so well that one becomes a model for others. Aristotle differentiated a craftsman from a standard bearer. The former does not guarantee the latter. One can strive to be a craftsman, but a standard bearer has such a title unofficially bestowed by the community itself. A person has some control over becoming a craftsman. Knowledge, skilled action, and love of the craft constitute the life of a craftsman. Only a community can offer the designation of standard bearer. "We" can call Bonhoeffer a standard bearer of a faith-centered communicative style. Bonhoeffer's integration of contraries such as conviction and pragmatic humility points the communicator toward textured readings of complex issues.

Bonhoeffer valued listening and was wary of seeking quick, simple answers to complex issues. For instance, if one wanted Bonhoeffer to reject a person or group of persons for "violation" of a particular moral position, one would be disappointed. Bonhoeffer offered a cautioned, careful, textured read that considered the "one" moral injunction under consideration and in addition would consider "other" moral injunctions related to the issue at hand, which would often bring principles into creative, responsive disagreement, shedding textured light upon the historical moment. Dietrich Bonhoeffer, a religious storyteller, integrated the paradox of conviction and humility. He is now a standard bearer—a trusted storyteller who engages us with humility that tempers conviction, recognizing that conviction can miss the texture and complexity of a given issue. Bonhoeffer is a religious storyteller working within the paradox of conviction and humility. His conviction is a standpoint or position situated in questioning and doubt; such a communicator rejects the temptation of communicative assurance identified with a "true believer" (Hoffer xii, 87).

Bonhoeffer's conviction is no less than that of a "true believer"; however, his conviction, tempered and restrained by humility, coupled with his willingness to listen to the Other, provides a unique, textured communicative style. This communicative standard bearer displayed a textured religious communication that embraced the interplay of communicative background and communicative foreground action.

Bonhoeffer, considered a premier "community theologian" of the twentieth century, was a craftsman of the community who did not seek to be a standard bearer. Such status is beyond self-promotion; however, Bonhoeffer did embrace the importance of commitment to the task similar to a craftsman. Bonhoeffer framed theory, practice, and the importance of a deep commitment to community.

A craftsman knows the theory, putting it into appropriate action, while also loving the craft. Bonhoeffer knew the theory of religious communication as witnessed in *The Communion of Saints* and *The Cost of Discipleship,* put into action as exemplified in *Life Together;* his love of the faith guided all his work. Bonhoeffer functioned as a craftsman of religious communication worthy of admiration as a communicative standard bearer for a religious community interested in encountering a world of difference in dialogue.

A standard bearer brings texture to a task and is acknowledged by others. From multiple angles, the work of a standard bearer illuminates and calls for our attention. Bonhoeffer's religious communication illuminates from multiple angles; his insights offer thoughtful texture that addresses a diverse and complex communicative environment. A community recognizes a standard bearer as bringing the "appropriate" sense of texture to a given craft in an exemplary fashion. Bonhoeffer's "ideal type" community is diverse enough that only textured readings and interpretations unify differences; this textured communicative wisdom pointed to by Dietrich Bonhoeffer permitted him to be a craftsman of service for the Other that became a standard for engaging diversity from a particular standpoint in a "world come of age."

8

THE PRACTICE OF COMMUNITY

Communicative Habits of the Heart

Alasdair MacIntyre on a fundamental social practice:

> [T]he distinction between secular atheistic man and Christian man is that the latter acknowledges his powerlessness in his concern for others. But what would it be like to do this in the world of today, of the welfare state and of the underdeveloped countries, facing the patterns of world revolution? One gets from Bonhoeffer's writings no clear picture of what type of action he would actually be recommending now, but one gets the clearest picture of what Bonhoeffer means if one sees it in the context out of which he wrote. For in Nazi Germany, and in the Europe of the 1930's, the Christian role was at best one of suffering witness. The Nazi regress to gods of race made relevant a Christian regress to a witness of the catacombs and of the martyrs. There was available then a simple form in which to relive Christ's passion. Bonhoeffer lived it. And in all situations where nothing else remains for Christians this remains. (*Against the Self* 18–19)

Dietrich Bonhoeffer on common tasks:

> Work plunges men into the world of things. The Christian steps out of the world of brotherly encounter into the world of impersonal things, the "it." [. . .] [F]or the "it"—world is only an instrument in the hand of God for the purification of Christians from all self-centeredness and self-seeking. The work of the world can be done only where a person forgets himself, where he loses himself in a cause, in reality, the task, the "it" [. . .]
>
> The work does not cease to be work; on the contrary, the hardness and rigor of the labor is really sought only by the one who knows what it does for him. The continuing struggle with the "it" remains. But at the same time the breakthrough is made; the unity of prayer and work, the unity of the day is discovered; for to find, back of the "it" of the day's work, the "Thou," which is God, is what Paul calls "praying without ceasing" (I Thess. 5.17). (*Life Together* 70–71)

MacIntyre and Bonhoeffer understand that social practices matter. Human communities live by actions toward and with one another. Religious communication situated within "habits of the heart" (Tocqueville 287;

Bellah, *Habits of the Heart,* xlii, 152–55) of the faith provides a sense of ground, a place from which to address and meet the Other. Bonhoeffer offers us a faith story with habits of the heart that unite the call of service and the inevitability of suffering. One cannot turn to Bonhoeffer for communicative habits of the heart that offer enhanced self-image or self-actualization or call forth a theology of glory. Bonhoeffer offers an alternative to conventional assumptions about a communicative "good life" that works to augment self-image, offering instead meaning emergent from responsiveness to the Other situated within a story of the faith.

> I also felt it to be an omission not to have carried out my long-cherished wish to attend the Lord's Supper with you. [. . .] I ask for your forgiveness, and yet I know that we have shared spiritually, although not physically, in the gift of confession, absolution, and communion, and that we may be quite happy and easy in our minds about it. (*Letters and Papers from Prison* 129)

What we do makes a difference in "life together"—our habits of the heart emerge from repetitive action. For a narrative to have life it must find support within social practices—communicative habits of the heart. The habits of the heart of a religious communicator are communicative social practices that sustain a given narrative.

Bonhoeffer points to communicative habits of the heart that provide a third alternative to sole reliance upon information or expressivism. Information works within a world of a priori control; information packages reality as if the information had no bias or standpoint. Expressivism works within a world of self-concern; expressivism does not seek to control bias but revels in subjective expression. Religious communication framed in the interplay of habits of the heart responsive to service and necessary sacrifice works within a world where control and individual expression remain secondary to responsiveness to the Other within the horizon of the faith story.

"Habits of the heart" are social practices that shape community life. A knowing commitment to a faith story requires movement from unreflective to reflective social practices. Understood "habits of the heart" require knowledge of the why and the how of given communicative social practices. The call to move to a world come of age requires one to shift from unreflective social practices to reflective awareness of social practices. Such action is praxis, theory-informed action, which in Bonhoeffer's case might more appropriately fit the description of religious story-informed "habits of the heart." A knowing commitment, an acceptance of theory, a deep knowledge of the faith story shapes the "habits of the heart" central to Bonhoeffer's religious communication.

This framework does not suggest standing above, but standing within, a story of the faith that encourages implementation of particular "habits of the heart." Theologically, the notion of the "fall" reveals the historical embeddedness that keeps one from seeing clearly. Once the person is in the world, not protected in a Garden of Eden, the ability to see, to understand, ceases. "Every attempt to make it understandable is merely an accusation which the creature hurls against the Creator. [. . .] The Fall affects the whole of the created world which is henceforth plundered of its creatureliness as it crashes blindly into infinite space" (Bonhoeffer, *Creation and Fall* 76). From a postmodern perspective, one contends with the religious overtones, but philosophically, the inability to see and comprehend with clarity guides Bonhoeffer's reading of the "fall."

In the field of communication, the term "habits" continues to have currency. For instance, it is the ongoing theme of Quentin Schultze's *Habits of the High-Tech Heart,* and the notion of "habits" rests at the heart of Karl Wallace's work. Wallace connects the story of democracy and communicative habits that engage the necessary social practices to protect democratic life: a "habit of search," a "habit of justice," a "habit of preferring public to private motivations," and a "habit of respect for descent" (1–9). From postwar reflection, Karl Wallace, in whose name the discipline gives the Karl R. Wallace Memorial Award each year, outlined the four above-named habits for democratic communication. He understood that "habits" are the heart of a story, in this case of democracy, accepting the wisdom of Tocqueville's understanding of "habits of the heart" that keep the story vibrant. In addition, Bellah recognized that "habits of the heart" are confused in a psychological culture, propelled more by individualism than by story. Stories require nourishing of "the common," a set of tacitly agreed upon presuppositions. Habits can form a common. Bonhoeffer pointed toward both the importance of the common and its limits in a world come of age, requiring rethinking of communicative habits of the heart for a world come of age, a postmodern moment of narrative and virtue contention.

The Common

Bonhoeffer pointed to the danger of control and expression unresponsive to habits of the heart, which offer revelation of the faith.

> After the fall of Adam, God never ceased to send his Word to sinful men. He sought after them in order to take them to himself. The whole purpose for which the Word came was to restore lost mankind to fellowship with God. The Word of God came both as a promise and as a law. It became weak and of no account for our sake. But men rejected the Word, refusing to be accepted by God. They offered sacrifices and performed works which they fondly imagined God would accept in place of themselves, but with these they wanted to buy themselves out. (*The Cost of Discipleship* 264)

The "fall" moved communicative life from a common, known Garden of Eden to self-expression outside the horizon of promise and law to efforts of informational control in packaged alms or sacrifices that ignored calls to service to Others. Communicative life lost a ground of common connection. The story of Adam and Eve expelled from the Garden is a story of lost communicative ground. Reliance upon information and expressivism exclusively ignores the call to reclaim a penultimate communicative Garden of the Common. Bonhoeffer implied a penultimate communicative commonplace of service and revelation in the midst of inevitable disappointed lives, finding life within communicative social practices—habits of the heart.

The notion of the common does not presuppose uniform understanding; the common requires minimal agreement on the symbols and ideas under discussion and interpretation. "The individual constantly experiences, thinks, and acts in a sphere of what is common, and only in it does he understand" (Buber, *The Knowledge of Man* 156). This view of the common links partners in communication. Communication between persons requires some agreed upon understanding of story, agents, ideas, and historical moment. Minimal knowledge of the common permits one to encounter the difference of the Other and discover a background, a limited agreed upon understanding.

For this form of communicative complexity to engage the Other, a first assumption that must be in place is the "common." The notion of the common, discussed above, suggests that making sense to another requires attending to the object or event. Interpretations vary, but sense making does not imply agreement; it only suggests that an object or event under discussion rests "in common." Making sense to another as one discusses the notion of a religious communication ethic requires the communicative partners to hold in common the importance of the faith story, or perhaps to hold in common the importance of understanding various approaches to communication ethics. What is common frames the ground of the communication.

Bonhoeffer's understanding of the common permits the possibility of transcendence, discovery of novel insight. Bonhoeffer suggests that communication becomes more demanding as the common becomes less clear. Bonhoeffer's fascination with creation and the creation story reminds us of a sense of void, losing a commonplace, and then eventually reclaiming a common place in Christ. The beginning of a commonplace is of little interest to Bonhoeffer; it is the ground it provides, not the sequence of creation relayed, that matters. The misplaced hope of finding "the" beginning "crumbles into dust, it runs aground upon itself" (Bonhoeffer, *Creation and Fall* 14). The common has no beginning or end, just invitation to join. The story of a "resurrected Christ" (20) fills a "false void" (20), for the common was never absent. Christ performed the role of visible reminder, providing ground, the common, a place upon which one could stand. Such ground made Bonhoeffer's task that of engagement from ground, not the effort to find the beginning or the end of the faith story/ground; but to be open to the revelatory uniqueness of that story in each temporal moment and situation.

Bonhoeffer's dialectical understanding of the common moves him from faith agreement alone. The common must live in the historical situation, not in abstraction. The act or focus of attention on God must simultaneously engage the Other in the unique historical situation. One brings ground or standpoint to the attention of the Other, and "being between" (Bonhoeffer, *Act and Being* 35) persons, the transcendence of being, manifests itself, permitting new insight from the Other, reshaping the "I." He frames a genuine "dialectics of Otherness" (Floyd 19).

Commonness in practical discourse invites the dialogue of a faith story and focus of attention upon the Other in a unique situation, providing an alternative to information accuracy or objectivity and focus on individual expression. This dialogic move finds life within communicative texture constituted by dialectic of interests: story, ideas, historical situation, and relationships within some minimal common agreement. In a world come of age, the minimal common agreement may be no more than the importance of the Other. Bonhoeffer brings communicative texture to the table of understanding and a realistic appraisal of the difficulty of meeting another in a world come of age. Bonhoeffer brings the common, the story of the faith, into encounter with everyday, changing historical demands.

> One can speak of "guidance" only on the other side of the twofold process, with God meeting us no longer as "Thou," but also "disguised" in the "It;" so in the last resort my question is how we are to find the "Thou" in this "It" (i.e. fate),

> or, in other words, how does "fate" really become "guidance?" It's therefore impossible to define the boundary between resistance and submission on abstract principles; but both of them must exist, and both must be practised. Faith demands this elasticity of behavior. Only so can we stand our ground in each situation as it arises, and turn it to gain. [. . .] [A] more flexible, livelier "theological" approach [. . .] is more in accord with reality. (*Letters and Papers from Prison* 217–18)

The common tempered by the historical moment guides Bonhoeffer into communication with another.

The notion of the common is an implicit center to Bonhoeffer's emphasis on a faith story tempered by communicative texture in the dialectic of the common and the historical moment, driven by interests situated within topic, persons, and standpoint. In an era of virtue contention and narrative disagreement, we look for the common in minimal places with minimal expectations, hoping to sustain communication long enough to invite a temporal sense of human community.

Dietrich Bonhoeffer implied a twofold understanding of the "common." First, from a Christian perspective, Bonhoeffer assumes the story of the faith as one engages another committed to the faith story. Second, in a world come of age, one might engage another on any ground possible. Assuming similar commitment to a faith narrative is problematic in a world come of age. In a postmodern age, assuming commitment to any narrative, whether religion or the notion of progress, is unwise. As the world shifts from an unreflective sense of agreement on the "common," the demands on a religious communicator, any communicator, increase.

Bonhoeffer understood the demise of a nineteen-hundred-year-old view of the faith. What no longer defined a world come of age was a "religious *a priori*" (Bonhoeffer, *Letters and Papers from Prison* 280). To deny this shift in worldview was, for Bonhoeffer, simply "intellectually dishonest" (280). The communicative task in a world come of age was honest meeting of the historical moment of change. Such is the continuing task of today.

The notion of a world come of age signaled the beginning of what we now call a postmodern moment. Bonhoeffer understood that the shifting world could no longer assume religion as the background narrative. Now we can no longer assume any one narrative as a common background. The common has simply become less common. Such is the reason that *sensus communis* detailed by Cicero (I.iii.12) no longer naturally accompanies life events. The emphasis on common sense arising out of the sense or habits of the heart of a community no longer comes assumed. Common sense lives within a common narrative and agreed-upon social practices. Without the common, we must work together to discern common sense in a given setting. Without the common, common sense becomes a commodity no longer taken for granted.

The "common" frames Bonhoeffer's religious communicative engagement. With agreement of Bonhoeffer's view of the "common," "discipleship" (*The Cost of Discipleship* 61–114), a faith story with a commitment to service to Others, religious communication takes on the importance of alterity over attentiveness to the self. Without a common of a faith story of service, there is no faith-centered communication ethic. Lack of a common, *sensus communis,* moves religious communication to the sharing of perspective and information. In typical dialectical fashion, to meet a world come of age of diversity, Bonhoeffer pointed to the ground of the common as the point of meeting. One meets difference from knowing ground—a common story of the faith or the common commitment to find temporal common ground between persons of difference.

For a religious communicator, the key is the story of the faith, but in a world come of age, one assumes that the Other will not necessarily concur with such a commitment. One searches for a minimal sense of a common story that permits one to engage the Other and the historical moment. The "common" is necessary for temporal agreement on communicative habits of the heart, permitting communicators to attend to the historical moment in a manner that makes sense to one another without necessarily suggesting agreement.

Acting in a sphere that is common does not mean agreement on how to address a given moment. On March 5, 1933, there was a common understanding of the historical situation in Germany as grave. The election announced differing interpretations of this crisis. Bonhoeffer voted for the Catholic Centre Party in hopes that their international connections could keep the "German factor" under control. The Nazis gained 44 percent of the vote and with the support of the German National Conservative Party, they took power. By March 24, the Enabling Act gave Hitler power above the constitution. By late June 1933, the Confessing Church formed in opposition to the German Evangelical Church. The common became the "grave situation." The communicative difference existed not in the reading of the common, but in response to that realization. No longer could the role of the church be the common connection between Christians in

Germany. The Barmen Conference and Declaration, May 29–31, made the opposition official. The declaration announced "the character of the resistance" (Robertson, *The Shame and the Sacrifice* 117). The notion of the common does not mean agreement on how to address a given situation; finding a minimal sense of the common is a task that a religious communicator cannot take for granted in a world of narrative and virtue contention.

In order to engage a world come of age, one must understand that communication needs to take on great flexibility and texture in meeting instability in a world of narrative contention. Calvin Schrag offers insight into a type of communicative understanding needed in a postmodern age with the notion of "communicative texture" (*Communicative Praxis* 17–111).

Communicative Texture

The phrase "communicative texture" embraces both the common and the different, framing interpretation for an era of narrative contention. The dialectic of the common and the different shapes a textured view of communication as opposed to information with its impulse for control and accuracy. Communicative texture lives outside self-expression and the realm of control and accuracy. Communicative texture suggests a complexity of communicative life within which we participate but do not direct or control.

The dialectical tension of common and different underscores the work of Calvin Schrag and the term "communicative texture" (*Communicative Praxis* 17–111); "in the end this may be the most important term" (23). What is the texture of a peach? What is the texture of sand? What is the texture of a "good" conversation? What is the texture of a "good" home? In each case, "texture" is difficult to define, but in the attempt, one learns about what one knows as one makes contact with another. Schrag takes us from "the privilege of seeing and the centrality of the eye" (22) to texture that can be understood only with and through extension of the senses. From feeling the texture in wood to hearing the texture in music, one senses a world beyond sight. For Schrag, this emphasis on texture slides into the focus on text, the "text as the narration of texture" (24).

Communicative texture is the complexity that makes a phenomenon what it is; to discuss the texture of a given phenomenon gives one better understanding of the idea, the event, the phenomenon at hand. Ask any graduate student who teaches whether he or she gains a greater understanding of the texture of his or her subject matter. Trying to explain what we know makes visible texture previously unnoticed or taken for granted.

Understanding communicative texture separates a communication technician from a communication engineer. The communication engineer uses the right communicative mode at the right time in the right manner, understanding the interconnection of varying combinations and styles of communicative engagement. A communication engineer responds to the setting and to the historical moment in a unique fashion using multiple communication tools. The inclusion of multiple communicative modes reflects Bonhoeffer's thoughtful and tempered understanding of religious communication ethics—enhancing the possibility of an appropriate response.

The title of this work begins with dialogue; however, Bonhoeffer's communication embraces a communicative texture beyond dialogue. Dialogue is one communicative mode central to Bonhoeffer. Dialogue shares the communicative stage with dialectic and with rhetoric. Bonhoeffer's communicative habits of the heart include dialogue, dialectic, and rhetoric. Bonhoeffer seems to suggest that one begins dialogue from a stance, in his case a faith story. One then meets the Other and the historical situation, seeking to learn from and understand that which is not one's own, tempering conviction of position with a dialectic of caution and, at times, doubt.

Finally, Bonhoeffer takes a rhetorical turn, offering comment on appropriate action, discerned in dialogue and through dialectical questioning. Bonhoeffer acted when he took a rhetorical turn to engagement of communicative texture that included a comprehensive use of communicative understandings. As Schrag suggests, a decentered subject works with the historical situation, attempting to understand its call. The mix of dialogue, dialectic, and rhetoric permitted Bonhoeffer to discern his response to common ground in a given historical moment with the best of discerned action. The rhetorical turn permitted Bonhoeffer to claim a sense of ground in a changing world and engage the world prophetically.

> [P]eople want to have fixed conceptions—despite everything. I'm eager to see what you've written to me. How do we Protestants avoid the actual surrender of "ground" from generation to generation or along the line (to put it crudely) [of] Barth-Bultmann-Bonhoeffer, which *in fact* has made tremendous progress in contrast to the liberal period, despite all new beginnings and restitutions? What has attracted people to Barth and to the Confessing Church? The feeling that they can find a certain hoard of truth here, "Old Testament, prophetic," the perception of a certain support of the oppressed? [. . .]
>
> So, what are we to do about making particular claims on "ground" in the world? (Bonhoeffer, *Letters and Papers from Prison* 318)

It is the communicative texture of Bonhoeffer, his use of dialogue, dialectic, and rhetoric, that permits his work to continue to speak to this historical moment.

The conviction level that propels Bonhoeffer's rhetoric found tempering in both the practical, in pastoral work, and in the academic, in use of dialectic. Both the pastoral and academic roles were part of Bonhoeffer's life, which contributed to a tempered, yet fully convicted, rhetoric. Milton Rokeach once warned, referring to Gandhi, not to confuse a person of supreme conviction with one of closure (60). Such is the manner in which one must understand Bonhoeffer. Even as Bonhoeffer embraced a prophetic tradition, his rhetorical framing of societal reform was tempered by pastoral and academic concerns for the Other and for fairness of inquiry.

Bonhoeffer tempered his rhetoric as he discussed the implications of *The Cost of Discipleship,* a book calling for pacifism, and his later participation in the assassination attempt on Hitler (*Letters and Papers from Prison* 369). Bonhoeffer later stood by the book but worried about the call to conviction that might propel one to take the righteousness of one's position too seriously. Bonhoeffer's rhetorical impulse propelled his desire to influence the world with full knowledge of his own limits.

> I discovered later, and I'm still discovering right up to this moment, that is it only by living completely in this world that one learns to have faith. One must completely abandon any attempt to make something of oneself, whether it be a saint, or a converted sinner, or a churchman (a so-called priestly type!), a righteous man or an unrighteous one, a sick man or a healthy one. By this-worldliness I mean living unreservedly in life's duties, problems, successes and failures, experiences and perplexities. In so doing we throw ourselves completely into the arms of God, taking seriously, not our own sufferings, but those of God in the world [. . .] How can success make us arrogant, or failure lead us astray, when we share in God's sufferings through a life of this kind? (*Letters and Papers from Prison* 369–70)

Rhetoric for a prophetic religious life requires the tempering of dialogue and dialectic within the story of the faith.

Bonhoeffer's stress on responsibility, discipleship, and deputyship within the story of the faith invites a particular view of dialogue, a dialogue situated within a rhetoric of the faith, questioned by an academic dialectic temperament. Such a view of dialogue rejects a "telling" style of communication that keeps the attention upon the self, while permitting a stance to begin the conversation. Bonhoeffer understood the notion of "being between" (*Act and Being* 35), as did Martin Buber through his idea of the "sphere of the 'between'" (*Between Man and Man* 203). The "being between" is a place where a glimpse of God guides and shapes the interaction. The being between provides a transcendental communicative glimpse, permitting the person to learn from the Other, which is only possible when one works from a stance that permits a sense of ground.

Dialogue-tempered religious rhetoric and dialectic work within three communicative social practices: conviction (rhetoric), discernment (dialectical analysis), and confession (dialogue). The interplay of multiple communicative modes and multiple communicative social practices frames a story-centered religious communication ethic uneasy with formulaic or doctrinal answers, responsive to the historical situation and ever cognizant of a particular focus of attention. Dialogue, dialectic, and rhetoric temper and enrich one another, unlike propaganda and expressivism. Bonhoeffer's communication stems from a moral story of the faith that met the test of Nazi struggle and embraced sophisticated texture of the interplay of dialogue, dialectic, and rhetoric.

Confession is the key link to the interplay of dialogue, dialectic, and rhetoric. First, as one hears the confession of another, or utters a confession to another, dialogue makes the disclosure possible. Second, listening to another's confession requires one to discern the information, looking at multiple sides of issues from a dialectical perspective, reminding oneself that disclosure of sin announces humanness and offers opportunity for new life. Finally, confession reconnects the Other and the confessor to the story of the faith; it is a rhetorical reminder of the story line of a faith-centered life. A psychologist engages the first two steps; the rhetoric of the faith story moves confession to a moral dimension based on criteria beyond the self.

> Only the Christian knows this. In the presence of a psychiatrist I can only be a sick man; in the presence of a Christian brother I can dare to be a sinner. [. . .] It is not lack of psychological knowledge but lack of love for the crucified Jesus Christ that makes us so poor and inefficient in brotherly confession. (Bonhoeffer, *Life Together* 119)

This three-fold communicative engagement frames Bonhoeffer's textured and thoughtful communicative connection with the Other and the historical moment before him, propelled by a confessional faith, a confessional understanding of one's limits, and a confessional sense of discernment.

Bonhoeffer's communicative social practices shape the interplay of rhetoric (conviction of the faith story), dialogue (attentiveness to the Other and historical situation), and dialectic (textured discernment of issues), framing a narrative of responsible texture contrary to ideological knowledge that embraces a priori assurance. A narrative guides. An ideology dictates without communicative texture, manifesting rigidity and stubborn persistence.

Narrative Beginnings

Narrative knowledge, in this case the faith story and the needs of the concrete moment, works dialectically to inform and temper. Responsible action requires attentiveness to both the narrative and the historical moment; responsible action requires "narrative fidelity" (Fisher 8) and attentiveness to the historical moment. Guilt emerges when one fails to engage a narrative or the historical moment appropriately. Confession is public admission of error that offers time to reconsider, to reexamine the story and the demands of the historical moment, requiring a reengagement of the narrative (faith story). This sequence, better understood as concentric circles that keep repeating a similar rhythm, increases knowledge, complexity, and texture. Narrative knowledge formed in the interplay of faith story, historical situation, and communicative modes and communicative actions offers a communicative model of interpretation responsive to multiple communicative elements.

Bonhoeffer entered a communicative setting with the story of the faith, a willingness to learn from Others and the historical moment, confidence to test ideas, and a teleology, a direction toward a social good—service to Others. Bonhoeffer offered a narrative glimpse of a story of faith-centered service in a world come of age. One may not agree with Bonhoeffer's religious story direction, but the clarity of engagement within his religious communication ethic made opposition to Nazi atrocity possible. Bonhoeffer knew "why" his faith story called for such opposition—in order to be of service to the Other. Bonhoeffer's textured communicative modes and actions brought a knowing sense of "why" capable of withstanding the test of the marketplace of everyday life.

Bonhoeffer walked into tests of the everyday with the support of textured narrative knowledge. He admitted the darker side of life without giving into its despair.

> Sickened by vermin
> that feed, in the side of the good,
> on envy, greed, and suspicion,
> by the snake-like hissing
> of venomous tongues

that fear and hate and revile
the mystery of free thought
and upright heart,
the spirit would cast aside all deceit,
open his heart to the spirit he trusts,
and unite with him freely as one.
Ungrudging, he will support,
will thank and acknowledge him,
and from him draw happiness and strength.

(*Letters and Papers from Prison* 390)

Bonhoeffer's textured and practical understanding of narrative knowledge permitted meeting darkness with story-filled assurance, ever mindful of difference without losing religious standpoint or a willingness to learn. Bonhoeffer points to a textured narrative that embraces a communicative dialectic of religious life of humble conviction, which can invite a sense of human community. When a given narrative is not held in common, communicative social practices shape a community and offer form to temporal narrative agreement.

Within Community

Bonhoeffer, a community theologian, understood theory and the necessity of practices. The metaphor of "habits of the heart" claims the importance of social practices for human community. Bellah and associates use the term "habits of the heart," coined by Alexis de Tocqueville in 1835 in *Democracy in America,* to understand how particular habits of the heart (communicative social practices) assisted or confounded the cultivation and sustaining of our contemporary versions of human community. Alexis de Tocqueville described the "habits of the heart" necessary for guiding a young democracy, and Bellah asks, "What are the necessary 'habits of the heart' for sustaining human community?" Each seeks an alternative to individualism, another term introduced by Tocqueville (506). The metaphor of "habits of the heart" understood within community offers guidance for the individual. This guidance comes from social practices taken seriously by the community. Such is the reason for Bonhoeffer's commitment to community as a scholar in *The Communion of Saints* and as a pastor of social practices illustrated in *Life Together.*

The notion of "habits of the heart" connects to the "natural" (*Ethics* 143–51), which Bonhoeffer understood as connected to Christ, while understanding the unnatural as moving away from Christ. He chastised the Protestant

Church for abandoning the natural. Catholic life keeps such a notion in place, guiding ethical conduct. In communication terms, the natural embodies social practices that keep one within the story of the everyday understanding of the faith. Natural practices guide as they remind one of the story of the faith.

> Natural life must not be understood simply as a preliminary to life with Christ. It is only from Christ Himself that it receives its validation. Christ Himself entered into the natural life, and it is only through the incarnation of Christ that the natural life becomes the penultimate which is directed towards the ultimate. Only through the incarnation of Christ do we have the right to call others to the natural life and to live the natural life ourselves.
>
> How does one recognize the natural? The natural is the form of life preserved by God for the fallen world and directed towards justification, redemption, and renewal through Christ. (Bonhoeffer, *Ethics* 145)

In a postmodern culture, we cannot expect agreement on the notion of the natural, a term tied more to narrative of the faith than to "natural events." The Christian story in a postmodern culture must vie for attention among multiple stories. Bonhoeffer worked within one story—a Christ-centered story that framed his view of the "natural"—but engaged a larger world. Today one must first accept the story of the faith, and then one can discern the natural situated within such a narrative.

Christ is the link to a Christian faith story. As one accepts this particular story, the actions become natural acts that are paradigmatic and story bound. When we join a story, certain readings become natural as one attends to calling and participation in the story. The metaphor of "natural" frames social practices and "habits of the heart" that become understandable within a faith story. Heidegger's famous line of language as constructing the "house of being" (217–18) makes sense in philosophy, but in communication the "house of being" is the story that offers a background for interpretive understanding. The story organizes the characteristics of the natural, of the "habits of the heart." The community shaped by habits of the heart or common social practices sustains members in practical life together. The old advice to beware of what one takes to heart is appropriate in the shaping of communities, people, and social practices.

> In the 1830s, the French social philosopher Alexis de Tocqueville offered the most comprehensive and penetrating analysis of the relationship between character and society [connected by social practices,] "habits of the heart" [that formed] American character. (Bellah et al. xlii)

"Habits of the heart" are the social practices that build character, shaping communities and persons.

Communicative Habits of the Heart

Communicative habits of the heart composed of dialectic, dialogue, and rhetoric support discernment, confession, and the courage of conviction. There is an ongoing interplay among Bonhoeffer's metaphors, such as "cheap grace" and "costly grace," the "penultimate" and the "ultimate," "Christocentric" and "world come of age," "worldliness" and "revelation," and "concrete obedience" and "deputyship"—each is equally responsive to the faith story and the needs of the historical situation.

It is difficult to find a major idea penned by Bonhoeffer that goes untouched by dialectical thinking. Dialectic is Bonhoeffer's entrance into God's world, offering a faith story responsive to textured discernment. He begins with position, then questions, then takes action, then questions again—ever using the notion of dialectic to guide him. Dialectic is a philosophical and practical tool for countering unreflective adherence to technique; dialectic is central to Bonhoeffer's life and work. Perhaps the only way to shape "habits of the heart" through knowing reflection is by dialectical tension, which permits one to learn from contradictions. Simply understood, the direction of "right" makes more sense with awareness that one can turn "left." North makes more sense with knowledge of south. A big house frames an understanding of a small house and vice versa. Dialectic brings together contraries that shed light upon one another, offering reciprocal clarity. In understanding Bonhoeffer's contribution to communication, dialectic is the Rosetta stone; dialectic is the beginning of a content rich communicative life. Bonhoeffer does not begin with expression, but rather with discernment guided by dialectic, offering entrance into a faith meeting a world come of age. Dialectic is the privileged key to communicative habits of the heart. Without dialectic, Bonhoeffer's textured view of confession would not be possible because it would miss the necessity of responsive application of the faith to the historical situation.

A person who assumes a position without knowing the dialectical tensions within a given stance embraces an unreflective or taken-for-granted ideology. The texture of the argument is lost. Dialectical questioning keeps theory and action thoughtful and informed, providing a knowing and reflective base of action that shapes communication. A commitment to dialectical inquiry does not insure correctness of decision but assists with ability to defend "why" a given idea or action is pursued. Dialectical thinking helps counter excess and deficiency of idea and action engagement.

Bonhoeffer works within a long tradition of scholars from Aristotle to Hegel who use the notion of dialectic to keep ideas in creative tension. Bonhoeffer's position on dialectic situates communication within texture and complexity, not easy answers and technique. The title of Hans-Georg Gadamer's *Truth and Method* points to the manner in which dialectic engaged by Bonhoeffer and Gadamer functions. Dialectic is not a method, but an intellectual and practical commitment to doing one's best to discern a textured understanding of what is "true" in a given historical situation.

The Dialectical Spirit of Dialogue

Dialectic has multiple renditions, more than one use, texturing dialogue. In *Dialogue and Dialectic: Eight Hermeneutical Studies on Plato,* Gadamer clarifies Hegel's work on dialectical thinking based in "contradictions" as a philosophical contribution ("Dialectic and Sophism in Plato's *Seventh Letter*" 93). However, Gadamer rejects dialectic that results in synthesis in which one idea subsumes another with a resultant synthesis furthering the knowledge of the Objective Spirit. A "spirit" of domination frames this view of dialectic. Bonhoeffer and Gadamer temper dialectic with dialogue, rejecting dialectic that seeks to dominate with the "strongest" idea over a "lesser" position.

The use of dialectic in Gadamer and Bonhoeffer situates dialectic within dialogue. Dialectic situated within dialogue has communicative purpose of tempering ideas, not finding the triumphant key. Communication between persons that brings dialectic and dialogue together rests in tempered understanding, a willingness to listen to Others and ideas of difference. Dialectic clarifies, making thoughtful contact with the Other/difference possible. The goal is to assist communication between persons as we bring thoughtful ideas to the communicative table; the goal is not to win or impress but to clarify and enrich.

Gadamer cites Plato's understanding of the interplay of dialectic and dialogue; the dialogues of Plato reveal the importance of understanding ideas in a complex fashion as we engage one another. Dialectic furthers the depth and thoughtfulness of a dialogue, and dialogue keeps dialectic within a communicative framework, outside an abstract view of "truth" in which the best idea trumps a lesser insight. Dialectic in the dialogues of Plato is not an end in itself, but a process for clarification of ideas that enhances thoughtful dialogue with another. Textured ideas from dialectical analysis in concert with dialogue lessen the chance of communication deteriorating into a form of proclamation, ideology, and propaganda.

One can suggest that understanding Bonhoeffer's contribution to religious communication rests on one primary privileged habit of the heart: the notion that dialectic textures understanding. This notion of understanding textured by dialectic permits Bonhoeffer to walk between the extremes of the story of the faith and the concrete demands of the secular world, the conceptual and the experiential, a commitment to community and a willingness to "dissolve" a community when necessary (Bonhoeffer, *Life Together* 35). Bonhoeffer, an aristocrat with genuine concern for the proletariat, naturally and philosophically used dialectical insight. He brought assurance of education, class, and privilege together into concern for the oppressed.

Bonhoeffer's commitment to dialectic and dialogue permits him to invite transcendental knowledge responsive to the historical situation. Floyd announces in the introduction to *Act and Being* the importance of dialectic and the kinship between Martin Buber's dialogue project and the work of Dietrich Bonhoeffer. Like Gadamer, Buber in *Between Man and Man* understands dialectic within the scope of communication and dialogue between persons. The notion of the between is a form of transcendence, permitting one to see beyond the view of self and other.

Dialectical Invitation of Transcendence

Dialectic tempered by dialogue seeks a textured understanding of ideas between persons, lessening the chance of communication becoming a sophistic exercise in which one simply delights in being contrary and triumphing over the Other.

Floyd states:

> A genuinely dialectical form of thinking is possible only to the extent that it sustains the reality of authentic Otherness.
>
> In Bonhoeffer's typology in *Act and Being,* therefore, both a genuine transcendental philosophy and a genuine ontology are dependent on philosophy being able to maintain the relationship between *both* the activity of thinking *and* something transcendent, *ein Tranzendentes,* to thought—ontologically distinct from the thinking subject—neither of which "swallows up" the other. Bonhoeffer's dialectical claim that "being between" that which is transcendent is "*Dasein*" brings to mind the dialogical philosophy of Martin Buber, whose work Bonhoeffer seems not to have known [. . .]. (10)

To misunderstand the dialectical character of Bonhoeffer's work is to miss the significance of his insights. As Floyd suggests, Bonhoeffer discusses "genuine transcendentalism" (*Act and Being* 34–35), understood only within dialectical terms. Bonhoeffer suggested textured and dialectical readings of transcendence.

> One may speak of genuine Transcendentalism so long as the resistance of transcendence to thinking is upheld, that is to say, so long as the thing-in-itself and transcendental apperception are understood as pure limiting concepts. (*Act and Being* 35)

Bonhoeffer united contrary ideas—the horizontal and the vertical, the universal and the particular. Bonhoeffer understood "being between" (*Act and Being* 35) as genuine transcendence. The metaphor of the between is central to Buber's dialogic project (*Between Man and Man* 202–3). Bonhoeffer adds a dialectically nourished dialogue that deliberately avoids easy answers, seeking insights between opposing ideas.

Only by attending to both the concrete Other/historical moment and a transcendental connection to God/the story of the faith is a genuine transcendence possible. Both God and person in dialectic interaction propel Bonhoeffer's understanding of genuine transcendence. To miss this dialectical move places Bonhoeffer within a transcendental view that he questions, deus ex machina (Bonhoeffer, *Letters and Papers from Prison* 282). Bonhoeffer does not embrace a transcendental connection to a God who fixes all. He understood the dialectic between God's will for human beings and the free will/responsibility of the person.

Bonhoeffer used dialectic to keep one concept (the story of the faith) from overwhelming the other (the demands of the concrete moment)—life and action lived as a "being between." Ideas become more complex with dialectical thinking. Genuine transcendence is the interplay of the horizontal and the vertical, God and the person, the faith and the historical moment intertwined and lived out as best one can, in religious communication.

Bonhoeffer used this dialectical approach of transcendence to temper both the "sociological" and "religious" community of the Church. The genuine transcendental alternative is the "community of spirit" (Bonhoeffer, *The Communion of Saints* 180–81) that is both sociological and religious. The Church is a community that is more than a sociological entity and more than a religious gathering. It is a dialectical third alternative where the spirit guides concrete interaction with one another. The dialectical interplay of faith and the secular world is central to Bonhoeffer and articulated by many interested in his work. For instance, James William McClendon Jr.'s 1986 book, *Systematic Theology Ethics,* quotes from Bonhoeffer's *Ethics:* "In Jesus Christ we have faith in the incarnate, crucified, and risen God. There could be no greater error than to tear these elements apart; for each of them comprises the whole" (16). The heart of a Christian faith story is claimed dialectically in the union of death and resurrection. One without the other is without sense. Bonhoeffer's wedding of dialogue and dialectic does not tear apart opposing elements but unites contraries to inform a third alternative.

Bonhoeffer's textured view of genuine transcendence frames his understanding of a key dialectical metaphor central to the Christian faith: death and resurrection. Death and resurrection in unity guided Bonhoeffer's understanding of the faith story. A theology that conceptualized only "the good" attempts to live in daily resurrection, and a person of despair perceives only death; both miss a faith dialectically textured with death and resurrection as the central ongoing metaphor of the story of the faith.

> The difference between the Christian hope of resurrection and the mythological hope is that the former sends a man back to his life on earth in a wholly new way which is even more sharply defined than it is in the Old Testament. The Christian, unlike the devotees of the redemption myths, has no last line of escape available from earthly tasks and difficulties into the eternal, but, like Christ himself ("My God, why hast thou forsaken me?"), he must drink the earthly cup to the dregs [. . .] Redemption myths arise from human boundary-experiences, but Christ takes hold of a man at the center of his life. (Bonhoeffer, *Letters and Papers from Prison* 336–37)

Bonhoeffer's dialectic took death as a propeller of life and responsibility. Resurrection lives in the faith that walks in the center of life, not away from burden and responsibility. Death and resurrection walk with Bonhoeffer within the faith story, making the reality of loss and new possibilities equally relevant to communicative life. Such texture points to a communicative life of cautious conviction—the possibility of death and new life walk side by side.

A Habit of Cautious Conviction

Bonhoeffer points to a communication that begins with dialectic tempered with dialogue. Situating dialectic within dialogue offers communication with a rich sense of texture, concerned for seeing multiple sides of ideas and responding to particular persons, a particular situation, from the stance of a particular faith. Discernment coupled with the humility of confession guides Bonhoeffer's entrance into decision making, into conviction, into the rhetorical task of engaging the Other from a standpoint of conviction.

Bonhoeffer's communicative habits of the heart frame a major caution helpful for understanding postmodern discourse—one must attend to differentiation by practicing slowness to suggest that "this" is simply "that." The impulse to say, "I understand. This is just like that" too often can discount difference in postmodern culture. Postmodernity offers a place of difference where contrary sociocultural standpoints on what constitutes a good life are commonplace. Yet, one must still take a stand, occupy a position, and work with conviction.

Bonhoeffer provided a faith-centered rhetoric tempered by a dialectic and dialogic framework. Such rhetoric assists us in a postmodern era of contending narrative structures. Bonhoeffer's religious rhetoric provides a communicative background intentionally enriched with dialectic and dialogue in order to take a thoughtful sense of communicative texture into his dialogic confession with the Other. Bonhoeffer communicated from a rhetorical stance of knowing honed by dialectic and deepened in texture and understanding, offering a dialogic confession. He was ever aware of his conviction and the possibility of error. Bonhoeffer's religious communication takes us through the discipline of communication from dialectic to dialogue to rhetoric to the continual rhythm of this textured cycle of discernment, confession, and commitment.

From Habits of the Heart to a Community of Memory

Bonhoeffer's communicative habits of the heart work within a story that did not run from the work of Nietzsche, who suggested, "God is dead" (12). In fact, Bonhoeffer had appreciation for some of Nietzsche's warnings. Bonhoeffer told a story in which immature reliance upon God was dead and that God now called us to responsibility, a mature sense of faith. "[I]t is God's will, revealed in Jesus Christ [. . .] has called man to [. . .] responsibility for the world" (Godsey 11). Bonhoeffer understood Nietzsche's communicative call to make a difference and the necessity to forego simple reliance upon God to fix a troubled world. The task of the Christian is to tend God's world; the faith is a plow, not a garden of plenty, in the story that Bonhoeffer offers.

Bonhoeffer understood that a good story finds life within a community, or what Robert Bellah termed a "community of memory" (*Habits of the Heart* 152–58, 333). A "community of memory" suggests a community of persons telling a story that reminds one another of action required by the "habits of the heart." At its best, the church is a "community of memory" in which members remind one another about the good and noble side of church life and the flaws and sins within themselves and the church. The story Bonhoeffer offers is a "community of memory" that works for fidelity with the faith. Dialectic and dialogue keep ideas textured without reliance upon ideology. Bringing the faith story to the arena of human action offers another test of fidelity. Encouraging confession when violation of the spirit of the faith story occurs is yet another test of fidelity. Bonhoeffer offers a story that frames a "community of memory" tested for fidelity by dialectic and dialogue in discernment and confession that prepares one for the "rhetorical turn" (Schrag, *Communicative Praxis* 179–214) of conviction and practical action.

Bonhoeffer's story of the faith is "realistically hopeful" (Lasch, *The True and Only* 80–81), situated within a story of a "community of memory" that reminds us of courage, hope, and faithfulness in spite of our flaws and caution in spite of a faith stance. Such a story embraces limitations and sin-making confession central to this story capable of shaping the "community of memory" of a people.

Alasdair MacIntyre offers insight into the importance of the test of ideas (a knowing sense of "why") and the test of actions (implementation). MacIntyre speaks about three generations. The first generation knows the "why" of value-laden ideas and the "how" (implementation strategies). The second generation has heard the stories of "why" and does the action. This generation has tired of the stories of "why." They know the stories and continue action without retelling the stories of "why" particular actions are worthy of doing. They do not pass on to the next generation a sense of "why" particular actions are worthy of implementation. The third generation provokes wrath from the second generation as it fails to do the expected; no longer do particular actions make sense without knowledge of "why." Without the sense of "why," some cease doing expected actions. The second generation then questions and wonders what went wrong with the third generation. Ironically, however, the generational sin rests with generation number two for not telling the story of "why." The second generation failed to keep the community of memory alive by providing a sense of "why" for the actions. The communicative task of each generation requires being a storyteller—a teller of the "why" of action guiding the community of memory. A "community of memory" keeps alive the story of a people by uniting social practices and the memory of action within a story that provides direction and insight. The communicative key of a storyteller is the uniting of social practices and action into a story worth remembering that offers guidance without dictate.

The uniting of social practices and ongoing action within a faith story strengthens a "community of memory" in a time of narrative contention and confusion. The additive component of a "community of memory" as Bonhoeffer understands the story of the faith requires a storyteller knowledgeable of the limits and flaws of persons and communities. Bonhoeffer's understanding of keeping the community of memory alive requires persons to live in the give and take of real life, not in the realm of the ideal. Innumerable times, an entire Christian community has broken down because it had sprung from a wish dream. The serious Christian, settling down for the first time in a Christian community, is likely to import a very definite idea of what Christian life together should be and to try to realize it. Nevertheless, God's grace speedily shatters such dreams. Just as surely as God desires to lead us to knowledge of genuine Christian fellowship, so surely must we be overwhelmed by a great disillusionment with others, with Christians in general, and, if we are fortunate, with ourselves.

> By sheer grace, God will not permit us to live even for a brief period in a dream world. He does not abandon us to those rapturous experiences and lofty moods that come over us like a dream. [. . .] Every wish dream that is injected into the Christian community is a hindrance to genuine community and must be banished if genuine community is to survive. (Bonhoeffer, *Life Together* 27)

A community of memory connects ideas of the faith story and the action of social practices. A storyteller works from a community of memory cognizant of disappointment and sin. Bonhoeffer points us toward a nonutopian community of memory. He understood the importance of working for the good and how demanding the pure can destroy a community of faith. Bonhoeffer offers us a story of the faith in the midst of human imperfection.

A story teller that unites social practices and the story of the faith invites a "community of faith" centered on the story of Christ's discipleship and suffering and the reality of our own sin and limitations. Christ abandoned and suffering guides a Christian community; a life of faith demands responsibility in the midst of suffering. The unique communication components in a "community of faith" begin and end with a common center—Christ, a realistic view of community, and the construction of the person. In *Act and Being,* Bonhoeffer offers a philosophical rationale for a "community of faith." The notion of "individual" is associated with being. However, the person of faith in a community of faith is shaped by act and being. The human being shaped in the action and situatedness of the faith community becomes a person.

> To speak of the human being as individual person and humanity, never in separation but always in unity, is only another way of talking about the human being as act and as being. [. . .] even if their being—humanity could be thought of as an abstraction that is of no concern to existence, such an idea would only break down in face of the historical reality of the community of faith of Christ and my belonging to it. (*Act and Being* 120–21)

Bonhoeffer's notion of person within a community of faith describes and points to a form of embedded agency, someone embedded within a story of faith. A person accepts such embeddedness, accepting freedom within restraint. The embeddedness of a community of memory that is a community of faith requires awareness of a suffering common center—Christ—who provides the "why" for continuing to work with a community with the reality of mistakes, flaws, and sin. The rhetorical power of a community of memory that accepts the further embeddedness of a community of faith comes from faith itself and from disciples or witnesses who display fidelity toward the story that invites others to join. The community of memory nourished by an empirical faith community walks a publicly proclaimed story into service of God's community, ever tempered by the communicative habits of dialectic and dialogue.

9
COMMUNICATIVE TURNING
Acknowledgment

James Hunter on forgotten moral narrative:

> [T]oday division is present; some have called it a time of "cultural warfare." [. . .] The Enlightenment *philosophies* long ago predicted that as societies advanced, modern individuals would outgrow their need for the comfort of religious "superstitions." One of the long-dreamed-for consequences of this would be the end to religiously motivated violence and division in society. [. . .] The end to which these hostilities tend is the domination of one cultural and moral ethos over all others. (*Culture Wars* 41–42)

Dietrich Bonhoeffer's warning:

> It is not good when the Church is anxious to praise itself too readily [or] to boast of its power and its influence too soon. It is only good when the Church humbly confesses its sins, allows itself to be forgiven and confesses its Lord. Daily must it receive the will of the incarnate, the humiliated and the exalted one. [. . .] Daily, it stumbles at the words afresh, "You will all be offended because of me" (Matt. 26.31). And daily it holds answer to the promise, "Blessed is he who is not offended in me" (Matt. 11.6). (*Christ the Center* 113)

Communicative turning claims one's focus of attention. The direction, to whom and what, one turns and attends shapes communicative content and energy. Communicative turning suggests that where one turns and to what one attends becomes the center of communicative life. Ironically, when communicative process becomes central one turns toward the abstract of communication, making process the privileged content supported by attentive energy.

Bonhoeffer was interested in communication but did not turn toward communicative process. His turning was to content, the faith-story, and engagement in the historical moment. Communicative process emerges as a by-product of engagement when the focus of attention is on content and meeting. Discussion of communication process has its place, but is of much less importance to Bonhoeffer. He embraced content and meeting as privileged keys to communicative turning.

Privileging a moral narrative of the faith avoids turning the communication process into an ultimate within the faith community. Turning to the communication process rather than to a moral narrative as first principle is consistent with what Jacques Ellul called the plague of a technocratic society—doing something because it *can* be done, not because it *should* be done (*Perspectives* 26). The communication process can assist in appropriate restraining, implementing, and engaging of a moral narrative only after one is clear about the content and a historical situation that calls forth a turning toward. Buber was correct in that turning toward is central to meeting: the content we bring to the communicative event and the unique demands of the moment make a difference.

Bonhoeffer sensed the danger of communication overemphasis. Bonhoeffer understood that a pastor sets the tone for communicative life within the church.

> The congregation is not the pastor's topic of conversation, but rather it is the flock of Christ to which he has been commissioned by his office and his responsibility. Whenever he does not observe this rule, he will find himself the congregation's topic of conversation! The pastor must also not discuss other pastors with the congregation. Gossip is usually the worst evil in a congregation. Gossip poisons all trust and destroys all constructive work. The parsonage must be the one place in the congregation in which others are not talked about. (*Spiritual Care* 40)

Too much focus upon the communication process can invite discussion of the persons involved in the communication. Bonhoeffer offered a warning: too much concentration upon the process misses the key to communication within the church—the moral narrative of the faith. Bonhoeffer warned of a contemporary Tower of Babel where the process becomes more important than the content that drives the communication. Bonhoeffer was content and application sensitive. It is not process as some form of technique that drives communication but content of the faith story and the importance of application.

A Contemporary Tower of Babel?

Bonhoeffer understood that the process of communication is not a panacea for ills within the church. The implications of Bonhoeffer's communicative insights suggest caution for churches caught between the extremes of authoritative pronouncements attempting to keep members in line and individual declarations that seemingly encourage anarchy. Both communication styles seek to control and manipulate. Unity calls for unreflective adherence to the group, and individual expression unrestrained is sensitive only to the self.

The intensity of group or individual success should generate long-term wariness on the part of a religious communicator. The "Tower of Babel" lives within indecision about what is and is not of primary importance. As Bonhoeffer stated: "For the Christian a life within the terms of a secular calling has a definite limit. It may well happen that after we have been called to a secular profession we shall be called upon to quit it" (*The Cost of Discipleship* 298). One must work to keep an ultimate focus of attention on the faith with a penultimate attentiveness to issues such as professional success. One of the functional ways in which a Tower of Babel becomes unimportant is by keeping focus of attention on first principles, even to the point of keeping career success at arm's length. Bonhoeffer followed such a path in his movement from academic life to the pastorate (Kelly and Nelson 35). He kept the first principle of calling as primary to his communicating about the faith; he kept the particular content of the faith first.

Bonhoeffer's Warning about the Tower of Babel

Bonhoeffer offered a number of warnings about the potential misuse of communication resulting in problematic directions for local congregations. He understood that a Tower of Babel composed of too much confidence in communication can be used for good as well as for mischief or evil. Communication is inherently a neutral component of life, available for contributing to the social good. Bonhoeffer points out in *Creation and Fall* and *Temptation* that the serpent is a voice of temptation, offering a quick and easy pleasure. At this point, the innocence of Adam and Eve makes them unable to offer opposition. They lack the insight, perception, and knowledge necessary to equip them in this struggle (Bonhoeffer, *Temptation* 102).

Unlike Adam and Eve, we do not have an excuse for our innocence about the value of communication. Too much confidence in communication is a temptation that a religious communicator must resist. Bonhoeffer's trust is in ultimate, not in penultimate, issues, such as communication between persons. Bonhoeffer understood that unrestrained expression is not constructive or helpful in building God's house. Bonhoeffer's warning about communication can be summarized thus: *Communication, yes, but not all types of expression, not at all times, and not the same communicative style for every person, relationship, problem, or moment.* Bonhoeffer rejects the notion of communication for communication's sake. The quickest way to miss the needs of a potentially caring moment is to find a formula or technique that offers an answer but is inattentive to the unique characteristics of a given moment or relationship. For Bonhoeffer, communication needs a time, place, appropriateness, and, most importantly, a connection to the faith story in order to make a long-term contribution to the community of the church.

For Bonhoeffer, religious communication rests in the guidance of the story of the faith and responsiveness. For such a reason, many answered the call of Jesus—but differently. Some left their jobs to follow, and others continued to work as before—but differently. The communicative call of the faith "never consists in this or that specific action: it is always a decision, either for or against Jesus Christ" (Bonhoeffer, *The Cost of Discipleship* 250). There is no technique, but there is necessary responsiveness to the story of the faith. Such faith-filled communication lessens the invitation of a Tower of Babel, requiring basic communicative assumptions that "interpret otherwise" than normative individualistic culture.

Basic Assumptions

A communication style responsive to a world come of age situated within a horizon of the faith that embraces dialectic, dialogue, and rhetoric in union suggests a hermeneutic stance akin to the work of Hans-Georg Gadamer. Bonhoeffer did what Gadamer called "philosophical hermeneutics" (*Philosophical Hermeneutics* 18). Georgia Warnke, in discussion of Gadamer, describes a rich, story-framed tradition from which Gadamer worked—as did Bonhoeffer.

> Hermeneutics, as Gadamer conceives of it [. . .] is no longer [. . .] a discourse on methods of "objective" understanding. [. . .] It no longer seeks to formulate a set of interpretive rules [. . .] "Philosophical hermeneutics" [. . .] turns to an account of the conditions of the possibility of understanding in general, conditions that in his view undermine faith in the ideas of both method and objectivity. Mythological approaches to both natural and human phenomena are rooted in history; they accept certain historical assumptions as to both what is to be studied and how it is to be approached. Understanding is therefore rooted in prejudice and the way in which we understand is thoroughly conditioned by the past or by what Gadamer calls "effective history." This influence of the past obtains in our aesthetic understanding, in our social and psychological self-understanding and in all forms of scientific understanding. The objectivity of

> our knowledge is therefore significantly curtailed by its dependence on tradition and this dependence is not one that method can in any way transcend. (Warnke qtd. in Gadamer, *Hermeneutics* 3)

Philosophical hermeneutics provides interpretive freedom with horizon or story limits. As one takes a communicative text seriously, one brings a story-rich tradition to the text. We limit interpretive vision by our situatedness, while we open possibilities due to our situatedness. Historicality and temporality are copresent companions to a story-laden tradition, resulting in interpretation unable to stand as a final answer, but representing one of many potential destinations. A story-laden tradition assists in framing questions that open a given text uniquely within a temporal moment (Weinsheimer and Marshall xvi–xviii).

Historicality of interpretation suggests a bias, a position from which one views or makes sense out of a topic. Paul, in his letter to the church at Rome, begins with a clear standpoint:

> This news is about the Son of God who, according to the human nature he took, was a descendant of David; it is about Jesus Christ our Lord who, in the order of the spirit, the spirit of holiness that was in him, was proclaimed Son of God in all his power through his resurrection from the dead. Through him we received grace and our apostolic mission to preach the obedience of faith. (*New Jerusalem Bible,* Rom. 1.3–6).

Paul's beginning statement to the church at Rome announces his position, framing a Christocentric viewpoint. This same Christocentric communicative focus guides the insight of Dietrich Bonhoeffer. Bonhoeffer, of course, works with texture and dialectical counter play that unite two additional assumptions with a Christocentric bias. Bonhoeffer's understanding of communicative disarray in the Church rests with his assumption that one can miss the content of Christ as Center by ignoring its story complexity. Bonhoeffer is ever-wary of extreme, single-minded positions that forego the admission of the need for texture and doubt in one's understanding.

Christ as Center

Bonhoeffer situated Christ as center. He was not only a "Christocentric" theologian, he was a Christocentric communicator. Bonhoeffer's "Christocentric" theology did not imply that one would use only "religious language," but rather that the spirit and mission of Christ's life and work should direct Christian life. He wanted communication moved by Christ to make a difference. Bonhoeffer worked to follow the "mind of Christ" with diligence, stating the following about St. John's words about Christ after his curing a blind man:

> As long as the day lasts I must carry out the work of the one who sent me; the night will soon be here when no one can work. As long as I am in the world I am the light of the world. (*New Jerusalem Bible,* John 9.4–5)

Such a guide offered direction for Bonhoeffer; he followed the one sent to assist God's people. Bonhoeffer was deeply upset as the church too quickly sided with the status quo, the Third Reich. He called the church back to a Christ-centered foundation, asking the church to attend to a higher calling than nationalist pride and church survival and growth. The doxology from Paul's letter to the Romans summarizes the message Bonhoeffer offered the church.

> Glory to him who is able to give you the strength to live according to the Good News I preach, and in which I proclaim Jesus Christ, the revelation of a mystery kept secret for endless ages, but now so clear that it must be broadcast to pagans everywhere to bring them to the obedience of faith. This is only what scripture has predicted, and it is all part of the way the eternal God wants things to be. He alone is wisdom; give glory therefore to him through Jesus Christ for ever and ever. Amen. (*New Jerusalem Bible,* Rom. 16.25–27)

Bonhoeffer took his Christocentric position into encounter with other stories that continued to enrich and inform his faith. A Christocentric position supplemented by knowledge of additional stories and insights guided Bonhoeffer's communicative life with others.

Stories

Bonhoeffer's love of Christ and the church took him into the daily struggles of life; his work and faith joined a full array of life's offerings from conversation to music and the arts to sports competition. Bonhoeffer brought a zest for life that included people and action, along with a commitment to reading, scholarship, and theological insight. Bonhoeffer's *Letters and Papers from Prison* reveals great intellectual breadth, a human being interested in music, art, and the lives of other people. In his correspondence with his parents and others, Bonhoeffer consistently minimized the dangers and inconvenience of his own incarceration, spending most of his time detailing what he had read and asking questions about the well being of others.

Dietrich Bonhoeffer's attentiveness to other stories permitted him to discern danger in Nazi Germany. Bonhoeffer's life and writing remind us that after the "fall" there is no way to return to the Garden of Eden; sin for

Bonhoeffer is ontological; it is part of being human. Sin becomes a fundamental part of the human story. Bonhoeffer lived with a deep sense of theological hope in God and God's world, but he was opposed to naive optimism that did not take the notions of "fall," "sin," and death seriously. Bonhoeffer rejected any story of human life that did not take seriously the struggles before us as flawed human beings.

Larry Rasmussen and Renate Bethge in *Dietrich Bonhoeffer—His Significance for North Americans* discuss the importance of Bonhoeffer's theology of the cross as central to Bonhoeffer's realistic sense of Christian hope.

> Against the North American theology of glory *(theologia gloriae)* of bourgeois optimism and its religion of legitimation and human "coping," the theology of the cross *(theologia crucis)* understands Christ existing as community as the church's societal vocation; and the way of the cross, especially in messianic suffering, is the strong musical line *(cantus firmus)* in a celebration of the full range of human experience. (145)

Bonhoeffer's conviction was that a theology of the cross required one to meet the inevitable hand of sin and evil in others and oneself. A Christocentric story sent one into the story of a world come of age, a flawed place calling for service and deputyship.

Bonhoeffer was aware that one of the sins of the "fall" was a hope of avoiding one's own death. One could envision the ideology of the Third Reich as an effort to avoid death through continuation of an "Aryan people." Ernest Becker offered a view of death avoidance in keeping with the communication misuse theme suggested by Bonhoeffer's project. He critiqued a psychology unresponsive to evil and death.

> I think that taking life seriously means something such as this: that whatever man does on this planet has to be done in the lived truth of the terror of creation, of the grotesque, of the rumble of panic underneath everything. Otherwise it is false. Whatever is achieved must be achieved from within the subjective energies of creatures, without deadening, with the full exercise of passion, of vision, of pain, of fear, and of sorrow. [. . .]
>
> Modern man is drinking and drugging himself out of awareness, or he spends his time shopping, which is the same thing. [. . .] [H]e buries himself in psychology in the belief that awareness all by itself will be some kind of magical cure for his problems. (283–84)

Bonhoeffer, like Becker, was wary of any form of communication that avoided awareness of the painful aspects of life. He wanted no part of a story that did not take the everyday praxis of human sin into account, thus rejecting the impulse to see the world through unrealistic and unduly optimistic lenses.

During Bonhoeffer's first eighteen months of his imprisonment in Tegel Prison in Berlin—April 5, 1943, to October 8, 1944—he reflected upon the human spirit and the flaws in himself, friends, and enemies. He wrote:

> Steady and firm we stand man against man;
> As the accused we accuse!
>
> Only before thee, source of all being,
> Before thee are we sinners.
>
> Afraid of suffering and poor in deeds,
> We have betrayed thee before man.
>
> We saw the lie raise its head,
> And we did not honour the truth.
>
> We saw brethren in direst need,
> And feared only our own death.
>
> ("Night Voices in Tegel" 23–24)

Bonhoeffer warned against any story that deceives by ignoring sin. Concentration on the communication process alone without beginning with a story of the faith responsive to the fallen world invites cynicism in those who eventually recognize the limits of their own and others' abilities to embody justice and right. Bonhoeffer's complexity of storylines reminds us that a religious communicator must meet sin and evil in a broken world and in one's own heart. One does so not with will power, but with the power of a Christocentric foundation.

For Bonhoeffer to get to what this work calls covenantal communication, he first embraces a Christocentric position, then meets the developing stories of the historical moment, and finally warns us against simplicity unable to accept "yes" and "no" in the same breath. Too much or too little emphasis on a given issue, such as communication or even community, can destroy a community of faith. Covenantal communication responsive to a Christocentric story and to a world come of age invites a religious communicator into a complex and demanding world of guidance and revelation responsive to the particular. The unity of faith story and response to the particular historical moment framed an ongoing question for Bonhoeffer. "What is bothering me incessantly is the question [. . .] who Christ really is, for us today?" (Bonhoeffer qtd. in Bethge, *Dietrich Bonhoeffer* 767). The communicative keys in Bonhoeffer's often-asked question are twofold: "Christ" and "us." The goal of a faith story is engagement with the Other—communication that rests under the story guidance of a covenant of faith.

Covenantal Communication

A covenant is an agreement between two parties requiring collective participation in a communicative commitment that transforms a life. The notion of covenant is somewhat enigmatic for us in this era of narrative and virtue contention. We live in a psychological age that encourages thinking in terms of effect on the individual person, not the notion of covenant between persons. Covenant is a sociocultural term, suggesting that life has an impact on us—you, the group, God, and me. The individual finds guidance within a covenant without being the center of existence. A covenant in religious terms binds us to the story of ourselves in relation to one another and God.

Bonhoeffer's attachment to a covenantal worldview distinguishes him from the ongoing main-line culture of individualism. Bonhoeffer rejected individualism for a sense of personhood situated within a complex set of concerns, including self, Other, and God. Such a position requires us to make demanding decisions less centered on "me" and more upon the historical situation, others, and our own faith commitment. The embedded person lives within a covenant, not as sufficient unto oneself.

A covenant is a reminder of obligation and responsibility beyond oneself. The Old Testament is a book about *The People of the Covenant,* with God and his people working to invite a place, a sense of home on this earth.

> Covenant is known when Yahweh rules over a devout people who live with the confidence of his sovereignty over history. Such an idea is the basis of Jesus' teaching about and the New Testament affirmation of a kingdom in which God reigns until the final day. (Flanders et al. 502)

Walter Brueggemann suggests that without a concrete feeling of being "at home" there is no fulfillment of a covenant. Instead, one feels in exile. Covenant suggests that persons with God have a place from which to live and make sense of the world, at times a physical place and always a theological position from which one can make sense of the world (107).

Anyone who has felt outside the covenant of a given church or body of people has felt in exile, outside the reach of God's people. In short, the notion of covenant is not just a law or a set of obligations; at best it is a feeling that offers a sense of being at home in God's world. Dietrich Bonhoeffer understood what it meant to live with a promise of physical covenant with family and people of the church.

Much of this work on dialogic confession relies upon the metaphors of story and narrative, but the notion of covenant takes on a different complexity—uniting reciprocity of commitment with a concrete set of people in a concrete place. A covenant is more than a story or a narrative; it lives in the foreground of a people in lived social practices. A narrative lives in the background giving direction, but a covenant lives in the foreground of a people. Only when the covenant lives in daily action and brings people together for action does its power guide.

The Biblical Covenant

The beginning of the covenant between God (Yahweh) and his people finds mention in four separate places in Genesis: 1) Genesis 8.20–9.17, in which life starts anew with Noah: "God said to Noah, 'This is the sign of the Covenant I have established between myself and every living thing that is found on the earth'" *(New Jerusalem Bible)*; 2) Genesis 10, the peopling of the earth through Noah's descendants; and 3) Genesis 11.10–32, in which Terah becomes the father of Abram; 4) and then in Genesis 12–26, when Yahweh makes his covenant with Abraham. Each covenant points to the covenant with Moses and God on Mt. Sinai (Exod. 19–20.20). At this time, a community and a people of Yahweh find life.

> For Israel the primary covenant was the covenant with Moses and all Israel at Mt. Sinai after the Exodus deliverance (Exod. 19–20.20). That covenant formed Israel both as a community and as the people of Yahweh, i.e., as "the people of the covenant," and, as the interpreters of Israel's prehistory point out, fulfilled the covenant promises made to Abraham. (Flanders et al. 105)

The communicative key of covenant is the concrete common center of commitment given a people. An agreed-upon common center permits one to have a sense of community. In religious life, it is the notion of covenant that shapes a community and gives the community a common center. The concrete nature of covenant is foregrounded, unlike the notion of narrative or story, which is backgrounded. For a covenant to work, it lives in our midst. Jesus, as the Christ, becomes the next step in this living covenant. Jesus becomes the living covenant, the common center of the faith.

Jesus as the Word made flesh is the New Testament fulfillment of the covenant. God sent his only son to care for his people. John the Baptist makes the continuing covenant clear in visible fashion.

> The next day, seeing Jesus coming towards him, John said, "Look, there is the Lamb of God that takes away the sins of the world. This is the one I spoke of when I said: 'a man is coming after me who ranks before me because he existed before me.' I did not know him myself, and yet it was to reveal him to Israel that I came baptizing with water." John also declared, "I saw the Spirit coming down on him from heaven like a dove and resting on him. I did not know him myself, but he who sent me to baptize with water had said to me, 'The man on whom you see the Spirit come down and rest is the one who is going to baptize with the Holy Spirit.' Yes, I have seen and I am the witness that he is the Chosen One of God." (*New Jerusalem Bible,* John 1.29–34)

Throughout Bonhoeffer's reading of the Old and New Testaments, he assumes a foundation of a special covenant between God and his people. As Bonhoeffer stated, "We belong to one another only through and in Jesus Christ" (*Life Together* 21). The common center of the Old Testament becomes the covenant and common center of Bonhoeffer's Christocentric theology.

The Significance of the Covenant

The notion of covenant is central to *Dialogic Confession* and to understanding Dietrich Bonhoeffer, who worked as a "covenantal theologian." For Bonhoeffer, "covenant" was not just an abstract issue; the concept suggested implications for living as a Christian.

In *The Cost of Discipleship,* Bonhoeffer states that Christ's covenant with his people is renewed daily. For a Christian, Christ lives in us. "Jesus Christ, incarnate, crucified and glorified, has entered my life and taken charge, 'To me to live is Christ'" (Bonhoeffer, *The Cost of Discipleship* 343). As Christ lives in us, the responsibility of our participating in covenant with God extends to others. In *Life Together,* Bonhoeffer reminds us that we go to one another through Christ, and where the spirit of Christ is forsaken, discord and problems emerge between brothers and sisters in a congregation. "Without Christ there is discord between God and man and between man and man" (*Life Together* 23).

Just as the Ten Commandments have statements of how to live both with and for God and also with other human beings, Bonhoeffer's understanding of covenant has both a horizontal dimension of concern for one another and a vertical dimension of commitment to God. We are required, as part of our participation in the covenant, to have concern for one another, not because we are good, but because Christ lives with us in the covenant.

If the notion of covenant involved only God, there would be little reason to examine how God fulfilled his obligations. There is a basic assumption of the faith that God does not break a covenant, although prophets such as Jeremiah certainly called Yahweh to task; it is we who ignore or violate the call of the covenant in our relation with God and our association with one another. We respond to the power of a call of a covenant even as we ignore or reject that covenant. Such overt contention against a covenant offers a strange form of witness about the power of the story of a given covenant. It is more difficult to see when a covenant fails due to the ignorance of good intentions—the irony of "good" intentions. It is possible to attempt to carry out a covenant in such a manner that one misses the mark and violates what one set out to do.

The Irony of Good Intentions

Sometimes covenants lose their power by intentionally evil action, but more often good people with good intentions take an idea too seriously, destroying the power of a given covenant. It is a demanding task to alter action cloaked in the garb of sincerity and good intentions. Meaning well can cause pain and problems, just as overt "evil" can. However, injury from people who appear "good" can invite a victim to ask the wrong question: "What is wrong with me?" A person giving the impression of living out a covenant in a manner that ignores the invitational responsibilities moves from the role of participant in a covenant to the possessor of the covenant, which seems best to rest in the hands of God alone.

Something happens when the social good of a given covenant lives in the hands of zealots who spin their own control, missing the invitational nature of the faith. God permits us to sin and to ignore the faith. To reject the possibility of this permission invites a greater sin of playing the role of "keeper" of the faith. Bonhoeffer's understanding of covenant points to the religious communicator as a servant of the faith, not a "keeper" of the faith.

Carrying out the rules in a legalistic manner misses the spirit of the faith, violating a covenant. Even a social good carried forth in an imperialistic fashion that seeks to dominate and control another (Brueggeman 127) breaks the covenant. Bonhoeffer suggests that such an effort at control only lends itself to eventual sin. "There is no longer any room for repentance, man can no longer obey. This way ends in idolatry. The God of grace has now become an idol, which I serve. This is clearly the tempting of God which provokes the wrath of God" (Bonhoeffer, *Temptation* 124). It is possible to become alienated from what one once believed and adhered to in public settings. Each of us at one time or another has believed something or someone, only to become disenchanted with what was formerly thought to be true. "Alienation occurs when the norms, as expressed in public practices, cease to hold our allegiance, when there is a growing sense of the disparity of what we take ourselves to be and forms of public life in which we find ourselves" (Bernstein, *Beyond Objectivism and Relativism* 173–74). Bonhoeffer points to what can happen when the social good of communication is misused; we begin to become alienated, wondering what went wrong with life together. Communication not only works to implement covenant in the church but loses its power in the excess of application.

Communicative Excess

Expressing oneself, of course, is of significant importance; the problem emerges when the process of expression masks lack of knowledge and forethought. "Expressivism" pushed to an extreme encourages us to work out what we think while speaking, relying on the communicative exchange to assist with the lucidity of our thoughts. For centuries we encouraged people to develop opinions through listening, reading, and thinking—the fertile soil for ideas to mature in before public display. The epistle of James calls us to "hold our tongue" before placing confidence in deliberate, thoughtful expression. Privileging communicative expression leads to what is suggested by the above subtitle, "communicative excess."

Jacques Ellul speaks of the importance of protecting the word in a day in which "the humiliation of the word" is so common, arguing that the tendency toward technique and easy answers typifies Western civilization. "Humiliation of the word" lives within too much reliance upon image, missing honest reflection of reality and interplay of faith story, historical situation, and uniqueness of the Other. Ellul states:

> The word is greatly mutilated, cadaverous, and almost dead, but we must become conscious of what this means: our whole civilization is loathed along with the word. The word signals our civilization's possible death and provides the channel through which the poison can get in. Anyone wishing to save humanity today must first of all save the word.
>
> The word is the place to begin. It is humiliated, crushed, and meaningless. We must restore its royal domain and its demands. The enormous mutation made possible by biblical revelation assures us that this effort does not amount to a pointless revelation or an attempt to try out a risky path. (*The Humiliation of the Word* 254)

In Bonhoeffer's terms, "expressivism" is "cheap grace." The bombardment of words cheapens and humiliates. I was amazed to hear a friend say he liked a particular speech, when the speaker had discussed a social policy he did not affirm. I asked my friend how he could listen to the speech and still want to vote for the candidate. His answer startled me: "He [the speaker] has to say those things to get the people off his case. I know he does not mean what he says, but it is necessary rhetoric if he is to be re-elected." Indeed, the word is humiliated when what we hear offers comfort not because we agree or understand, but because we assume the speaker lacks the conviction ever to generate policy around such ideas!

For Bonhoeffer, communicative excess occurs when hearing one's own voice becomes more important than hearing the Word of God. The Word works to keep us restrained within the limits of faith. Unleashing our own expression without restraint humiliates the Word, twisting it to our own advantage, leaving us outside the moral story of the faith. In *Life Together,* Bonhoeffer speaks of our need for reliance on the Word. "If somebody asks him, where is your salvation, your righteousness? he can never point to himself. He points to the Word of God in Jesus Christ [. . .] the redeeming Word" (22). Communicative excess embraces our own expression as more important than the restraining call of the faith through the Word of God. God's moral story offered through the Word of the scriptures points to how we are to live with one another in faith and how sin finds restraint by the Word. Communicative excess and humiliation of the word places undue confidence in ourselves, forgetting the restraining and shaping power of the Word. Expressivism can encourage complaint that does not seek to assist or heal. Robert Bellah provides an alternative in his discussion of healing and "broken covenants."

The Broken Covenant

The other side of "expressivism" is a "culture of silence" (Freire 13) where issues go unattended that need expression. Restraint does not suggest elimination of discussion; such a communicative posture simply calls for deliberation first, keeping God, not one's own voice, as primary. Unthinking expression invites problems by confusing babble with the Word. "When one person is struck by the Word, he speaks it to others [. . .] Without Christ there is discord between God and man and between man and man" (Bonhoeffer, *Life Together* 23).

Robert Bellah, in *The Broken Covenant,* offers a common-sense perception of the consequences of a broken covenant. He states that the Old Testament view of covenant was corporate—between a people and God and among the people themselves. A covenant has obligations and responsibilities toward others that bind us together. When we add an individualistic tone to a covenant, it breaks down, unable to guide one's responsibilities and obligations to others. Covenants do not work well in a "me-ism culture." A covenant by definition is a corporate commitment, not an individual statement.

A "broken covenant" is something quite different from a neglected covenant that simply needs more attention (Bellah 139–51). A "broken covenant" is a violated covenant, violated by the people, by contrary action. Bonhoeffer assumed that when Christ is no longer the center of the church, we break the covenant. In place of the covenant between God and the person, which calls us to care about one another, we have tried to place hope in interpersonal interaction with one another and in our own expression.

The "broken covenant," as I am using the term, is a forgetting of Christ as the center of the church, forgetting the *why* and the *how* of our interaction with one another. As Ralph Ross has stated, what makes religion is not just a connection with God, but a changed connection, a concerned connection, with one another (195). Our communicative connection with one another puts at risk the center of the faith when our own breath guides the communication with too much assurance. Bonhoeffer's warning is for the church to keep its faith story, refusing to substitute the process of communication for the substance of the faith:

> In the presence of a psychiatrist I can only be a sick man; in the presence of a Christian brother I can dare to be a sinner. [. . .] The Christian brother knows when I come to him: here is a sinner like myself, a godless man who wants to confess and yearns for God's forgiveness. (*Life Together* 119)

Bonhoeffer's warning is for us not to forget the moral story of the faith that guides our communicative interaction with one another. Instead of misuse of communication, where communication is primary, Bonhoeffer understands communication as a vehicle for carrying the faith story—a story of transcendence. Broken covenants find healing in restrained and thoughtful dialogue situated within a known narrative structure. Bonhoeffer's interest in dialogue and the I-Thou relationship suggests an ongoing commitment to transcendence and revelation. One can transcend brokenness through dialogue with the Other.

I-Thou

The idea of an I-Thou as dialogic relation often falls within discussion of Martin Buber. Buber outlined the lineage of I-Thou in an essay entitled "The History of the Dialogic Principle" (*Between Man and Man* 209–24).

The importance of this essay is that therein Buber provided historical background on dialogue, reminding us of the tradition of this scholarship.

Buber stated that "in essential reciprocity man becomes revealed as man" (*Between Man and Man* 209). "In 1775, Friedrich Heinrich Jacoby writes in a letter about the inseparability of I and Thou. Jacoby later writes: The I is impossible without the Thou" (209). A half-century later Ludwig Feuerbach states: "'The consciousness of the world is mediated for the I through the consciousness of the Thou'" (qtd. in *Between Man and Man* 210). Kierkegaard then limits the I-Thou relation to a connection with God. Herman Cohen and his disciple Franz Rosenzweig reconnect the I and Thou to persons in early 1900s. Then Buber suggested that a Catholic schoolteacher discusses the "solitude of the I" (*Between Man and Man* 213) when closed off from the Thou, again limiting the connection to God. Not mentioning all Buber's points of contact, he reminds us of the work of Gabriel Marcel, Theodor Litt's *Individuum und Gemeinschaft; Grundfragen der Sozialen Theorie und Ethik,* Karl Lowith's *Das Individuum in der Rolle des Mitmenschen,* and the work of Karl Jaspers. He then goes to Barth, who situates the "I" within the Christology of Jesus, which Buber rejected; Buber situated the "I" emergent in the ontology of the "between."

This abbreviated summary of Buber's dialogic lineage is important for four major reasons. First, one can see the interplay of Thou resting with God and with the Other person. Second, Buber worked most closely with Feuerbach but was familiar with the work of Barth, the major theological mentor of Bonhoeffer, who, like Bonhoeffer, situates the "I" within a Christocentric story. Third, many of the dialogic writers cited by Buber are quoted within Bonhoeffer's work. Finally, the dialectic of separateness and connection lives within both Buber's and Bonhoeffer's views of the I-Thou.

Buber framed the dialogic principle within a complex lineage—one strand assumes a God as an eternal Thou and another situates the Thou only with persons. Buber's work rests between these two traditions as does the work of Bonhoeffer. The difference is that Bonhoeffer's contribution relies more keenly upon the insight of Barth and a Christocentric story. Both Buber and Bonhoeffer assume distance for understanding the uniqueness of the Other. What separates these two traditions is the particular Eternal Thou and the particular assumptions that undergird the faith story that accompanies the dialogue. Bonhoeffer's work rests within a dialogic tradition that presupposes the importance of a Christocentric faith as one meets the Other. Bonhoeffer suggested:

> No man can of himself make the other into an I, into a moral person conscious of responsibility. God, or the Holy Spirit, comes to the concrete Thou, only by his action does the other become a Thou for me, from which my I arises. In other words, every human Thou is an image of the divine Thou. [. . .] The other man is Thou only in so far as God makes him this. It is only in God that the claim of the other resides; but for this very reason it is the claim of the other. (*The Communion of Saints* 36)

Bonhoeffer's language frames his position on dialogue within a Christocentric assumption. Situating oneself within the story of the faith gives one a reason, a "why," to attend to the Other, who then calls out one's responsible "I."

In Bonhoeffer's case the phenomenology of the Other shapes the "I." Sin keeps the focus off phenomenological reality before us and within the "I." We work at fooling ourselves into the importance of the "I" while minimizing the importance of the Other. This act of an "I" focus does not begin with the phenomenological reality of the "I" but functions as an act of "bad faith" (Sartre 86–116). Bonhoeffer adds the Christocentric story of the faith as a "why" to attend to a phenomenological reality, which aligns itself with a theological presupposition of the human created in the image of God—in the image of the Other.

Bonhoeffer's understanding of dialogue as supported by a Christocentric story and his commitment to confession as the beginning of change and a call to reconnection to the faith story point to similar foundations—the faith story guides Bonhoeffer. It is the strength of this narrative foundation that permits Bonhoeffer to "interpret otherwise" (Manning 7), offering a view of the world that does not begin with the "I," but finds the "I" called forth into responsible action. Bonhoeffer, like Levinas and Buber, offers a critique of Western culture that begins with agency, the "I." The creation of this alternative position resulted in postmodern scholarship expressing heightened interest in Levinas (Eaglestone 7). This work suggests that Bonhoeffer offers a similar critique from the standpoint of a public Christocentric bias that calls one to attend to the Other and to one's responsibility to the Other.

The dialogic principle has a tradition, and Bonhoeffer participates in a strand of that tradition. He situates the Thou or person within a Christocentric story of the faith. He adapts Barth's faith bias on dialogue; additionally, Bonhoeffer takes the notion of the I-Thou into encounter with others. Bonhoeffer wrote: "The individual exists only through the 'other.' The individual is not solitary. For the individual to exist, 'others' must also exist. If I call the individual the concrete 'I,' then the other is the concrete Thou" (*The Communion of Saints* 32). The importance of situating the "I" within the Christocentric story permits Bonhoeffer to understand the transformation of the "I" as individual to the "I" as person situated with the story of the faith that shapes a "moral person" (*The Communion of Saints* 36). When person meets person within the story of the faith, transcendence happens between persons that calls one to a story-informed sense of responsibility—responsibility informed by the story of the faith.

The I-Thou is a phenomenological fact, finding transformation within the meeting of the Christocentric story, historical situation, and persons in dialogue. Buber and Bonhoeffer begin with stories (faith presuppositions) that call the "I" into personhood. Moral faith stories offer a call that transforms the individual into a person within the movement into dialogue with the Other. The act of dialogic confession acknowledges this dual movement of connection to the faith story and the Other. Dialogic confession seeks to address or meet the Other with the guiding reminder of a sense of "why," a faith story that calls one to attend to the Other and the historical situation, offering a life of responsibility. Dialogic confession offers the possibility of interpersonal transcendence, permitting us momentarily to see difference through the eyes of the Other.

Public Acknowledgment

Bonhoeffer centers *confession* as the beginning public acknowledgment of one's own position. Acknowledging a position is the first step to dialogue. Centering confession in a dialogic faith sensitive to one's own position and that of the Other offers the beginning gesture of dialogue. Bonhoeffer's confession began in scholarship with his dissertation, eventually published as *The Communion of Saints: A Dogmatic Inquiry into the Sociology of the Church,* wherein he rejected two foundations for faith: blind commitment to institutional religion and interpersonal warmth used to cover the ignored presence of Christ. Both the institutional Church and personal connections "disguise the absence of the essential thing" God who centers "community of saints" and attempts to replace the genuine and required center of the faith and Christian community. Bonhoeffer sought the uncertain demands of dialogue, faith, and confession, walking away from the temptation of institutional and interpersonal assurance. Bonhoeffer's insight points us to dialogue between persons outside the extremes of institutional conviction and interpersonal warmth—a story-laden and story-guided understanding of dialogue.

Stories order information, providing a sense of "why." Ricoeur's trilogy, *Time and Narrative,* works with the importance of ordering, providing a sense of plot for information. Ricoeur understands narrative as the ordering process of information. In a postmodern age of random information, the narrative process, the ability to tell a coherent story, takes on increasing significance. Dialogic confession grounds the storytelling process of mutual confession, which orders the communication within a common space invited by a temporally reciprocal act.

The metaphor of dialogic confession points to a story beyond provinciality. In a time of diversity, provinciality or attachment to a sense of place often generates a response of disrespect from those hoping to function from a more "cosmopolitan" position. For many, the alternative to a sense of place is attentiveness to the self. Yet this move is but another form of provinciality, the notion of "self." The self becomes a modern sense of place, offering a "hometown advantage" of one! There is a third alternative to the notions of place and self, pointed to by dialogic confession that reminds one of stories that guide interlocutors. Dialogue, guided by the confession of a story, a given standpoint, provides an alternative to the provincial attachments of place and self.

Bonhoeffer, as a theologian and pastor, knew the faith pointed to a third alternative—not to a provincial place, nor the modern form of provinciality of the self, but to a story about God and concern for the neighbor. A modern perspective does not want to understand faith beyond provinciality of place, and a "cosmopolitan" perspective that lives within the self misses the importance of a story that takes one beyond place and self. Bonhoeffer's move beyond provinciality does not fall prey to a private form of provinciality, the self; he kept before us the possibility of story. Bonhoeffer situates confession within the faith. Confession reconnects one to the ultimate, the faith story. Bonhoeffer's "world come of age" permits a metaphor such as dialogic confession to embrace the dialectic of faith and the necessity of reaching those of contrary standpoints.

Confession does not center on information or the self. Confession is a third alternative, akin to dialogue. Technical dialogue centers on "information—questions and answers" (Buber, *Between Man and Man* 19). Monologue is self-talk. Both are necessary at times and both make dialogue possible. Additionally, mandated dialogue is a contradiction in terms, as is mandated confession.

Confession as a penultimate is a momentary common ground upon which persons make contact with one another; it is a third alternative to information accuracy and expressivism. Confession, like dialogue, is a penultimate. Confession and dialogue work as alternatives to the technical processing of information and discourse meant to enhance the image of the self. Dialogic confession takes us in a "world come of age" to the importance of the Other.

Bonhoeffer was committed to historically appropriate applications of a knowing faith taken into communicative action of everyday life. He stated, "There can be no evangelical message without knowledge of the present" (*Ethics* 192). Meeting the demands of the present assumes the dialectic of faith knowledge and the historical moment tested in communicative action—constituting a three-fold communicative act. First, a communicator must know that communicator's own faith position. Second, a communicator takes this knowledge into dialectical encounter with the unique demands of a given historical situation. Third, confession requires testing the synthesis of faith and historical moment in public communicative action. Confession requires a knowing faith meeting the historical situation with the resultant combination tested in everyday communicative life.

Confession lives within a set of restraints similar to those of dialogue; confession forced upon a person or a situation becomes confession in name only. Both confession and dialogue require discernment, with imposition as a contrary act. The commonplace of confession needs appropriate ground, similar to the invitation of dialogue. Paulo Freire consistently underscored the warning that dialogue cannot find a place in each relationship; sometimes, inordinate structural power differences make dialogue impossible (Freire 73–74). When the Other attends to protection of the self, the focus of attention does not rest "between" partners, but within one's own image. The result is the appearance of doing or attending to confession that misses the actual act of confession.

Bonhoeffer understood the importance of confession linked with dialogue. Confession without a dialogic character invites self-serving disclosure. Confession as psychic relief alone does not provide a stance from which one enters into conversation with the Other. Bonhoeffer's understanding of confession is inherently dialogical. Bonhoeffer's project points to the importance of confession in dialogic encounter as one meets the historical situation, God, persons, and the human community.

Confession, as opposed to telling, is central to the interpretive framework of Bonhoeffer. Confession, not telling, offers a commonplace that begins with listening to the confession of the Other. Bonhoeffer's notion of confession foregoes the impulse to tell, embracing listening even while speaking. Confession makes public what began in silence. To confess involves three-fold listening: to the story, which guides interpretation, to the historical moment, and to caution in evaluating ideas and actions; such listening gathers insight for the act of confession. Confession understood as a gestalt where the whole is greater than the sum of the parts involves background listening that shapes the moment of communicative disclosure.

The public act of confession invites the Other into conversation that begins in silence, in listening that frames a position, which openly invites the Other into the act of confession. The impulse of telling rather than listening turns confession into "bad faith," lying to oneself (Sartre 86–116). As Bonhoeffer stated,

> Many people are looking for an ear that will listen. They do not find it among Christians, because these Christians are telling where they should be listening. But he who can no longer listen to his brother will soon no longer be listening to God either; he will be doing nothing but prattle in the presence of God too. (*Life Together* 98)

Confession requires listening to one's understanding of a guiding story and the historical situation before speaking and listening to the Other. Dialogic confession becomes common ground when both parties listen in confession that begins in silence, permitting the act, not the content of the confession, to offer temporal common ground.

Bonhoeffer discovered power that reconnected him to the story of the faith in silence. Perhaps the key to Bonhoeffer's connection of the faith to secular theory and the particulars of application was silence. With silence and listening, he worked under dire circumstances of great danger and hardship. The last letter received from Bonhoeffer announces the power of silence and listening that redirected him to the story of the faith and to concern for the Other.

> [T]he quieter it is around me, the clearer do I feel the connection to you. It is as though in solitude the soul develops senses which we hardly know in everyday life. Therefore I have not felt lonely or abandoned for one moment. You, the parents, all of you, the friends and students of mine at the front, all are constantly present to me. [. . .] Therefore you must not think that I am unhappy. What is happiness and unhappiness? It depends so little on the circumstances; it depends really only on that which happens inside a person. I am grateful every day that I have you, and that makes me happy (19 December 1944). (*Letters and Papers from Prison* 419)

On April 9, 1945, Dietrich Bonhoeffer lost his physical life to the Nazis. The uniform statement from those imprisoned with him was that his generosity of spirit and dignity did not leave him as he met death. He understood the importance of silence and listening, keeping connected to the faith story. Bonhoeffer accepted silence and listening as keys to confession, reconnecting one to a faith story, offering a "why" for engaging the demands of the historical situation before us.

Bonhoeffer warns of three misuses of confession: 1) the feeling of self-righteousness while listening, keeping the focus upon oneself, not the words of the Other; 2) indiscriminate confession, in which one only wants to tell, not worrying about the identity of the recipient of the information; and 3) confession to someone unwilling to engage in confession (*Life Together 119–23*). Such concern for the Other points to possibility of dialogic confession between strangers. "In truth, freedom is relationship between two persons. Being free means 'being free for the other,' because the other has bound me to him. Only in relationship with the other am I free" (Bonhoeffer, *Creation and Fall* 37). The freedom of being bound to the Other permits us to work with both those with whom we are in agreement and those with whom we are not in agreement. Dialogic confession as a penultimate makes sense as an act of freedom—freedom bound in relationships with those with whom we agree and disagree. This confessional freedom takes us from self-righteous listening, indiscriminate telling, and set-apart listening that shares a similar focal point, the self, to common ground between persons—to dialogic confession, the penultimate link back to a story-laden sense of ground.

10

MEETING THE OTHER
Communication Ethics in a "World Come of Age"

Emmanuel Levinas on the Other:

> It is banal to say we never exist in the singular. We are surrounded by beings and things with which we maintain relations. Through sight, touch, sympathy and common work we are *with* others. All these relations are transitive. I touch an object, I see the other; but I *am* not the other. (*Ethics and Infinity* 58)

Dietrich Bonhoeffer on nourishing the "why" of meeting the Other:

> Even the responsible, serious, and faithful pastor may be driven to external or internal perplexity. This can be a pure lack of faith. In the end, perplexity leads to insensitivity. The load is too heavy to bear alone. We need someone who will help us use our powers in ministry correctly, someone who will defend us against our own lack of faith. The activist and the resigned, lazy pastor are flip sides of the same coin and are equally dispensable: both of them lack silent, ordered prayer and spiritual care. If the pastor has no one to offer him spiritual care, then he will have to seek someone out. Only through prayer will mission and skill come together in an orderly relationship. (*Spiritual Care* 67)

Dialogic confession is a bridge to the Other, a way of engaging a communication ethic—among persons working from the same story structure—and communication ethics—among persons working from differing story structures with dissimilar narrative and virtue assumptions. Bonhoeffer works from a communication ethic that points to the manner of engagement of a communication ethic of conviction with other communication ethics in a world come of age.

Communication ethics, differentiated from philosophical ethics and codes, informs us about what is ethical, bringing philosophy and information into direct contact with persons and the historical situation. Communication ethics requires *phronesis* (Aristotle 1141a20–1142a), practical wisdom that communicates an ethical framework "appropriate" and "right" for persons in a given historical situation. Those seeking legalistic assurance will not find such a view adequate. A priori knowledge of an ethical story guides with final action resultant of story, situation, and person in interactive response. Communication ethics lives in interactive action, not in abstract theory—situated within *phronesis.* Dialogic confession is a communication ethic, responsive to story, persons, and the historical situation.

Such a view of communication ethics guides without a priori clarity; communication ethics offers "fuzzy clarity," responsive to the immediate moment. On the other hand, communication ethics should not be confused with "situational ethics." Bonhoeffer points to ethics as a form of dialogic confession embracing the horizon of a Christocentric faith, responsive to the historical situation and to the Other. Bonhoeffer's ongoing commitment to dialectic rejects both objectivism and relativism. Few would confuse Bonhoeffer's ethics with objectivism; thus, attentiveness to how his work is not relativistic requires attention. Due to potential confusion of Bonhoeffer's position with a "situational ethic," it is necessary to revisit "situational ethics," differentiating this approach from communication ethics.

The Christocentric

The term "situational ethics" is now part of popular conversation, different from its founding moment in Joseph Fletcher's *Situation Ethics: The New Morality* of 1966. Fletcher's work generated conversation and controversy in the mid-twentieth century. Today, the term would not turn a head. What might surprise people is who Fletcher was, an Episcopal priest and a professor of social ethics. The founder of the popular term "situational ethics" was a pastor and religious academic. Fletcher even cites Bonhoeffer's *Ethics:* "The conscience which has been set free is not timid like the conscience which is bound by the law, but it stands wide open for our neighbor and for his concrete distress" (Bonhoeffer qtd. in Fletcher, *Moral Responsibility* 8).

Fletcher connects situational ethics to the notion of "love." Of Fletcher's six propositions that outline situational ethics, the first four refer to "love" (*Situation Ethics* 14–28). Bonhoeffer, on the other hand, situates all his work within a Christocentric "first principle."

Bonhoeffer states:

> Already in the possibility of the knowledge of good and evil Christian ethics discerns a falling away from the origin. Man at his origin knows only one thing: God. It is only in the unity of his knowledge of God that he knows of other men, of things, and of himself. He knows all things only in God, and God in

> all things. The knowledge of good and evil shows that he is no longer at one with this origin. (*Ethics* 17)

This work does not intend to critique Fletcher, but to suggest that the two approaches to the historical moment or the concrete situation are quite different. Fletcher situates love as a Christian first principle. Bonhoeffer places God as "first principle." Love moves one to a relational model of ethics with persons and situation privileged. Bonhoeffer moves his ethics to persons and situation in dialectical tension with a Christocentric worldview, or with what this work calls a story-centered view of the faith. The story begins with Christ; Christ is the "why" for the action of love. Fletcher presupposes a "why," moving to discussion of love. Bonhoeffer reminds us of a more specific first principle for religious communicators attentive to the faith story he frames—a Christocentric "why" for a particular communication ethic. Bonhoeffer's story of the faith with the "why" of Christ as "first principle" suggests love as an action, not the reason for ethical behavior.

Fletcher was the product of a modern world in which agreed-upon assumptions carried actions. If we have similar assumptions, a related sense of "why," the focus can be on action alone. In a postmodern culture of multiple narrative structures and contentious virtue positions, we must make the "why" of action public. We cannot assume that others begin with the same "first principles." Bonhoeffer's clarity about "first principles" permits his religious communication ethic to engage a postmodern world of diversity, while Fletcher's situational ethics assumes a modern position of agreement on the notion of love; love loses its practical and historical import when understood within universal or metanarrative agreement. Bonhoeffer's position is more specific and more able to meet a postmodern world of communication ethics. Bonhoeffer claims a specific petite narrative, while Fletcher assumes a much broader sense of agreement. Modernity permitted global assumptions that postmodernity and world come of age assumed practically impossible.

A Christocentric perspective has a particular story. The notion of love has many stories that situate its significance. Fletcher placed the metaphor of love within a Christian context; however, over time, the Christian story was lost and the notion of "situation" remained. Bonhoeffer's Christocentric story, on the other hand, vies for attention in a postmodern world from a position of limits. Bonhoeffer's ethics engage a postmodern world; they do not require universal acceptance to be in conversation with this historical moment. The emphasis on love calls for universal acceptance. Ironically, the inclusiveness of Fletcher's work moves it to a universal, deemed inadequate to meet the historical situation of today. The particularity of Bonhoeffer's story permits its telling and significance in a world of multiple narrative and virtue commitments. Bonhoeffer's story begins with limits, which ironically keeps it available for consideration in a world of multiplicity. The penultimate sometimes moves one to less than perfect solutions.

Situational ethics connects love to agency, decision making, and individual action. Dialogic confession, on the other hand, works not for the ideal, but for what Bonhoeffer called the "penultimate" (*Ethics* 125–43). What is the best we can do in this historical situation with these persons in conjunction with a particular ethical story? Both require agency, but the tone of the "penultimate" has a questioning framework, not assuming that one has the ultimate answer. Focus upon love for the other takes on a sense of assurance unknown by the questioning commitment to a penultimate act that is the best one can do. Dialogic confession, framed in the penultimate reading of the historical situation, simply does the best one can do in a given moment, guided by the interplay of the story of the faith and the moment at hand. There is no sense of heroic assurance that one knows the right answer out of love; there is no ultimate answer. We live as flawed persons doing our best to connect the faith story and the historical situation.

Communication Ethics as Penultimate

Dialogic confession is a communicative penultimate. It begins with confessing a stance and then takes in new information from the Other and the historical situation, permitting the reshaping of the position and, at the very least, the testing of a given stance. Dialogic confession, as a penultimate, assumes responsiveness to persons, historical situation, and narrative guidelines. The privileged key of dialogic confession is not information telling, but responsive change within the horizon of a Christocentric story.

Religious communication ethics framed within the metaphor of dialogic confession begins with the philosophical and practical tool of dialectic, situating action in humble conviction, not abstract theory about "what is" ethical. The act of communication moves ethics from evaluation of standard and behavior to the interplay of narrative framework, behavior (social practices), the historical situation, and impact upon the Other. Communication ethics involves principles coming from a narrative framework and particulars emergent from the historical moment. Principles guide behavior; additionally, particulars guide and temper behavior. The particulars—communicative relationships and the historical moment—in interplay with narrative principles form communication ethics. The following classically cited example from Bonhoeffer points to a form of dialogic confession, a communication ethic that informs in attentiveness to the particular.

> For example, a teacher asks a child in front of the class whether it is true that his father often comes home drunk. It is true, but the child denies it. The teacher's question has placed him in a situation for which he is not yet prepared. He feels only that what is taking place is an unjustified interference in the order of the family and that he must oppose it. What goes on in the family is not for the ears of the class in school. The family has its own secret and must preserve it. The teacher has failed to respect the reality of this institution. The child ought now to find a way of answering which would comply with both the rule of the family and the rule of the school. But he is not yet able to do this. He lacks experience, knowledge, and the ability to express himself in the right way. As a simple no to the teacher's question the child's answer is certainly untrue; yet at the same time it nevertheless gives expression to the truth that the family is an institution *sui generis* and that the teacher had no right to interfere in it. The child's answer can indeed be called a lie; yet this lie contains more truth, that is to say, it is more in accordance with reality than would have been the case if the child had betrayed his father's weakness in front of the class. (*Ethics* 367–68)

This interplay of a Christocentric story and particulars unites a form of communication ethics responsive to the unique historical situation and human relationships.

Bonhoeffer did not write on communication ethics explicitly; his posthumously published work called *Ethics* engaged the notion of dialectic and dialogue, offering a textured understanding of what this author calls Bonhoeffer's implicit commitment to religious *communication* ethics—a dialogic confession. Philosophical ethics are marked by abstract clarity unavailable in Bonhoeffer's communication ethics. Bonhoeffer's communication ethic connects to a narrative standard of the faith moderated by attention to person, topic, historical moment, and the Other. Bonhoeffer's communication ethic begins in dialectic and moves to rhetorical application *(phronesis),* meeting the Other and the historical moment. Bonhoeffer's ethics project rejects an abstract philosophical ethics, which embodies clarity only when behavior is in agreement with a previously agreed-upon public standard. Actions judged in accordance with consistency with a preset standard do not rest within a textured use of dialectic. The phrase "faith story historically and appropriately applied to life's events" fits Bonhoeffer better than the notion of consistency of application. Bonhoeffer continuously points to something beyond philosophical and abstract ethics—a communication ethic.

A communication ethic is the dialectical interplay between two basic sets of assumptions: 1) ethics emerge in the between of a faith story and responsiveness to the historical moment, and 2) communication ethics emerge between the elements above and relational attentiveness to particular people in a particular situation. This approach to communication ethics rides between extremes—universality and historicity. Like Bonhoeffer's understanding of genuine transcendence, a religious communication ethic must rest between the transcendental and the horizontal, or the story of the faith and the historical implementation of ideas.

This understanding of Bonhoeffer's work is consistent with the insights of Seyla Benhabib (330–69). She does not forego the importance of the universal, while she rejects equating any one system with universal applicability. The notion of the universal must simultaneously meet the importance of the historical moment. She is unwilling to claim a victor in the dialectic of universal or the particular. Bonhoeffer worked from similar complexity; this work uses dialogic confession as a form of religious communication ethics that keeps moral conversation going, ever responsive to the particulars of a given historical situation and commitment to an ultimate faith story. Bonhoeffer would say "yes" and "no" to both extremes (universality that can stop a conversation—"no", and an ultimate commitment—"yes." His responsiveness to the particular keeps a conversation going—"yes," and he rejects a pure relativism, knowing that at times, one must stop the conversation and act, even to violate the demands of the community. Yet, both goals (universal and particular) are laudable and appropriate as one meets the concrete demands of everyday life with the two held in tension. Benhabib works dialectically, like Bonhoeffer, aiming for what she considers a "dialogically reformulated universalist ethical theory" (334).

> A serious exchange between such a universalist ethical theory, which suggests neither from the methodological individualism nor from the ahistoricism of traditional Kantian ethics, and a hermeneutically inspired neo-Aristotelianism can lead us to see that some traditional oppositions and exclusions in moral philosophy are no longer convincing. Such oppositions as between universalism and historicity, and ethics of principle and judgment in context, or ethical cognition and moral motivation, within the confines of which much recent discussion has run, are no longer compelling. (334)

The dialogic effort to attend to the dialectical unity of contrasting ethical extremes is at the heart of Bonhoeffer's work. His courage was both practical and intellectual, refusing to offer artificial solace with easy, formulaic answers.

Bonhoeffer suggested that the church must live in and with two contrasting sayings of Jesus—one that reminds us of the stories of the faith and the other responsive to the historical moment of secular life.

> These two sayings ["he that is not with us is against us" and "He that is not against us is for us"] necessarily belong together as the two claims of Jesus Christ, the claim to exclusiveness and the claim to totality. The greater the exclusiveness, the greater the freedom. But in isolation the claim to exclusiveness leads to fanaticism and to slavery; and in isolation the claim to totality leads to secularization and self-abandonment of the Church. The more exclusively we acknowledge and confess Christ as our Lord, the more fully the wide range of His dominion will be disclosed to us. (*Ethics* 58)

One hears repeatedly in Bonhoeffer the dialectics of principles/particulars and the story of the faith/secular life. In this interplay, ethical life emerges, not within one extreme, but between contraries. Bonhoeffer goes so far as to state that God does not love the ideal man or the ideal world, but the world as it is: "God sides with the real man" (*Ethics* 71). Bonhoeffer's religious communication ethic brings us into the center of life guided by a story of the faith.

This view of religious communication ethics as dialogic confession rests upon three assumptions that provide both stability and flexibility/responsiveness to the historical moment. A religious communication ethic inspired by Bonhoeffer tempers conviction with question and question with conviction. Such a communication ethic understands life as involving risk, mistakes, and change, keeping the metaphor of death and resurrection as central in daily living. Finally, a religious communication ethic uses confession as an action metaphor that calls or summons one back into the story of the faith. Confession links death and resurrection as we admit mistakes and move to new possibilities. Confession is the dialectical bridge that guides a faith (story)-centered communication ethic. Bonhoeffer suggests not just a religious communication ethic, but also the ingredients for a story-centered communication ethic. Bonhoeffer offers a story-centered communication ethic that invites dialogic confession in interpersonal engagement—framing a bridge to the Other without forgetting that walls shape a person's position or stance.

Dialectic as Bridge

Bonhoeffer used dialectic as a bridge for opening dialogue between persons. Answers lie in the center of the bridge, not on one extreme pillar or the other. "Bridges" is the guiding theme that underscores Dietrich Bonhoeffer's implied understanding of interpersonal communication ethics. Dialogic confession assumes walls or standpoints of the two communicators, which connect a temporal bridge of confession that brings the two walls, standpoints, or narrative positions into conversation. Bonhoeffer's ethical position of dialectical "bridges" provides a temporal ground for learning.

Bonhoeffer's Christocentric framework might turn away readers reluctant to encounter God-centered language. Yet Bonhoeffer himself articulated a cautious position on religious piety and language use, discussing "religionless Christianity" (*Letters and Papers from Prison* 280–82) in a "world come of age" (326–29), as well as stating his own frustration with the church's unwillingness to stand against the growing menace of the Third Reich ("The Question of the Boundaries of the Church and Church Union" 158–67).

Consistent with his work, Bonhoeffer used dialectic to temper extreme positions on either side—too much assurance and too much openness. His struggle against the Nazis reveals a life counter to relativism, and his consistent rejection of deus ex machina (*Letters and Papers from Prison* 282), a Supreme Being who comes down from the heavens to pull humans out of difficult moments, announced his wariness of undue assurance. Bonhoeffer used the term "religionless Christianity" as a way to detail his commitment to the faith historically engaged, not piety privately observed.

> I often ask myself why a "Christian instinct" often draws me more to religionless people than to the religious, by which I don't in the least mean with any evangelizing intention, but [. . .] "in brotherhood." [. . .] I'm often reluctant to mention God by name to religious people [. . .] Religious people speak of God when human knowledge [. . .] has come to an end, or when human resources fail—in fact it is always the *deus ex machina* that they bring on the scene [. . .] How this religionless Christianity looks, what form it takes, is something that I'm thinking about a great deal, and I shall be writing to you again about it soon. (*Letters and Papers from Prison* 281–82)

Bonhoeffer's view of Christ-centered language embraces Christian service, requiring us to become more interested in what we can do for others than what God should do for us. Bonhoeffer was a Christian deeply interested in God and the importance of responsible, caring action for God's world; he refused to use God as a tool to enhance himself or as a weapon to fend off and ignore those personally, culturally, and religiously different than himself and other Christians.

Bonhoeffer's view of an interpersonal communication ethic suggests a "common center" (Buber, *The Knowledge of Man* 110) that ties us to something larger and more significant than the individual self. Using the words of Christopher Lasch, Bonhoeffer was aware that "the culture of narcissism" and "the minimal self" existed prior to the titles penned years later; he understood that when decision making without a common center becomes normative, diverse people can no longer pull together: they fall to the temptation of the self. Instead of a common center of God and the scriptures, we discover the individual self as the center of existence.

Bonhoeffer, of course, considered the common center of the church to be a God-centered faith, not one in which God was required to be a servant to us, but one in which the human is called to live out the faith in service to God. Bonhoeffer might suggest that numerous institutions have lost their common centers for long-term participation in the marketplace. For business, the common center needs to be commitment to increasing the quality of products responsive to the historical situation in which people live, not campaigns to convince one to use the unhelpful. When one meets a historical need, the advertising comes with an implicit "why" the product is important, permitting one to tell about the improvements in the product. For college campuses, the common center needs to be learning and teaching, not marketing of caring and friendship. The latter is a by-product of a commitment to the Other, but something vile happens when one markets caring (Arnett, *Dialogic Education* 194). In politics, the common center needs to be concern for the common good, not the survival of one's own perspective or merely one's reelection at any cost. Each of the above non–common center issues is of importance in its own right, but an organization gathers its soul from the common center around that which it organizes.

Advertising, marketing, friendship, and reelection are all helpful as long as each facilitates the common center, rather than masking the loss of an institutional identity and direction. The notion of a common center is the heart of a particular institution. Bonhoeffer's work reminds each particular organization to understand the common center that legitimizes its unique existence, assembling people around a central theme. The common center provides the walls of a given organization. It gives ground and assurance to those living in, working for, and assisting the common center. The metaphor of "bridges," central to *Bridges Not Walls,* by John Stewart, points to the notion of bridge as an ethical common center other than the self.

Constructing Bridges

Bridges Not Walls: A Book about Interpersonal Communication, edited by John Stewart, is arguably the most important interpersonal communication text grounded in the relational perspective: the book first appeared in 1973, now transformed through eight editions. The title *Bridges Not Walls* reminds us of the importance of reaching out to another. For Bonhoeffer, the metaphor of bridge has dialogic resonance, connecting opposing pillars of universal and particular, self and other, faith story and secular life, the eternal and temporal, summarized by the notion of "ultimate" and "penultimate." As a "community theologian," Bonhoeffer was concerned with the interpersonal ethics without "cheap grace" of facile relationships; he rejected relational openness that failed to recognize both pillars—the Other and what one brings to discourse in story-laden commitments.

Relational Openness

A focus on relational openness coincided with the humanistic movement in psychology and communication, aiding us in the examination of the importance of "bridges" between one another. The goal of relational openness was timely, helpful, and appropriate for the historical moment of a Vietnam War and Civil Rights era of mistrust and walls between persons of differing positions.

The goal of bridging one's way to another was laudable and needed. The vocabulary of this movement impacted all phases of life. Ironically, as relational openness became more normative in discourse, the focus on self increased in emphasis. The therapeutic worldview dominated much of everyday life in the latter part of the twentieth century, framing the self as an alternative to the transcendent. The success of the movement invited excess, leading to ongoing scholarly critiques of the danger of too much focus upon the self in the work of Philip Reiff *(The Feeling Intellect: Selected Writings),* Alasdair MacIntyre *(After Virtue: A Study in Moral Theory),* and Robert Bellah et al. *(Habits of the Heart: Individualism and Commitment in American Life).* Their collective insight was akin to Alexis de Tocqueville's warning about the danger of "individualism," a term he coined (506). Simply put, such a focus limits attentiveness to narrative life, placing false confidence in the self, the individual unguided by narrative structures. Tocqueville understood this danger in 1835. The therapeutic movement questioned traditional moral authorities, substituting the self for the transcendent guidance of a narrative of the faith. What was missed was Stewart's insight. It is not the self, but the bridge that makes relational life possible.

Robert Bellah et al. outlined the limits of a therapeutic view of the self in opposition to a moral narrative, which also has therapeutic possibilities.

> This therapeutic view not only refuses to take a moral stand, it actively distrusts "morality" and sees therapeutic contractualism as a more adequate framework for viewing human action. [. . .] Unfortunately, in all existing societies, traditional social practices and the moral standards that govern them are subject to just these distortions. But the therapeutically inclined are wrong to think that morality itself is the culprit, that moral standards are inherently authoritarian and in the service of domination. (129, 140)

The therapeutic movement challenged an old moral order, decreasing its story-laden influence. Bonhoeffer would accept this act but would counter with a reminder that life is lived within stories, not the "self." A story suggests the beginning of a relational bridge. A bridge needs a pillar upon which to stand. The story provides such a pillar and the bridge is the action metaphor that permits embedded agents to meet one another in dialogue.

In Bonhoeffer's *Ethics,* there is an alternative to the focus upon the self; Bonhoeffer pointed to a narrative of faith-shaped responsibility to the Other.

> Only when it has become selfless in this obligation does a life stand in the freedom of a man's truly own life and action. The obligation assumes the form of deputyship and of correspondence with reality; freedom displays itself in the self-examination of life and of action and in the venture of a concrete decision. This gives us the arrangement for our discussion of the structure of responsible life. (224)

Bonhoeffer underscored responsibility for the world and the Other. He suggested not a mystical call to responsibility, but a concrete call to action propelled by the story of a Christocentric faith. The center of decision making is the text or story and the particular moment, not the individual or the self alone. He understood that the irony of self-development is that it begins in attentiveness to life outside the self. The total liberty, liberty without restraint, of the human leads to "self destruction" (Bonhoeffer, *Ethics* 102). For Bonhoeffer, the key is not freedom from restraint, but the particular restraint within which one enacts freedom. The narrative of the faith restricts while guiding, giving direction without dictating the answer to another, permitting freedom of engagement in the world.

Alternatives to an Old Moral Order

The therapeutic movement accurately sensed a declining metanarrative, a collapse of conventionally agreed-upon meaning, the old moral order crumbling. The therapeutic movement offered an alternative to a dying moral order in which an agreed-upon narrative no longer offered guidance in decision making. Individuals had to rely on conversation with others and upon the self. The Enlightenment critique of tradition had become part of everyday interpersonal life. The focus on the self became normative, a natural extension of the enlightenment project.

The constructive side of this movement from metanarrative was the call to responsibility. The unreflective dangerous side was placing too much communicative confidence in the self for figuring out responsibility without narrative guidance. The self-focus bypassed learning for telling and discernment for expression. Modernity's love affair with the self offered false confidence that we had arrived, opening a door to the self and to telling in a historical moment that seemed to call for implementation, not sorting through and discerning narrative direction. Modernity presupposed a narrative direction in which progress and implementation guided decision making and life together.

The unknowing dark side of the therapeutic revolution substituted the self for learning and the act of self-expression for discernment. Robert Bellah and associates in *Habits of the Heart* contend that this orientation has developed "an acute concern for the monitoring and managing of inner feelings and emphasizes their expression in open communication" (138). Bellah understood the limits of MacIntyre's "expressivism" (*After Virtue* 11–14, 16–35), and Stanley Hauerwas in his discussion of the need for virtue guidelines outlines the danger of seeking answers through "emotivism" and attempts to encourage a sense of hope and patience rooted in the Biblical story, as people look for answers in troubled contemporary life (111–28). Hauerwas understood "emotivism," decision making by personal preference, as the decision-making key to a focus on the self. Hauerwas agreed with Alasdair MacIntyre that "emotivism is the doctrine that all evaluative judgments and more specifically all moral judgments are nothing but expressions of preference, expressions of feeling, insofar as they are moral or evaluative in character" (*After Virtue* 13–14). Emotivism is the result of the self living without a guiding story that can offer direction or limits, encouraging the expression of views based more on personal preference than documented deliberation (MacIntyre, *After Virtue* 30–31).

Bonhoeffer understood the limits of self-driven decision making. He called for discernment responsive to a guiding moral story. In *Life Together,* Bonhoeffer stated:

> How often we hear innumerable arguments "from life" and "from experience" put forward as the basis for most crucial decisions, but the argument of Scrip-

> ture is missing. [. . .] It is not surprising, of course, that the person who attempts to cast discredit upon their wisdom should be the one who himself does not seriously read, know, and study the Scriptures. (55)

Bonhoeffer reminded us of the importance of learning as opposed to babble that renders opinion by the force of self-expression.

Vernard Eller critiqued communication based on privatism and individualism that was responsive merely to one's own "pathos" or emotions. Such language calls for "self-identity, self-worth, self-fulfillment, and authentic selfhood—as feeling good about oneself, as being liberated, as experiencing rightness" (Eller 18). Like Bellah, Eller understood that when an old moral system is torn down and reveals only therapeutic language, we lose "habits of the heart," a commitment to a sense of community and values that transcend our emotive perceptions. Therapeutic language carries the language of "self" and personal preference, not the language of commitment that invites one to participate in and contribute to an ongoing moral story or narrative. Philip Reiff in *The Triumph of the Therapeutic: Uses of Faith after Freud* reminded us that modernity was a deconversion from the restrictions of a Judeo-Christian value system to the therapeutic. "[M]odern culture is unique in having given birth to such elaborately argued antireligions, all aiming to confirm us in our devastating illusions of individuality and freedom" (10).

The therapeutic movement gave us emotivism and expressivism. "Expressivism" in communication attempts to protect the "Royal me," the authentic feelings of the self (Hart and Burks, "Rhetorical Sensitivity" 5). "Expressivism" emerged, according to Richard Bernstein, with the work of Hegel (*Philosophical Profiles* 162). Charles Taylor uses the term "expressivism" in his discussion of Hegel, defining the term as a "sense in which we speak of expression as giving vent to, a realizing in external reality of something we feel or desire" (qtd. in Bernstein, *Philosophical Profiles* 162).

Howard Kirschenbaum, in his biography of Carl Rogers, profiles why so much attention has been placed on expression by those of us contributing to the "triumph of the therapeutic." Many understood the old moral stories as too restrictive and unresponsive, unable to suggest direction for a complex and diverse set of struggles. Kirschenbaum says of Rogers:

> The last of the "less deep" therapies which Rogers employed during his Rochester years was "Expressive therapy" or "release." He was more intrigued by the possibilities of this approach than by those already mentioned. To "talk out" one's feelings, to ventilate one's conflicts, to unburden oneself of concerns, anxieties

> and problems, Rogers felt, had considerable therapeutic value. "Such a catharsis," he wrote then, "even where the therapist is a listener only has a constructive effect, since the child clarifies his feelings by verbalizing them." (81)

Rogers pointed to expressivism as the center of communicative life, as a way out of a dying metanarrative. In defense of this approach, it was an effort to meet metanarrative decline with the tools of self, emotivism, and expressivism. What was missing was the search for and discovery of petite narratives that could inform and assist the person in liberation from a moment of metanarrative decline, an alternative to the answer of the self.

Liberation

When an old moral order is degenerating and dying, it is understandable that liberation efforts emerge. In Western culture, the philosophical cornerstone alternative to the old corrupt moral order was the call to *liberty.* J. S. Mill, in *On Liberty,* suggested, "The struggle between liberty and authority is the most conspicuous feature in the portions of history (59). Mill understood the importance of unleashing the person to search out new options when an old moral system is under question. The philosophical and political work of Mill lives in the therapeutic revolution that placed primary confidence in the self. The therapeutic revolution is the offspring of the Enlightenment project.

Bonhoeffer discussed liberty in his *Ethics.* His response to the Enlightenment and the French Revolution's movement toward liberty was to remind the person of the faith of a more fundamental common center. He understood the importance of affirming the "limitation of earthly powers by the sovereignty of God" (104). It is easy to see how Bonhoeffer feared "fanaticism," which so typified the speeches and actions of Hitler (*Ethics* 66). Bonhoeffer's Germany revealed the danger of unrestrained earthly power, and the excess of the French revolution announced the problematic of extremes of individual liberty. Bonhoeffer's Christocentric theology announced another form of liberty. The common center of God and the story of the faith faded in memory and power, and individual initiative built great and glorious structures. Offering absolute loyalty to earthly structures invited what Bonhoeffer called a "genuine decay" (*Ethics* 108) in Western civilization.

Bonhoeffer witnessed fascism, communism, and consumerism; each competes for loyalty of the hearts of the people. As Bonhoeffer wrote: "But the spiritual force is lacking. The question is: What protects us against the menace of organization?" (*Letters and Papers from Prison* 380). Bonhoeffer understood that organizations centered on a nonspiritual set of moral codes did not necessarily result in a "better" moral system, particularly when the call for almost blind devotion and loyalty was a major requirement for participation in the organization. The excess of liberty and the excess of organizational power engage a similar error—both miss the spirit of the faith that must shape individual liberty and organizational life.

Bonhoeffer understood an even more subtle way to undercut liberty than the call for blind adherence to the group—making the notion of liberty itself into an absolute. Bonhoeffer warned against the tendency to make good ideas into harmful practices through extreme application. Most of us have known someone whose ideas are on target, but the effort to apply those good ideas results in an opposite effect.

Bonhoeffer called for restraint, without which one finds the seeds of destruction in liberty.

> With the destruction of the Biblical faith in God and of all divine commands and ordinances, man destroys himself. There arises an unrestrained vitalism which involves the dissolution of all values and achieves its goal only in final self-destruction, in the void. (*Ethics* 103)

Individual liberty works best as a "penultimate," requiring constraints to avoid taking on the image of an "ultimate." As Bonhoeffer stated in *Life Together:*

> Where Christ bids me to maintain fellowship for the sake of love, I will maintain it. Where his truth enjoins me to dissolve a fellowship for love's sake, then I will dissolve it, despite all the protests of my human love. (35)

Sometimes acts of individual liberty against a social structure calling for loyalty are essential. In other words, Bonhoeffer recognized the danger of too much blind loyalty.

Bonhoeffer's philosophical and theological system was deeply indebted to an understanding of the importance of limits; no term can be constructive if pushed too far, from liberty to the notion of salvation. Extreme use of a concept too often moves it from social good to an extreme that contradicts the original aim.

> [E]ven the word of salvation has its limits. He has neither power nor right to force it on other men in season and out of season. Every attempt to impose the gospel by force, to run after people and proselytize them, to use our own resources to arrange the salvation of other people, is both futile and dangerous. [. . .] Our easy trafficking with the word of cheap grace simply bores the world to disgust [. . .] (Bonhoeffer, *The Cost of Discipleship* 206–07)

The only way to counter misuse of terms such as *liberty* and *organizational loyalty,* and even theological terms, is to buffer them within dialectical caution.

Bonhoeffer's Dialectic—The Restraint of Liberty and Group Loyalty

Bonhoeffer worked in a deliberate dialectical fashion, inviting a "polemical unity" (*Ethics* 199). Bonhoeffer believed that when liberty is made into an absolute or an "ultimate," the result is the deification of the person, unleashing even more violence and unrestrained self-expression on the world.

Every "penultimate" requires a set of constraints or it will be over stressed and vie for the status of an "ultimate." Liberty, like any of a large number of important "penultimates," needs constraints as a reminder that it is a means to a greater end. For Bonhoeffer, the "ultimate," reserved for God alone, consists of all that a human must do to invite life to reflect the image of God in everyday interaction (*Ethics* 120–43). The "penultimate" needs restraint. In *Ethics,* Bonhoeffer suggests:

> And the "restrainer" is the force which takes effect within history through God's governance of the world, and which sets due limits to evil. The "restrainer" itself is not God; it is not without guilt; but God makes use of it in order to preserve the world from destruction. (108)

Bonhoeffer's view of liberty, like Martin Buber's understanding of freedom, had a positive and a cautious tone—trusting liberty or freedom with one hand and mistrusting it with the other (Buber, *Way of Response* 166).

As stated above, Bonhoeffer was supportive of liberation, and he was concerned about the mistake of making any notion into an absolute; the "penultimate" restrained from appearance as the "ultimate" situates Bonhoeffer more aptly within the metaphor of "walls with bridges." He understands that one must begin with a position that restrains individual liberty and confidence in the self.

"Distance"

Bonhoeffer would have agreed that "distance" begins the invitation to engagement. Buber privileged distance and eschewed closeness that emerges too quickly—warning us about "overrunning reality" (Buber qtd. in Friedman, *The Hidden Human Image* 301). Four basic protections of distance frame the life of a person, an individual situated within a moral story: privacy, a moral story of a God-centered faith, Christian community, and family.

Privacy. Bonhoeffer supported the right to human privacy. Bonhoeffer stated this need for privacy walls in firm fashion.

> And as every man still has a private sphere somewhere, that is where he was thought to be most vulnerable. The secrets known to a man's valet—that is, to put it crudely, the range of his intimate life, from prayer to his sexual life—have become the hunting-ground of modern pastoral workers. In that way they resemble (though with quite different intentions) the dirtiest gutter journalists [. . .] In the one case it's social, financial, or political blackmail and in the other, religious blackmail. Forgive me, but I can't put it more mildly. (*Letters and Papers from Prison* 344)

Bonhoeffer would not approve of the blurring of public/private information so common in contemporary culture and personified in sharpest form by midday talk shows. His critique would not center as much on the topic as it would on the inappropriate discussion of private and intimate information in a public setting.

Bonhoeffer's remarks are similar to Reiff's assertion in *The Triumph of the Therapeutic:*

> We are, I fear, getting to know one another. Reticence, secrecy, concealments of self have been transformed into social problems; once they were aspects of civility, when the great Western formulary summed up in the creedal phrase "Know thyself" encouraged obedience to communal purposes rather than suspicion of them. (22)

We are not entitled to all information about another; it is possible to cross the line between caring about another and communicative voyeurism, where we are more interested in the titillation factor than the information itself.

Bonhoeffer contends that "the primal relationship of man to man is a giving one, in the state of sin is purely demanding" (*The Communion of Saints* 71). When we demand that another's privacy come down to fit our version of "good interpersonal communication," we do not invite an ethic that Bonhoeffer affirms but rather open the door to sin of communicative voyeurism.

In *Ethics,* Bonhoeffer quoted with approval Nietzsche's statement that profound minds need masks. He critiqued Kant, who, when caught praying, felt so bad that he felt compelled to argue against prayer. Bonhoeffer stated that instead of giving up prayer, Kant needed to articulate the importance of privacy; not all parts of life are for public viewing and discussion (*Ethics* 60).

Moral story of the faith. Bonhoeffer's life and scholarship provide a moral story of the faith, with God as the common center of life. Bonhoeffer, within the tradition of the Old Testament prophets, attempted to assist people in understanding the crisis, chaos, and destruction that threatened the walls of Christian culture and life in that war-saturated world. The struggle and unrelenting assault of Bonhoeffer on the forces of evil around him placed him within the Old Testament prophetic tradition.

> Jeremiah, Ezekiel, and 2 Isaiah [. . .] This literature is from a period when the "known world" of Jerusalem was assaulted and finally disbanded. In 587 Jerusalem was destroyed, and with it the symbols and props which held life together. (Brueggeman 1)

Bonhoeffer functioned as a storyteller, as a pastor, as a teacher, as a head of a seminary and even as a prisoner. In each case, he was able to keep God, not himself, at the center of the story. Perhaps the importance of the story of the faith echoes in Bonhoeffer's last hours:

> Bonhoeffer's last weeks were spent with prisoners drawn from all over Europe. Among them was Payne Best, an English officer. In his book, *The Venlo Incident,* Best writes [. . .] The following day, Sunday, April 8th, 1945, Pastor Bonhoeffer held a little service and spoke to us in a manner which reached the hearts of all, finding just the right words to express the spirit of our imprisonment and the thoughts and resolutions which it had brought. He had hardly finished his last prayers when the door opened and two evil-looking men in civilian clothes came in and said: "Prisoner Bonhoeffer, get ready to come with us." Those words "come with us"—for all prisoners they had come to mean one thing only—the scaffold. We bade him goodbye—he drew me aside—"This is the end," he said. "For me the beginning of life" [. . .] Next day, at Flossenburg, he was hanged. (Bethge, *Dietrich Bonhoeffer* 11)

Bonhoeffer spoke at a time when the foundations of German Christianity were under significant siege. He spoke with conviction in his life, attempting to keep the walls of a Christian-life centered around a moral story of God and God's people:

> It is with the Christ who is persecuted and who suffers in His Church that justice, truth, humanity and freedom must now seek refuge; it is with the Christ who found no shelter in the world, the Christ who was cast out from the world, the Christ of the crib and the cross, under whose protection they now seek sanctuary [. . .] (*Ethics* 59)

Bonhoeffer worked to keep the faith strong in a time when Nazi officials were using both legitimate and illegitimate means of influence that invited the tearing down of walls and the building of bridges with the Third Reich.

The church community and family. The Christian community and that of family provided the base for an ecumenical "bridge" and for attentiveness to others in acts of "deputyship," acts of service for others outside the immediate biological family. Bonhoeffer's family was important to him. *Letters and Papers from Prison* finds life in letters written primarily to family or to those who might become family. Bonhoeffer's family provided a place from which he could meet the power and danger of the moment before him. Bonhoeffer's family of educators and lovers of the arts gave him a family story composed of ancestors with commitments to service and educational excellence. "The rich world of his ancestors set the standards for Dietrich Bonhoeffer's own life" (Bethge, *Dietrich Bonhoeffer* 928). Bonhoeffer lived in the best of an aristocratic world with education and service providing the background music of family life. Such a family provided a strong narrative framework from which to meet the world.

Story-laden meeting. Again, consistent with Bonhoeffer's dialectical orientation, he could have, but did not, make a fetish out of any one of the above walls that provide distance that must be spanned by a "bridge" that would reach out to others. For individual privacy, he offered the importance of "confession" with one another as temporal bridge. For a God-centered moral story, he suggested a "bridge" of "religionless Christianity," which understood the danger of making religion into words without corresponding action, permitting him to make genuine contact with those outside the church and realizing the potential sin of those within the church. Even for his emphasis on family he reminded us that this is God's world and framed a Christocentric theology.

Bonhoeffer embraced a story of a relational human framework that is the dialectical companion to his focus on a God-centered moral story. In *The Communion of Saints,* he uses I-Thou language in much the same way it is used by Martin Buber. He suggests, "The individual is not solitary. For the individual to exist, 'others' must also exist" (32). Bonhoeffer wrote in a time when it was dangerous to offer "bridges" to another too quickly and when it was necessary to keep the "walls" of the house of God firm. In such a time of attack on values, he knew that openness to another could carry severe consequences, even death.

Dietrich Bonhoeffer believed in a tradition that permitted and in fact encouraged the withholding of "bridges." Bonhoeffer, while in prison, wrote a fictional novel in which Christoph is in conversation with his uncle. With this quotation, one can get the flavor of the seriousness of the time and the difficulty of inviting "bridges" between persons. This exchange explicitly connects communication with those who misuse power and disregard common assumptions of civility.

> [. . .] Christoph began, "it seemed as though the ground were being taken from under my feet, as though I were to walk upon the sea. You call love of real life, living together and getting along, the ultimate lessons of history and life. But what happens if there are already forces at work which render impossible, intentionally, any living and getting along together? What if a struggle has already been proclaimed to us in which there is no communication, only victory or defeat? What if a power rises up against us—like a monster that has been sleeping—which seeks to annihilate all that has made life valuable and significant to us?" (*Novel* 124)

Bonhoeffer's interpersonal ethic of dialogic confession reaches out to others while firmly surrounded by a story that connects one to others through the "bridges" of service and awareness of other perspectives. His interpersonal ethic is neither an absolute unleashing of individual liberty nor a desperate clinging to an old moral system, but an interpersonal life guided by a center that reaches out to others, supported by conviction and extended by the cautionary act of lowering "bridges." This "unity of contraries" approach that guides his interpersonal ethic requires the strength and courage to know where one stands and to reach out to others, offering "bridges" where persons of difference can meet for conversation and work together. In a postmodern age, Bonhoeffer offers the following confession: begin with a position, walls that sustain ground for narrative life, and then reach out to the Other in this historical moment of diversity, of a "world come of age." Bonhoeffer offers insight into the "how" of taking walls into a world of diversity only to discover the pragmatic necessity of learning, which offers the bridge for the twenty-first century.

WORKS CITED

INDEX

WORKS CITED

Arendt, Hannah. *The Human Condition.* 2nd ed. Chicago: U of Chicago P, 1998.

Aristotle. *Nicomachean Ethics.* Trans. W. D. Ross. *Introduction to Aristotle.* Ed. Richard McKeon. New York: Modern Library, 1992. 316–579.

Arnett, Ronald C. *Communication and Community: Implications of Martin Buber's Dialogue.* Carbondale: Southern Illinois UP, 1986.

———. "Communication and Community in an Age of Diversity." *Communication Ethics in an Age of Diversity.* Ed. Josina M. Makau and Ronald C. Arnett. Urbana: U of Illinois P, 1997. 27–47.

———. "Dialogic Civility as Pragmatic Ethical *Praxis:* An Interpersonal Metaphor for the Public Domain." *Communication Theory* 11 (2001): 315–38.

———. *Dialogic Education: Conversation About Ideas and Between Persons.* Carbondale: Southern Illinois UP, 1992.

———. "Existential Homelessness: A Contemporary Case for Dialogue." *The Reach of Dialogue: Confirmation, Voice, and Community.* Ed. Rob Anderson, Kenneth N. Cissna, and Ronald C. Arnett. Cresskill: Hampton, 1994. 229–45.

———. "Paulo Freire's Revolutionary Pedagogy: From a Story-Centered to a Narrative-Centered Communication Ethic." *Qualitative Inquiry* 8 (2002): 489–510.

———. "Technicians of Goodness: Ignoring the Narrative Life of Dialogue." *Responsible Communication: Ethical Issues in Business, Industry, and the Professions.* Ed. James J. Jaksa and Michael S. Pritchard. Cresskill: Hampton, 1996. 339–55.

Arnett, Ronald C., and Pat Arneson. *Dialogical Civility in a Cynical Age: Community, Hope, and Interpersonal Relationships.* Albany: State U of New York P, 1999.

Bakhtin, Mikhail M. *Speech Genres and Other Late Essays.* Trans. Vern W. McGee. Ed. Caryl Emerson and Michael Holquist. U of Texas P Slavic Series 8. Austin: U of Texas P, 1986.

Becker, Ernest. *The Denial of Death.* New York: Free, 1975.

Bell, Daniel. *The Coming of Post-Industrial Society: A Venture in Social Forecasting.* New York: Basic, 1973.

Bellah, Robert N. *The Broken Covenant: American Civil Religion in Time of Trial.* 2nd ed. Chicago: U of Chicago P, 1992.

Bellah, Robert N., et al. *Habits of the Heart: Individualism and Commitment in American Life.* Berkeley: U of California P, 1985.

Benhabib, Seyla. "Afterword: Communicative Ethics and Contemporary Controversies in Practical Philosophy." *The Communicative Ethics Controversy.* Ed. Seyla Benhabib and Fred Dallmayr. Cambridge: MIT P, 1990. 330–69.

Bernstein, Richard J. *Beyond Objectivism and Relativism: Science, Hermeneutics and Praxis.* Philadelphia: U of Pennsylvania P, 1983.

———. *Philosophical Profiles: Essays in a Pragmatic Mode.* Philadelphia: U of Pennsylvania P, 1986.

Bethge, Eberhard. *Bonhoeffer: Exile and Martyr.* Ed. John W. de Gruchy. London: Collins, 1975.

———. *Dietrich Bonhoeffer: A Biography.* Rev ed. Ed. Victoria J. Barnett. Minneapolis: Fortress, 2000.

Bethge, Renate, and Eberhard Bethge. Introduction. *Fiction from Prison: Gathering Up the Past.* By Dietrich Bonhoeffer. Trans. Ursula Hoffmann. Ed. Renate Bethge, Eberhard Bethge, and Clifford Green. Philadelphia: Fortress, 1981.

Bok, Sissela. *Common Values.* Columbia: U of Missouri P, 1995.

Bonhoeffer, Dietrich. *Act and Being: Transcendental Philosophy and Ontology in Systematic Theology.* Trans. H. Martin Rumscheidt. Ed. Hans-Richard Reuter and Wayne Whitson Floyd Jr. *Dietrich Bonhoeffer Works.* Vol. 2. Minneapolis: Fortress, 1996.

———. "Christians and Pagans." *Prayers from Prison.* Philadelphia: Fortress, 1978. 26.

———. *Christ the Center.* Trans. Edwin H. Robertson. New York: Harper and Row, 1978.

———. *The Communion of Saints: A Dogmatic Inquiry into the Sociology of the Church.* Trans. R. Gregor Smith. New York: Harper and Row, 1963.

———. *The Cost of Discipleship.* Trans. Irmgard Booth. New York: Macmillan, 1963.

———. *Creation and Fall: A Theological Interpretation of Genesis 1–3.* Trans. John C. Fletcher. *Creation and Fall/Temptation: Two Biblical Studies.* New York: Macmillan, 1959. 11–94.

———. *Drama.* Trans. Ursula Hoffmann. *Fiction from Prison: Gathering Up the Past.* Ed. Renate Bethge, Eberhard Bethge and Clifford Green. Philadelphia: Fortress, 1981. 13–47.

———. *Ethics.* Trans. Neville Horton Smith. Ed. Eberhard Bethge. New York: Macmillan, 1955.

———. "The First Table of the Ten Commandments." *Preface to Bonhoeffer: The Man and Two of His Shorter Writings.* By John D. Godsey. Philadelphia: Fortress, 1965. 49–67.

———. "The Friend." *Prayers from Prison.* Philadelphia: Fortress, 1978. 29–32.

———. *Letters and Papers from Prison: The Enlarged Edition.* Trans. Christian Kaiser Verlag. Ed. Eberhard Bethge. New York: Macmillan, 1972.

———. *Life Together.* Trans. John W. Doberstein. New York: Harper and Row, 1954.

———. "Meditation on Psalm 119." *Meditating on the Word.* Trans. and ed. David McI. Gracie. Cambridge: Cowley, 1986. 101–45.

———. "Night Voices in Tegel." *Prayers from Prison.* Philadelphia: Fortress, 1978. 19–25.

———. *Novel.* Trans. Ursula Hoffmann. *Fiction from Prison: Gathering Up the Past.* Ed. Renate Bethge, Eberhard Bethge and Clifford Green. Philadelphia: Fortress, 1981. 49–130.

———. "On Meditation." *Meditating on the Word.* Trans. and ed. David McI. Gracie. Cambridge: Cowley, 1986. 27–53.

———. "Our Way According to the Testimony of Scripture." *A Testament to Freedom: The Essential Writings of Dietrich Bonhoeffer.* Rev ed. Ed. Geffrey B. Kelly and F. Burton Nelson. New York: Harper, 1995. 168–71.

———. "The Question of the Boundaries of the Church and Church Union." *A Testament to Freedom: The Essential Writings of Dietrich Bonhoeffer.* Rev ed. Ed. Geffrey B. Kelly and F. Burton Nelson. New York: Harper, 1995. 158–67.

———. *Spiritual Care.* Trans. Jay C. Rochelle. Philadelphia: Fortress, 1985.

———. *Temptation.* Trans. Kathleen Downham. *Creation and Fall/Temptation: Two Biblical Studies.* Ed. Eberhard Bethge. New York: Macmillan, 1959. 97–128.

———. "Thy Kingdom Come: The Prayer for the Church for God's Kingdom on Earth." *A Testament to Freedom: The Essential Writings of Dietrich Bonhoeffer.* Rev. ed. Ed. Geffrey B. Kelly and F. Burton Nelson. New York: Harper, 1995. 88–92.

———. "Who Am I?" *Prayers from Prison.* Philadelphia: Fortress, 1978. 17–18.

Brueggemann, Walter. *Hopeful Imagination: Prophetic Voices In Exile.* Philadelphia: Fortress, 1977.

Buber, Martin. *Between Man and Man.* New York: Macmillan, 1965.

———. "Books and Men." *Meetings.* La Salle: Open Court, 1973.

———. *I and Thou.* 2nd ed. Trans. Walter Kaufmann. New York: Scribner's, 1958.

———. *The Knowledge of Man: A Philosophy of the Interhuman.* New York: Harper, 1966.

———. *The Way of Response: Martin Buber; Selections From His Writings.* Ed. Nahum N. Glatzer. New York: Schocken, 1966.

Camus, Albert. *L'Etranger.* Paris: Gallimard, 1942.

Cicero, Marcus Tullius. *De Oratore.* Trans. E. W. Sutton and H. Rackham. 2 vols. Cambridge: Harvard UP, 1959–60.

Cohen, Richard A. Translator's Introduction. *Ethics and Infinity: Conversations with Philippe Nemo.* By Emmanuel Levinas. Trans. Richard A. Cohen. Pittsburgh: Duquesne UP, 1985. 1–15.

Coles, Robert. *The Spiritual Life of Children.* Boston: Houghton, 1990.

Dickens, Charles. *Hard Times.* 1854. New York: Penguin Putnam, 1997.

Dumas, André. "Religion and Reality in the Work of Bonhoeffer." *A Bonhoeffer Legacy: Essays in Understanding.* Ed. A. J. Klassen. Grand Rapids: Eerdmans, 1981. 258–67.

Eaglestone, Robert. *Ethical Criticism: Reading after Levinas.* Edinburgh: Edinburgh UP, 1997.

Eller, Vernard. *Towering Babble: God's People Without God's Word.* Elgin: Brethren, 1983.

Ellul, Jacques. *The Humiliation of the Word.* Grand Rapids: Eerdmans, 1985.

———. *Perspectives on Our Age: Jacques Ellul Speaks on His life and Work.* Ed. William H. Vanderburg. Toronto: Anansi, 1997.

———. *The Technological Society.* New York: Knopf, 1964.

Engels, Friedrich. *The Condition of the Working Class in England: From Personal Observations and Authentic Sources.* 1844. London: Lawrence and Wishart, 1977.

Feil, Ernest. "Dietrich Bonhoeffer's Understanding of the World." *A Bonhoeffer Legacy: Essays in Understanding.* Ed. A. J. Klassen. Grand Rapids: Eerdmans, 1981. 237–55.

Fisher, Walter R. "Narration as a Human Communication Paradigm: The Case of Public Moral Argument." *Communication Monographs* 51 (1984): 1–22.

Flanders, Henry Jackson, et al. *The People of the Covenant: An Introduction to the Hebrew Bible.* 4th ed. Oxford: Oxford UP, 1996.

Fletcher, Joseph. *Moral Responsibility: Situation Ethics at Work.* Philadelphia: Westminster, 1967.

———. *Situation Ethics: The New Morality.* Philadelphia: Westminster, 1966.

Floyd, Wayne Whitson, Jr. Editor's Introduction to the English Edition. *Act and Being: Transcendental Philosophy and Ontology in Systematic Theology.* By Dietrich Bonhoeffer. Trans. H. Martin Rumscheidt. Ed. Hans-Richard Reuter and Wayne Whitson Floyd Jr. *Dietrich Bonhoeffer Works.* Vol. 2. Minneapolis: Fortress, 1996. 1–24.

Frankl, Viktor. *Man's Search for Meaning: An Introduction to Logotherapy.* New York: Pocket, 1974.

———. *Psychotherapy and Existentialism: Selected Papers on Logotherapy.* New York: Simon, 1967.

Freire, Paulo. *Pedagogy of the Oppressed.* Trans. Myra Bergman Ramos. New York: Seabury, 1974.

Friedman, Maurice. *The Hidden Human Image.* New York: Dell, 1974.

———. *Martin Buber: The Life of Dialogue.* Chicago: U of Chicago P, 1976.

Gadamer, Hans-Georg. "Dialectic and Sophism in Plato's *Seventh Letter.*" Trans. P. Christopher Smith. *Dialogue and Dialectic: Eight Hermeneutical Studies on Plato.* New Haven: Yale UP, 1980. 93–123.

———. *Hermeneutics, Tradition, and Reason.* Trans. Georgia Warnke. Stanford: Stanford UP, 1987.

———. "*Logos* and *Ergon* in Plato's *Lysis.*" Trans. P. Christopher Smith. *Dialogue and Dialectic: Eight Hermeneutical Studies on Plato.* New Haven: Yale UP, 1980. 1–20.

———. *Philosophical Hermeneutics.* Trans. and ed. David E. Linge. Berkeley: U of California P, 1976.

———. *Truth and Method.* 2nd rev. ed. Trans. Joel Weinsheimer and Donald G. Marshall. New York: Continuum, 1999.

Geertz, Clifford. *The Interpretation of Cultures.* New York: Basic, 1973.

Godsey, John D. "Bonhoeffer the Man." *Preface to Bonhoeffer: The Man and Two of His Shorter Writings.* By John D. Godsey. Philadelphia: Fortress, 1965. 1–26.

Hart, Roderick P., and Don Burks. "Rhetorical Sensitivity and Social Interaction." *Speech Monograph* 39 (1972): 75–91.

Hauerwas, Stanley. *A Community of Character: Toward a Constructive Christian Social Ethic.* Notre Dame: U of Notre Dame P, 1977.

Hawthorne, Nathaniel. "The Great Stone Face." 1850. *Hawthorne's Short Stories.* Ed. Newton Arvin. New York: Vintage, 1946. 291–311.

Heidegger, Martin. "Letter on Humanism." *Basic Writings: From Being and Time (1927) to The Task of Thinking (1964).* Rev. and expanded ed. Ed. David Farrell Krell. San Francisco: Harper, 1993. 213–66.

Hesse, Hermann. *Beneath the Wheel.* Trans. Michael Roloff. New York: Farrar, 1968.

———. *The Glass Bead Game: Magister Ludi.* Trans. Richard Winston and Clara Winston. New York: Holt, 1969.

"History Place Holocaust Timeline, The." <http://www.historyplace.com/worldwar2/holocaust/timeline.html>. March 10, 2003.

Hoffer, Eric. *The True Believer: Thoughts on the Nature of Mass Movements.* New York: Harper, 1951.

Hoy, David Couzens. *The Critical Circle: Literature, History, and Philosophical Hermeneutics.* Berkeley: U of California P, 1978.

Hunter, James Davison. *Culture Wars: The Struggle to Define America.* New York: Basic, 1991.

Husserl, Edmund. *Ideas: General Introduction to Pure Phenomenology.* Trans. W. R. Boyce Gibson. New York: Collier, 1962.

James, William. *Pragmatism: A New Name for Some Old Ways of Thinking. Pragmatism and The Meaning of Truth.* Cambridge: Harvard UP, 1975. 1–166.

Jefferson, Thomas. *Thomas Jefferson, Revolutionary Philosopher: A Selection of Writings.* Ed. John S. Pancake and N. Sharon Summers. Woodbury: Barron, 1976.

Johannesen, Richard L. *Ethics in Human Communication.* 5th ed. Prospect Heights: Waveland, 2002.

Kelly, Geffrey B., and F. Burton Nelson. Editors' Introduction. *A Testament to Freedom: The Essential Writings of Dietrich Bonhoeffer.* Rev. ed. Ed. Geffrey B. Kelly and F. Burton Nelson. New York: Harper, 1995. 1–44.

Kierkegaard, Soren. *Fear and Trembling.* Trans. and ed. Howard V. Hong and Edna H. Hong. Princeton: Princeton UP, 1983.

King, Martin Luther, Jr. *A Testament of Hope: The Essential Writings of Martin Luther King, Jr.* Ed. James Melvin Washington. San Francisco: Harper, 1986.

Kirschenbaum, Howard. *On Becoming Carl Rogers.* New York: Delta, 1979.

Kushner, Harold S. *When Bad Things Happen to Good People.* New York: Schocken, 1981.

Lasch, Christopher. *The Culture of Narcissism: American Life in a Time of Diminishing Expectations.* New York: Norton, 1979.
———. *The Minimal Self: Psychic Survival in Troubled Times.* New York: Norton, 1984.
———. *The True and Only Heaven: Progress and Its Critics.* New York: Norton, 1991.
Levinas, Emmanuel. *Ethics and Infinity: Conversations with Philippe Nemo.* Trans. Richard A. Cohen. Pittsburgh: Duquesne UP, 1985.
———. *Time and the Other.* Trans. Richard A. Cohen. Pittsburgh: Duquesne UP, 1987.
———. *Totality and Infinity: An Essay on Exteriority.* Trans. Alphonso Lingis. Pittsburgh: Duquesne UP, 1969.
Litt, Theodor. *Individuum und Gemeinschaft; Grundfragen der Sozialen Theorie und Ethik.* Leipzig and Berlin: B. G. Teubner, 1919.
Lowith, Karl. *Das Individuum in der Rolle des Mitmenschen.* Munich: Drei Masken Verlag, 1928.
Lyotard, Jean-François. *The Postmodern Condition: A Report on Knowledge.* Trans. Geoff Bennington and Brian Massumi. Vol. 10 of *Theory and History of Literature.* Minneapolis: U of Minnesota P, 1984.
MacIntyre, Alasdair. *After Virtue: A Study in Moral Theory.* 2nd ed. Notre Dame: U of Notre Dame P, 1984.
———. *Against the Self-Images of the Age: Essays on Ideology and Philosophy.* New York: Schocken, 1971.
———. *Dependent Rational Animals: Why Human Beings Need the Virtues.* Chicago: Open Court, 1999.
The Majestic. Dir. Frank Darabont. Perf. Jim Carrey, Martin Landau. Warner, 2001.
Manning, Robert John Sheffler. *Interpreting Otherwise than Heidegger: Emmanuel Levinas's Ethics as First Philosophy.* Pittsburgh: Duquesne UP, 1993.
Marx, Karl. *Capital: A Critique of Political Economy.* Ed. Frederick Engels. 3 vols. New York: International, 1967.
Mayer, Rainer. "Christology: The Genuine Form of Transcendence." *A Bonhoeffer Legacy: Essays in Understanding.* Ed. A. J. Klassen. Grand Rapids: Eerdmans, 1981. 179–92.
McClendon, James William, Jr. *Systematic Theology Ethics.* Nashville: Abingdon, 1986.
Mead, George Herbert. *Mind, Self, and Society from the Standpoint of a Social Behaviorist.* Ed. Charles W. Morris. Chicago: U of Chicago P, 1934.
Mill, John Stuart. *On Liberty.* 1859. Ed. Gertrude Himelfarb. New York: Penguin, 1974.
Naisbitt, John. *Megatrends: Ten New Directions Transforming Our Lives.* New York: Warner, 1984.
The New Jerusalem Bible. Gen. ed. Henry Wansbrough. New York: Doubleday, 1985.
The New Oxford Annotated Bible: New Revised Standard Version. Ed. Bruce M. Metzger and Roland E. Murphy. Oxford: Oxford UP, 1994.
Niebuhr, Reinhold. *The Irony of American History.* New York: Scribner's, 1952.

———. *The Nature and Destiny of Man: A Christian Interpretation.* Vol. 1. New York: Scribner, 1964. 2 vols.

Nietzsche, Friedrich. *Thus Spoke Zarathustra: A Book for None and All.* Trans. Walter Kaufmann. New York: Penguin, 1954.

Plato. *Phaedo.* Trans. W. H. D. Rouse. *Great Dialogues of Plato.* Ed. Eric H. Warmington and Philip G. Rouse. New York: Mentor, 1984. 460–521.

Pleasantville. Screenplay by Gary Ross. Dir. Gary Ross. Perf. Joan Allen, Jeff Daniels. New Line, 1998.

Postman, Neil. *Amusing Ourselves to Death: Public Discourse in the Age of Show Business.* New York: Viking, 1985.

———. *Building a Bridge to the Eighteenth Century: How the Past Can Improve Our Future.* New York: Vintage, 1999.

Postman, Neil, and Charles Weingartner. *Teaching as Subversive Activity.* New York: Dell, 1969.

Rasmussen, Larry, and Renate Bethge. *Dietrich Bonhoeffer—His Significance for North Americans.* Minneapolis: Fortress, 1990.

Reiff, Philip. *The Feeling Intellect: Selected Writings.* Chicago: U of Chicago P, 1990.

———. *The Triumph of the Therapeutic: Uses of Faith after Freud.* Chicago: U of Chicago P, 1987.

Ricoeur, Paul. *Oneself as Another.* Trans. Kathleen Blamey. Chicago: U of Chicago P, 1992.

———. *Time and Narrative.* Trans. Kathleen McLaughlin and David Pellauer. Vol 1. Chicago: U of Chicago P, 1984. 3 vols.

Robertson, Edwin. *Bonhoeffer's Legacy: The Christian Way in a World Without Religion.* New York: Collier, 1989.

———. *The Shame and the Sacrifice: The Life and Martyrdom of Dietrich Bonhoeffer.* New York: 1988.

Rokeach, Milton. *The Open and Closed Mind.* New York: Basic, 1960.

Sartre, Jean-Paul. *Being and Nothingness: An Essay on Phenomenological Ontology.* Trans. Hazel E. Barnes. New York: Washington Square, 1953.

Schlesinger, Arthur M., Jr. *The Disuniting of America.* New York: Norton, 1992.

Schrag, Calvin O. *Communicative Praxis and the Space of Subjectivity.* Bloomington: Indiana UP, 1986.

———. *The Self after Postmodernity.* New Haven: Yale UP, 1997.

Schultze, Quentin J. *Habits of the High-Tech Heart: Living Virtuously in the Information Age.* Grand Rapids: Baker, 2002.

Sennett, Richard. *Authority.* New York: Knopf, 1980.

———. *The Fall of Public Man.* New York: Norton, 1992.

Shakespeare, William. *The Rape of Lucrece. The Yale Shakespeare: The Complete Works.* Ed. Wilbur L. Cross and Tucker Brooke. New York: Barnes and Noble, 1993. 1453–72.

Shirer, William L. *The Rise and Fall of the Third Reich: A History of Nazi Germany.* New York: Simon, 1960.

Simmel, Georg. *Conflict and the Web of Group-Affiliations.* Trans. Kurt H. Wolff and Reinhard Bendix. New York: Free, 1955.

Sinclair, Upton. *The Jungle.* 1906. New York: New American Library, 1960.

Stewart, John Robert, ed. *Bridges Not Walls: A Book about Interpersonal Communication.* 8th ed. Boston: McGraw, 2001.

Tocqueville, Alexis de. *Democracy in America.* Trans. George Lawrence. Ed. J. P. Mayer. New York: Doubleday, 1969.

Tolkein, J. R. R. *The Fellowship of the Ring: Being the First Part of The Lord of the Rings.* 2nd ed. Boston: Houghton, 1994.

Vannorsdall, John. Afterword. *Meditating on the Word.* By Dietrich Bonhoeffer. Trans. and ed. David McI. Gracie. Cambridge: Cowley, 1986. 147–49.

Wallace, Karl R. "An Ethical Basis of Communication." *Communication Education* 4 (1955): 1–9.

Weinsheimer, Joel and Donald G. Marshall. Translators' Preface. *Truth and Method.* 2nd rev. ed. By Hans-Georg Gadamer. Trans. Joel Weinsheimer and Donald G. Marshall. New York: Continuum, 1999. xi–xix.

Zerner, Ruth. "Dietrich Bonhoeffer's Prison Fiction: A Commentary." *Fiction from Prison: Gathering Up the Past.* By Dietrich Bonhoeffer. Trans. Ursula Hoffmann. Ed. Renate Bethge, Eberhard Bethge and Clifford Green. Philadelphia: Fortress, 1981. 139–67.

Žižek, Slavoj. *The Fragile Absolute, Or, Why Is the Christian Legacy Worth Fighting For?* New York: Verso, 2000.

INDEX

Ronald C. Arnett is the chair of and a professor in the Department of Communication and Rhetorical Studies at Duquesne University. He has edited two books and authored four others, including *Dialogic Education: Conversations About Ideas and Between Persons* (1992), *Dialogic Civility in a Cynical Age: Community, Hope, and Interpersonal Relationships* (with Pat Arneson, 1999), and *Communication and Community* (1986), which earned the 1988 Religious Speech Communication Association Book Award. His article "Interpersonal Praxis: The Interplay of Religious Narrative, Historicality, and Metaphor" won the 1999 Religious Speech Communication Association Article of the Year Award, and his "Self-Fulfillment and Interpersonal Communication" won the 1979 Religious Speech Communication Association Outstanding Article Award. He is a former president of the Religious Communication Association.